Praise for

AMERICA LAST

"[Jacob] Heilbrunn isn't the first to tell the story of the right's barely submerged affinity for Hitler. Philip Roth's great counterfactual novel, *The Plot Against America*, takes this affinity as its premise—and as does Rachel Maddow's recently published history, *Prequel*. But it's always bracing to be reminded of how former President Herbert Hoover made excuses for Hitler before the war and how the press baron William Randolph Hearst commissioned stories by him. . . . Heilbrunn's book opens with verve. . . . Foreign dictators are now thoroughly attuned to the tendency that *America Last* describes. . . . [W]hat makes Heilbrunn's history, ultimately, so poignant is that the American right no longer needs to project its displaced desires onto leaders in other countries. It doesn't have to shop abroad for a tribune who channels the movement's deepest, most subversive desires. Trump is the foreign dictator that they craved all along."

—Franklin Foer, *Atlantic*

"*America Last* offers a lively—if grim—historical tour of the American right's fondness for foreign strongmen. . . . [It] showcases many of the more revolting moments in the right's history of autocrat worship. . . . [A] fast-paced and readable book, full of carefully constructed vignettes and telling anecdotes, and Heilbrunn deftly details the many ways in which the right's admiration for foreign autocrats dovetailed with authoritarian leanings here at home."

—Rosa Brooks, *Washington Monthly*

"Heilbrunn draws on the large body of scholarship documenting the Nazi sympathies of figures like Henry Ford, Charles Lindbergh, Father Coughlin, and the America Firsters of the late 1930s. And once again, he draws our attention to the elite pedigree of this movement. . . . If Trump wins and continues to pursue a foreign policy that rewards authoritarians and alienates liberal democracies, Jacob Heilbrunn's *America Last* will have provided us with a spirited and clear-eyed warning of how ideas, impulses, and resentments on the American Right can lead to disasters for the United States and the world."

—Jeffrey Herf, *Quillette*

"As Jacob Heilbrunn successfully argues in his new book, *America Last: The Right's Century-Long Romance With Foreign Dictators*, [conservatives across the U.S.] created a blueprint for how foreign dictators even decades later could cultivate conservative communities to their cause—and could, by the early 21st century, help propel one as far as the presidency. The story of the Americans who worshipped Wilhelm is just one of a range of pro-dictatorship efforts that Heilbrunn excavates, threading a century-long conservative infatuation with right-wing dictators. It's not only a corrective to the voluminous (if also accurate) investigations on how communist tyrannies fostered leftist supporters in the U.S., but also an able—and wildly timely— effort to stitch together nominally disparate views, from different epochs and eras. It all adds up to a convincing conclusion: that Trump, in 'lavishing praise on Putin and other dictators . . . wasn't creating a new style of right-wing politics,' Heilbrunn, editor of *The National Interest* and author of a previously acclaimed book on the history of neoconservatives, writes. Instead, he was building on a long-standing tradition."

—Casey Michel, *New York*

"*America Last* addresses the growing danger of authoritarianism—in the United States from the Trumpist Republican party, and abroad from the likes of Hungary's Viktor Orbán and his allies among Europe's populist parties. Heilbrunn searches for the historical roots of the right wing's interest in authoritarianism. . . . In our fight against illiberal democracy, Jacob Heilbrunn has given us a history of what he concludes is the 'long and melancholy saga of the American Right's self-abasement before foreign tyrants.' Those who still think of themselves as conservatives should read this book and learn about what some of the leaders they admire have in store for our country."

—Ronald Radosh, *Bulwark*

"Heilbrunn's book provides an essential, eye-opening perspective in which it is clear that Trump's flirtation with monsters and monstrous policies has deep roots that extend back to the original 'America First' movement and Hitler sympathizers like Charles Lindbergh."

—David Rothkopf, *Daily Beast*

"Trumpism is much bigger, we now know, than Donald Trump himself. But how did the movement come into being? Who are its true founders? And where may it be headed next? Jacob Heilbrunn, our foremost chronicler of the New Right, has the answers—and they are as chilling as they are surprising. *America Last* is a tour de force of historical investigation written with the verve of a first-rate political thriller." —Sam Tanenhaus, author of *The Death of Conservatism: The Movement and Its Consequences*

"Jacob Heilbrunn is Washington's shrewdest and most perceptive neocon-trarian. He now trains his sights on the American Right's historical bromancing of foreign dictators, a deplorable pageant currently featuring their pin-up, Hungary's leader Viktor Orbán, and his number-one fanboy, Tucker Carlson. This is an important book, and a warning for what could lie ahead beginning on January 20, 2025."

—Christopher Buckley, no relation to the William F. Buckley Jr. mentioned on pages 41, 137–63, 166–67, 175, 185–86, 191, 196, 200, 207, 218, and 220

"In *America Last*, Jacob Heilbrunn examines the convoluted line of thinking that draws so many on the Right to the illiberalism of Viktor Orbán and Vladimir Putin. He brings to this task a talent for illuminating the dark side of—and a deep understanding of—his subject, acquired over decades of editing such publications as the *New Republic*, the *National Interest*, and the *Los Angeles Times*. In one respect, *America Last* is an extension of Heilbrunn's celebrated 2008 book, *They Knew They Were Right: The Rise of the Neocons*, but, more importantly, *America Last* reveals how a key wing of the conservative movement has become, in effect, anti-American."

—Thomas Byrne Edsall, author of *The Point of No Return: American Democracy at the Crossroads*

"Jacob Heilbrunn's new book, *America Last*, is quite simply a must-read. This is history as revelation, and unfortunately it is all too relevant to understanding America's present-day politics."

—Susan Glasser, staff writer for *The New Yorker* and coauthor of *The Divider: Trump in the White House, 2017–2021*

"Though they love to wrap themselves in the flag and boast of their patriotism, the ugly truth is that American conservatives have long valorized, and even sought to emulate, dictators and autocrats abroad, from Mussolini to Pinochet up to Viktor Orbán today. In this elegantly written history of the Right's infatuation with the forces of illiberalism and foes of democracy, Jacob Heilbrunn helps us grasp the full dimensions of the threat today's conservatives, and the political party that represents them, pose to achieving a more decent, humane, and democratic United States."

—Matthew Sitman, cohost of the podcast *Know Your Enemy*

"As we focus on the perilous state of American democracy, Jacob Heilbrunn provides a lucid and original examination of just how the right wing descended to its current antidemocratic depths. Combining a historian's mastery of the past with vivid storytelling, Heilbrunn traces how a small but ruthlessly determined group silenced the rational center of the Republican Party. Read Heilbrunn's sobering but urgently important book."

—Kati Marton, author of *Enemies of the People:*
My Family's Journey to America and
The Chancellor: The Remarkable Odyssey of Angela Merkel

AMERICA LAST

ALSO BY JACOB HEILBRUNN

They Knew They Were Right:
The Rise of the Neocons

AMERICA LAST

The Right's Century-Long Romance with Foreign Dictators

Jacob Heilbrunn

Liveright Publishing Corporation

A Division of W. W. Norton & Company
Independent Publishers Since 1923

For information about permission to reproduce selections from this book, write to
Permissions, Liveright Publishing Corporation, a division of
W. W. Norton & Company, Inc., 500 Fifth Avenue, New York, NY 10110

For information about special discounts for bulk purchases, please contact
W. W. Norton Special Sales at specialsales@wwnorton.com or 800-233-4830

Manufacturing by Lakeside Book Company
Book design by Daniel Lagin
Production manager: Anna Oler

Library of Congress Control Number: 2024938278

ISBN 978-1-324-09567-5 pbk.

Liveright Publishing Corporation, 500 Fifth Avenue, New York, N.Y. 10110
www.wwnorton.com

W. W. Norton & Company Ltd., 15 Carlisle Street, London W1D 3BS

10 9 8 7 6 5 4 3 2 1

To my father

The tender respect of Augustus for a free constitution
which he had destroyed, can only be explained by an attentive
consideration of the character of that subtle tyrant.

—Edward Gibbon,
The Decline and Fall of the Roman Empire

CONTENTS

AMERICA LAST

INTRODUCTION

When the Heritage Foundation celebrated its fiftieth anniversary in April 2023 with a two-day conference and lavish party at Mount Vernon, it invited a number of leading conservative politicians, including Senators Tim Scott, J. D. Vance, Mike Lee, Rick Scott, and Josh Hawley, as well as Florida governor Ron DeSantis, who had not yet announced his bid for the presidency. But one guest speaker's name stuck out on the program—that of Balázs Orbán, a thirty-eight-year-old Hungarian parliamentarian and political director for Prime Minister Viktor Orbán (they are not related). Balázs Orbán spoke right after Vance, who decried Ukraine as the most corrupt government in the world: "Get America out of Ukraine!" Hostility to Ukraine and respect for Russian president Vladimir Putin as a foe of "woke" Western liberalism are widespread on the Right. At the same time, Hungary's government enjoys considerable favor for its crusade on behalf of traditional family values, its crackdown on liberal institutions, and its simple hatred for migrants. Orbán was appearing as part of a panel,

"Strengthening Our Cultural Institutions," that discussed transgender rights, among other things. "A man is a man, and a woman is a woman," Orbán said. "It's in the Constitution. End of discussion."

He meant, of course, the Hungarian Constitution, which Orbán's Fidesz party modified in March 2014 to weaken the country's democracy. With his allusions to Renaissance paintings, French novelists, and the decline and fall of the Roman Empire, the bespectacled Orbán gave off an academic air, but he delivered a dispatch from the front lines of the culture wars in Hungary, which has created an illiberal democracy. Orbán received an ecstatic response for his comments about so-called gender ideology, seeming to elicit not only rapt attention but also a degree of envy from his fellow panelists and the audience alike.

No Hungarian official has worked more assiduously to forge ties with a variety of conservative organizations and the Republican Party than Balázs Orbán. While Viktor Orbán swoops in for high-profile addresses to the Conservative Political Action Conference, it's the younger man who engages most frequently with the American Right. American government officials in Hungary call him "the puppet master." His time in America was not limited to the Heritage conference. Orbán was everywhere, flogging his book *The Hungarian Way of Strategy* in a meeting with the New York Young Republican Club, appearing on *Tucker Carlson Tonight*, and meeting Vance at his office in the Dirksen Building for a photo op. He tweeted a resulting picture with the words, "Thank you for being a good friend of #Hungary and for standing up for our shared values!" Back home, where his visit was widely reported on in state media, Orbán's high-profile itinerary was touted as affirmation of the prominent place that Hungary occupies on the American political landscape. One Heritage official excitedly told me, "I'm definitely going to make the pilgrimage to Budapest."

During the panel discussion, Orbán was treated like a visiting dignitary by the moderator, Delano Squires, a research fellow at the foundation's Helen DeVos Center for Life, Religion, and Family. Like a talk show host soliciting advice from a self-help guru, Squires was palpably eager to learn what lessons Orbán could convey from his battles to defend Western civilization. And Orbán seemed happy to oblige. After joking that he has the same "scary" last name as Viktor Orbán, Balázs lauded the "cooperation between Hungary and Heritage." He explained that Hungary had become a "conservative safe space" where traditional family values were strictly observed. Hungary, he claimed, had slashed abortion and divorce rates in half—an essential component of its efforts in a "geopolitical competition" with non-Western nations that are outstripping the West in birthrates. To safeguard your national identity, he said, you could surrender by allowing in vast numbers of migrants, or you could adopt pronatalist policies, including financial incentives and property subsidies. He didn't have to add which course he recommended for America.

Why were the America Firsters at the Heritage Foundation—the think tank that is the crown jewel of the conservative movement—looking to a Hungarian parliamentarian as a guide to navigating the culture wars? How had a small, landlocked country—with half the population of Florida and dependent on economic subsidies from Brussels—emerged as a model for the proud American Right, those supposed believers in American exceptionalism?

How, in short, did Hungary become the future that works for this country's conservatives?

Over the past decade or so, I've had numerous opportunities to observe the conservative fascination with foreign autocrats firsthand. As editor of *The National Interest*, a magazine that was founded by the neoconservative godfather Irving Kristol and that published Francis Fukuyama's essay "The End of History?," I have come into contact with a wide variety of figures on the Right, a number of whom ended up in Donald Trump's orbit. After graduating from Oberlin College, I became an assistant editor at the magazine in 1989, the year the Eastern Bloc crumbled, before attending graduate school at Georgetown University. As an editor at *The New Republic*, I coined the term "theocon" in a cover story in 1996 about intellectual radicals on the Right. After writing a book about neoconservatism and the Iraq War, I ended up returning, in 2008, to *The National Interest*, which Kristol had sold in the interim to the Canadian media mogul Conrad Black and the Nixon Center for Peace and Freedom in 2001. In 2007, Black was convicted of mail fraud and obstruction of justice. (In May 2019 President Trump granted Black, the author of *Donald J. Trump: A President Like No Other* [2018], a full pardon.)

Black ceded full control of the magazine to the Nixon Center's president and CEO, Dimitri K. Simes. Simes was a controversial figure in Washington. A hulking man who had emigrated from Russia to the United States in January 1973 as a twenty-six-year-old, he had worked as a researcher for Yevgeny Primakov, who became Russia's prime minister, at the Communist Party's most influential think tank, the Institute of World Economy and International Relations, where he also served as acting secretary for the institute's Komsomol, or Communist Youth League, branch. His mother, Dina Kaminskaya, was a defense attorney, or "advocate," in Moscow who represented Soviet dissidents such as Yuli Daniel and Vladimir Bukovsky. Her husband, Konstantin Simis, was an expert on Soviet constitutional law. They were expelled from the Soviet Union in 1977. "It's not a story of immigration," Simis told the *Washington Post*. "It's a story of exile. We did not want to leave our country."[1] In 1982 Kaminskaya published a memoir, *Final Judgment: My Life as a Soviet Defense Attorney*. Simis wrote a book titled *USSR: The Corrupt Society* that appeared the same year. "My intention was to prepare an encyclopedia of Soviet society and state at all levels, from streetwalkers to Politburo members," he said. "The corruption of the ruling machine corrupts the people, too."

While his courageous parents worked to expose the true nature of the Soviet system, Simes followed a different tack. He called for détente with the evil empire. In 1979 Simes published an essay in *Foreign Policy* that raised eyebrows around Washington, particularly among the neoconservatives who became his lifelong enemies. It was called "The Anti-Soviet Brigade." Simes complained that unrepentant cold warriors were peddling "half-truths and lies about Soviet behavior at home and abroad" and that Washington was moving away from accepting Moscow as a "legitimate equal" in world affairs. Instead, what was needed when it came to the Kremlin was "dialogue." Simes would make the same argument, decade after decade, Russian regime after Russian regime. Whether Brezhnev, Chernenko, Andropov, Gorbachev, Yeltsin, or Putin were in charge, his counsel remained steadfast—America should cater to the Kremlin's sensitivities. By September 2018, he was ensconced in Moscow as the host of a television show on Russian state television Channel One about foreign affairs called *Bolshaya igra*—"The Big Game." After Ukrainian president Volodymyr Zelensky made a historic appearance before the US Congress on December 21, 2022, Simes went on the Russian propagandist Vladimir Solovyov's radio show, *Full Contact*, to denounce him. "As I watched the TV coverage," Simes said, "I also thought of comparisons to Churchill—not of Zelensky, but Putin. . . . This was a speech worthy of Churchill! The speech of President Vladimir Putin."[2] His remarks did not go unnoticed. In January 2023, Adrian Karatnycky, a former president of Freedom House, wrote an op-ed in the *Wall Street Journal* that dubbed Simes one of "Putin's American Cheerleaders."[3] In June 2023, Simes moderated a plenary session at the St. Petersburg International Economic Forum with Putin and his Algerian counterpart Abdelmadjid Tebboune, prompting one observer to tell the *Moscow Times* that "his job there is to play the role of the 'model American,' to show viewers that there is another, 'normal' America. So he's been thanked and promoted to the honorary role of moderator."[4]

Simes initially rose to prominence as director of the Soviet and East European Research Center at the Johns Hopkins School of Advanced International Studies. In 1983 he joined the Carnegie Endowment for International Peace as a senior associate. In an August 1984 op-ed, he alluded to Nixon's missteps during Watergate but summed him up as "not only a very impressive president, but also in an important way . . . an honorable statesman." He met the former president for the first time in 1985 at his office in lower Manhattan and went on to become his postpresidential adviser on Russian affairs.[5] Nixon had a long-standing fascination with Russia, dating back to his first visit in July 1959, as Dwight D. Eisenhower's vice president, when he conducted the famous "kitchen cabinet" debate with Soviet premier Nikita Khrushchev at the American National Exhibition in Moscow's Sokolniki Park. After Nixon died in 1994, Simes became the president of the Nixon Center for Peace and Freedom, a position he occupied until 2022 (in 1998 it changed its name to The Nixon Center, then in 2011 the Center for the National Interest[6]). Throughout, Simes boasted what were surely the most intimate ties of any American private citizen to the Kremlin.

The extensive nature of those ties started to become apparent to me when I encountered a young redheaded woman named Maria Butina at a small Center for the National Interest event. A Russian exchange student at American University, Butina was connected to Aleksandr Torshin, the rubicund former deputy governor of Russia's Central Bank, and she was later arrested by the Justice Department as an unregistered foreign agent. On June 8, 2015, Simes emailed her to relate that "I will mention to him that he may get a piece from you."[7] "Him" was me. Later that day Butina sent me an op-ed she had drafted about how the Russian bear and the American elephant could cooperate in the interests of world peace. Her main thrust was that American conservatives should stop demonizing poor, misunderstood Putin. It was time for an alliance between the Russian and American Right. I was bemused, emailing her that I looked forward to publishing the "audacious" essay. It seemed far-fetched, to say the least. That conservative Republicans would cozy up to Putin? No way.

With Trump's candidacy for the presidency, however, the very scenario that had seemed so improbable to me increasingly began to resemble reality. In early 2016, shortly before the start of the Republican primaries, Simes summoned me to his office. "Guess who I've just been talking to," he bragged. "Donald Trump, the next president of the United States!"

A lunch meeting with Henry Kissinger followed that spring in the boardroom of the Time Warner Center in New York. Jared Kushner, in his trademark dark suit, white shirt, no tie, and white tennis shoes, took part. The subject was artificial intelligence. I vividly recall the look of astonishment on Kushner's otherwise impassive face after the meeting adjourned and Simes made a bee-line for him, announcing that he viewed Trump favorably. "You do?" Kushner said.

Kushner may have been incredulous, but the bond was forged. In coming months, Simes bragged to me that he was speaking regularly with Trump, though he was careful to note that it wasn't any-thing like discussing foreign affairs with Nixon. After protracted negotiations with the Trump campaign, Simes hosted Trump's sole foreign policy speech during the primaries at the Mayflower Hotel in April 2016. A day or so before the speech, Simes came into my office and sat down on the white leather couch opposite my desk. He explained—really, decreed—that the magazine would be the speech's sponsor so that it could pass muster as a press event.

At the private reception before the speech, where everyone from Senator Jeff Sessions to the Russian ambassador Sergei Kis-lyak was circulating, Trump bounded in and exclaimed, "Hello, everybody!" His sole criterion for interest in a particular person was celebrity. "You're famous!" he shouted when former Reagan national security adviser Robert McFarlane shook his hand. By con-trast, I received a quizzical stare. Soon enough it was time for the speech itself in the Mayflower ballroom. After announcing to the audience that Trump would appear shortly, I took my seat behind that of his campaign manager Paul Manafort, and watched from up close as the future president clutched the lectern in a death grip, bellowing about "America First."

Trump didn't make any rhetorical bows to the foreign policy establishment. Quite the contrary. Like Senator Joe McCarthy condemning the State Department's traitorous "bright young men who are born with silver spoons in their mouths" at Wheeling, West Virginia, in 1950, Trump sneered at the so-called foreign policy experts with their "perfect résumés" who had "nothing to brag about." That evening I wrote a piece for *Politico* that enraged the Trump campaign. It was subtitled, "After his son-in-law contacted us, we decided to give him a chance to deliver, at last, a coherent view of the world. I wasn't converted."

When Trump won the presidency in November 2016, I thought of the credo of Saul Bellow's protagonist Moses Herzog: "If I am out of my mind, it's all right with me." Robert Mueller, after he was brought on as special counsel in May 2017 to investigate Russian interference in the election, took a long look at the Center for the National Interest's hosting of the Trump speech; he was eager to learn what, if any, contact had taken place between Kislyak and Sessions, who became Trump's first attorney general. Like a number of others affiliated with the center, I testified before the commission. In the end, the Mueller report found that Simes and the center had extensive contacts with the Trump campaign but that no wrongdoing occurred. *Washington Post* columnist Josh Rogin summed up the mess in a column titled, "Dimitri Simes flew too close to Trump, and his think tank got burned."[8]

There was no question that things had changed in Washington. Where the neocons had once counseled intervention everywhere, the new advance guard was declaring that it should take place nowhere. It was Trump's bargain basement version of foreign policy realism—America's allies are moochers, we have no national interest in maintaining alliances in Asia or Europe, Ukraine belongs to Putin's sphere of influence, dictators are worthy of emulation, and so on—that was turning into the new foreign policy gospel, at least in Republican circles. As Washington descended into a moronic inferno, something unprecedented was taking shape.

Or was it?

The longer I've listened to conservatives today talk about Hungary, Russia, "wokeness," "the deep state," abortion, immigration, and media bias, the more I've become convinced that many of their arguments are not novel. If anything, the opposite is true: these arguments represent an act of conservation, preserving in a kind of rhetorical alembic grievances and apprehensions that can be traced all the way back to World War I, when intellectuals on the Right displayed an unease with mass democracy that manifested itself in a hankering for authoritarian leaders abroad. In the 1920s and 1930s, this set of beliefs, or habit of mind, became even more pronounced as Hitler and Mussolini attracted a variety of American devotees, including the newspaper tycoon William Randolph Hearst and the aviator Charles Lindbergh as well as outright fascists such as the publicist Lawrence J. Dennis and the New York financier Merwin K. Hart. Throughout the Cold War, the Right evinced a fondness for autocrats such as Francisco Franco and Augusto Pinochet, even as some wrote revisionist accounts of the Third Reich—which wasn't so bad, after all.

Today, a Hungarian strongman who is peddling völkisch ethnonational thought as a replacement pan-European ideology— the pretense being that the unelected bureaucrats running the European Union have supplanted the Soviet Union as the threatening totalitarian power—is the latest object of the Right's dictator worship. Balázs Orbán has traveled to the US to make his pitch and to forge connections. But American politicians and intellectuals and talk show hosts also now flock to Budapest to celebrate and emulate his boss. The contemporary Left might look to the Nordic social democracies for policy inspiration, but it engages in nothing as coordinated or systematic as the Right's polemics on behalf of Orbán and other authoritarians.

Its aims are expansive. Liberalism, conservatives say, stands for totalitarianism, democracy for injustice, and rights for decadence. Conservatives have a different formula. They wish to protect freedom in the name of limiting it. They aspire to create a revolution to preserve tradition, to capture the future by returning to a mythical past. Right-wing intellectuals profess to subscribe to foreign policy realism, which they argue means allying with warmongers abroad in order to preserve peace at home. But the tradition this book excavates is not based on realism or pragmatism. It is rooted, rather, in a sincere affinity. Its advocates avow, or at least intimate, that authoritarianism, in one form or other, is superior to democracy. They don't quite say that: even as they disparage liberals who invoke "liberty" and "justice" and "history" and "democracy," conservatives use the same terms as rhetorical cudgels. Their aim is to turn the language of liberalism on its head. They denounce "cancel culture," but are busily canceling anything that nettles them, from books to beer. They define freedom as the ability to suppress the views and beliefs, ranging from transgender rights to an independent media, that they revile. At bottom, they are advocating ethno-nationalism in the guise of a set of principles. That the US is the rare nation founded on universalist ideals and that this has been the key difference between the US and those foreign, authoritarian nations they have long revered—scarcely seems to occur to them.

This book does not argue that all conservatives are fascists or that all fascists are conservatives. Nor does it attempt to provide a comprehensive history of the American Right. Instead, it provides a guide for the perplexed, identifying and tracing a persuasion— what might be called the illiberal imagination—that has persisted for over a century on the Right. At the outset of the cold war, George Orwell, in a classic essay in 1946 about the writings of James Burnham, a former Trotskyist who moved to the right, diagnosed the power worship in the intellectual class that prompted it to treat totalitarian societies as invincible and democratic ones as feeble. The intelligentsia, Orwell wrote, harbored a secret wish to "usher in a hierarchical society where the intellectual can at last get his hands on the whip." In *1984*, Orwell created just such a figure. For O'Brien, a member of the Inner Party who works at the Ministry of Truth, it is a source of sadistic satisfaction to wield terror as an instrument of purification, to torture Winston Smith, a minor functionary, into recanting his heresies and treating him as his savior.

Neither the Left nor the Right has been immune to the power

worship that Orwell discerned. Perhaps because conservatives have often professed to hold something of a patent on patriotism, the illusions of the Left about communist tyranny have tended to receive more attention than those of the Right. The political pilgrims to communist countries have become a byword for human credulity or cynicism, but the Right possesses its own tradition of homage to authoritarian regimes masquerading as defenders of Western civilization.

In examining the record of the latter, I realized that very much like the fellow travelers on the Left who celebrated Stalin, Mao, and Fidel Castro as prophetic figures, a variety of intellectuals and politicians on the Right, too, have regularly embarked upon quixotic quests for a utopia abroad, whether in Kaiser Wilhelm's Germany or Mussolini's Italy, in Augusto Pinochet's Chile or Viktor Orbán's Hungary. The desire to live in a personal dream palace has repeatedly manifested itself over the decades, and usually ended in blaming rather than celebrating America first. Aggrieved, or at least disappointed, by what they perceived as their own society's failings—its liberalism, its tolerance, its increasing secularism—conservatives have searched for a paradise abroad that can serve as a model at home.

This deification of foreign dictators is not "un-American," as the Right has long professed about liberals and the Left. To make such a claim would be to ignore a tradition of homegrown authoritarianism in this country. The most obvious expression of that tradition, if one doesn't count slavery itself, is the Jim Crow South—which helped inspire, as did the dispossession of Native Americans, none other than Hitler. As James Q. Whitman documented in *Hitler's American Model* (2017), the Führer drew on

American citizenship and anti-miscegenation laws for the 1935 Nuremberg Race Laws.

In fact, a proclivity for authoritarianism is American to its core. While much of the story that follows focuses on the "revisionist" history that conservatives regularly espouse, the Right has been right all along, so to speak. Its members don't despise America; they loath the America they cannot bludgeon into submission. To justify their power grab, they turn American political history on its head.[9] America, they say, is a republic, not a democracy—ignoring that the Founding Fathers favored a republican government not to promote minority rule, but to avert what James Madison in *Federalist* No. 10 referred to as "the spectacles of turbulence and contention" of mob rule. Today, nothing less than regime change to replace a liberal American ruling class with a "pre-postmodern" conservative aristocracy, we are told by an ambitious American political theorist and votary of Viktor Orbán, can reverse our expulsion from a political Eden.[10] It is an openly (and frighteningly) anti-democratic claim from those who have noisily demanded strict fidelity to the American Constitution.

Yet the Right's hostility to democracy is not new. It never went away in the first place. And this is where that story begins.

Chapter 1

COURTING KAISER WILHELM

Poet and propagandist George Sylvester Viereck visiting Berlin in 1911. Three decades later he was arrested and prosecuted by Franklin Roosevelt's Justice Department as a Nazi agent.

At the turn of the twentieth century, Prussia was the premier modern illiberal state in Europe. After defeating France and achieving unification in 1871, it compensated for its late arrival to great power status by demanding what German chancellor Bernhard von Bülow famously called its "place in the sun." Imperial Germany's phenomenal population and economic growth—by 1913, coal production equaled Great Britain's and steel production was more than twice Britain's—prompted it to embark not only on colonial expansion but also a naval arms race with the island nation for world supremacy. The fork-bearded Admiral Alfred von Tirpitz stated that expansion was "as irresistible as a law of nature." Meanwhile, the professoriate declared that Germany had a unique cultural mission to oppose Western liberalism, championing war as a morally elevating enterprise. The historian Heinrich von Treitschke, the author of a five-volume history of Germany and a leading anti-Semite, instructed his students at Humboldt University in Berlin that "The State is not an Academy of Art. It is Power!"[1] And at the head of this Teutonic military colossus was a most unusual ruler.

Kaiser Wilhelm II was a monster. When he assumed power in 1888 at age twenty-nine, Wilhelm immediately had the imperial residence of his mother Vicky, the eldest daughter of Queen Victoria, searched by his soldiers. He trampled over the German Reichstag, or parliament. He sought to restore the medieval Divine Right of the Kaiser in order to rule Germany as he saw fit. "There is only one person who is master in this empire and I am not going to tolerate any other," he said. He was a compulsive liar who constantly threatened Germany's neighbors.[2] He presided over a strutting military clique that espoused racial nationalism and contempt for democracy. Wilhelm, who had 120 military uniforms, fostered a petulant nationalistic spirit that Heinrich Mann lacerated in his novel *The Loyal Subject* as "the Power which transcends us and whose hooves we kiss." In 1900 Wilhelm delivered what became known as the "Hun speech," instructing a German expeditionary force sent to help defeat the Boxer Rebellion in China that it should take no prisoners alive, thereby ensuring that "no Chinese will ever again dare to look cross-eyed at a German." He embarked upon a squalid and vicious colonization campaign, perpetrating genocide against the Herero people in Namibia in 1904, a policy that has been seen as a precursor of Hitler's own war of racial conquest.[3] His jealousy of Great Britain impelled him to pursue policies that led directly to World War I. Amid that war, in April 1917, he dispatched Vladimir Lenin to Russia in a sealed boxcar, thereby abetting the rise of the Bolshevik dictatorship in Russia. After he forfeited his throne in November 1918 and fled to Holland, he shirked all responsibility for the German catastrophe, declaring that it was the Jews who were culpable for Germany's defeat and that they should be gassed to death.[4] He and his three sons, in contrast to the Habsburg royals in Austria, embraced Hitler, viewing him as a welcome ally who might restore the Hohenzollerns to the vacant throne.[5] More than any other European monarch, the Kaiser set the twentieth century on its path to strife, bloodshed, and calamity.

In America, however, "Kaiser Bill," as he was known, enjoyed numerous admirers. They saw him as a wronged figure, an upholder of traditional values who had been vilified by the Western powers. They did not simply defend Kaiser Wilhelm; they venerated him. They regarded Britain, not Germany, as the main threat to world peace. And they depicted Woodrow Wilson, not Kaiser Wilhelm, as the truly unhinged leader.

Among the Americans who revered Kaiser Wilhelm were two young men who claimed descent, respectively, from German chancellor Otto von Bismarck and Kaiser Wilhelm I. Both lauded the son, Kaiser Wilhelm II. Both read and spoke German. Both were writers. Both revered German culture and believed it was superior to America's. Both corresponded with and visited the Kaiser in his exile in Roon, Holland, after he abdicated in November 1918. Both would decry American intervention not only in World War I but also World War II. And Henry Louis Mencken and George Sylvester Viereck both propounded many of the arguments that future generations of American apologists for authoritarian leaders would deploy.

Those arguments came in a variety of forms. Mencken and Viereck engaged in whataboutism, scorned Western liberalism as a bankrupt ideology, and elevated authoritarianism above democracy. Instead of forcing it to capitulate on the battlefield, and instead of trying to force it to adopt debased and corrupt Western liberal values, they suggested that America and Great Britain should have accommodated Germany's wholly legitimate aspiration to safeguard its own unique, anti-Western culture. In essence, Mencken and Viereck inverted reality, converting Kaiser Wilhelm into a crusader for freedom and Wilson into a barbaric warmonger.

In adopting this stance, they went far beyond the wider anti-war movement in the US, which advocated neutrality, not a pro-German position. It included everyone from the social worker Jane Addams, who won the Nobel Peace Prize, to Wisconsin senator Robert La Follette, who voted against authorizing American entry into the war. They opposed militarism and maintained that entry into the war would destroy Wilson's domestic reform program. It did. After he led the US into the war in April 1917, Wilson rapidly established a surveillance state to quash domestic dissent and whipped up a good deal of hysteria about the loyalty of German Americans. In his 2017 book *War Against War* celebrating the anti-war movement, the historian Michael Kazin speculated that had Wilson declined to intervene, the outcome would have been far superior for America and Europe—no Treaty of Versailles, no stab-in-the-back myth, and "no rise, much less triumph, of Hitler and his National Socialist Party."[6]

If only. What Kazin called the "anti-warriors" had legitimate grounds for balking at American involvement in Europe's horrific war, but they refused to recognize that it would have been tantamount to abandoning Europe to German tyranny, an outcome that would only have heightened the Kaiser's desire for world supremacy and, eventually, led to a direct military confrontation between Berlin and Washington. For all the criticisms directed at Wilson for his conduct of the war and its aftermath, he had it right. Wilson realized that a modus vivendi with an imperial Germany intent on world conquest was a nonstarter. In maintaining a balance of power in Europe, Wilson, far from being an idealistic dreamer, proved in many ways to be the ultimate foreign policy realist. His intervention provided Germany with the opportunity, however slender, to become a successful democracy after World War I.

It was precisely the emergence of a democratic as opposed to a monarchical Germany after World War I that H. L. Mencken deplored. A columnist, satirist, and lexicographer with an omnipresent cigar dangling from his mouth, Mencken was a professional curmudgeon—and the leading journalist of his era. He invented the op-ed, established *The American Mercury* magazine, and promoted the careers of numerous novelists, including Theodore Dreiser, who inscribed one book, "To H. L. Mencken, my oldest living enemy," and F. Scott Fitzgerald, who declared, "Mencken has done more for national letters than any man alive." Mencken's only fear was being boring. He waded into America's culture wars, covering the 1925 Scopes Monkey Trial in Dayton, Tennessee, to ridicule the "theologic bilge" of William Jennings Bryan, the three-time Democratic presidential candidate and defender of fundamentalist Christianity.

At bottom, Mencken was an aristocratic wannabe who viewed America with contempt and Germany with worship. Had it not been crushed during the Civil War, Mencken believed, the Old South might have created a genuine aristocracy. As for the northern business plutocracy, it was "based on money alone—individuals of great wealth were really just members of the ignorant mob who happened to have gotten rich."[7] At the same time, Mencken condemned the rise of an administrative state under Wilson as an intolerable infringement on American liberties. He never reconciled his ardor for Prussia—a highly developed bureaucratic powerhouse—with his condemnation of big government in America.

With his innate conservatism—his disdain for the common man, his opposition to suffrage for women, his belief in an elite, his anti-Semitism, and his racism—Mencken served as one of the godfathers of what has become known as the Old Right, a diffuse collection of libertarian intellectuals who formed an elite that started on the Left but recoiled at the outcome of World War I and the rise of the New Deal. Mencken's influence has, in one way or another, lingered down to today: in 2006, Ann Coulter declared on CNN, "I am the new right-wing Mencken" and the scholar Paul Gottfried, a leading figure among so-called paleoconservatives, coined the term "alt-right" at a 2008 meeting of the H. L. Mencken Society, which was founded by Gottfried and the white nationalists Richard Spencer and William Regnery.[8]

Mencken, who boasted German descent on both sides of his family, grew up in Baltimore. He delighted in the fact that in 1715 his ancestor Johann Burkhard Mencken, who earned a degree at the University of Leipzig, wrote a widely read book titled *The Charlatanry of the Learned* that was translated into Dutch, French, German, and Italian. "It gave me a shock," Mencken observed. "All my stock in trade was there—loud assertions, heavy buffooneries, slashing attacks on professors. It was really uncanny."[9] His grandfather, Burkhard Ludwig Mencken, emigrated from Saxony to America after the failed democratic 1848 revolution in Germany, which many historians see as a decisive moment in its failure to adopt enduring liberal institutions. Not Mencken. He praised King Friedrich Wilhelm IV—who spurned the entreaties of the Frankfurt liberals to become Emperor of the Germans—for crushing the uprising with military force.

In 1875, Mencken's father, August, who wore a diamond stud pin and a Masonic watch charm, established a cigar factory whose boxes bore a Mencken coat of arms. A staunch conservative, he regarded taxes and the labor movement alike with alarm. August left it to his wife, Anna Abhau, to initiate Henry into German high culture. "The immigrant Germans whom I saw at home as a boy all affected a certain aloof superiority towards America and everything American," Mencken said. "To say anything was American, in my family circle, was to hint that it was cheap and trashy."[10] He never budged from this snobbish conviction. "I inherited," he said, "a bias against the rabble."[11] He was also influenced by the Australian writer Ida Alexa Ross Wylie's personal account of a year in Germany, *The Germans*. It featured a frontispiece of Kaiser Wilhelm in full dress uniform, deplored the "inherited prejudices" of the British toward Germany, and extolled the innate Teutonic attachment to discipline and learning.[12]

Mencken first visited Germany in 1908, the same year that Kaiser Wilhelm created an international furor during an interview with the *Daily Telegraph* in which he declared, "You English are mad, mad, mad as March hares. What has come over you that you are so completely given over to suspicions quite unworthy of a great nation?" According to his biographer Marion Elizabeth Rogers, "With a glinting seidel of Spatenbrau before him in Munich's Hofbräuhaus"—where Hitler, incidentally, would launch his abortive November 1923 Beer Hall Putsch—"Mencken felt in his element. Every time Mencken returned to the United States, he noticed the cultural difference between the two countries."[13] He did indeed. Mencken prided himself on his superiority to most other Americans, and though he admired tradition and what he saw as the glories of the American past, he also thought of himself as forward-looking. He would confront the harsh truths that others shrank from confronting. Not for him the consoling pieties of the Rotarians or the palaver about a crusade for democracy that Wilson purveyed. "Like Nietzsche," he wrote, "I console myself with the hope that I am the man of the future, emancipated from the prevailing delusions and superstitions, and gone beyond nationalism."[14]

There can be no doubting that Nietzsche's iconoclasm, hostility to religion, and contempt for the masses left a lasting mark on Mencken. His worship of Nietzsche extended to his views of women; Mencken voiced his apprehension that a prolonged marriage carried with it the danger of leaving a trace of the feminine outlook on a husband. In 1908 Mencken published a pioneering work, *The Philosophy of Friedrich Nietzsche*. Mencken saw the Nietzsche he wanted to see—a successor to the Social Darwinists he admired such as Charles Graham Sumner and Herbert Spencer. Democracy was in his gunsights. After he attended the 1912 Democratic National Convention, which was held in Baltimore, Mencken expressed his antipathy toward the hurly-burly of American politics by pointing to the superior example of Germany. Aristocrats could take a lofty and objective view of their nation's true interests, while democratic politicians had to cater to the superstitions of the common man. "Such a mountebank as the Hon. William Jennings Bryan," Mencken claimed, "with his astounding repertoire of bogus remedies, would be almost unimaginable in Germany."[15]

Mencken, you could even say, was a fellow traveler of autocracy who reveled in trolling the political establishment. He laid the foundations for the Right's attacks on liberal presidents. He said that Wilson was a clueless professor. He said that the American government was engaging in a massive propaganda campaign to deceive its citizens about Germany's true nature and ambitions. He said that the Western allies had encircled a fearful Germany that felt compelled to go to war to protect itself. And he said that Wilson was exploiting the war to use the federal government to cow Americans into obedience. Like Kaiser Wilhelm, Mencken viewed liberal democracy as tantamount to mob rule, a conviction that led him to espouse "a kind of libertarian fascism."[16] The literary critic Alfred Kazin pointed to the "intellectual brutality in Mencken's makeup."[17] Nowhere did it emerge more conspicuously than in his fealty to Germany.

His first real chance to display his zeal for imperial Germany for a national audience arrived at the outset of World War I. In August 1914, Mencken received a letter from Ellery Sedgwick, the editor of *The Atlantic*, which was based in Boston and a faithful expositor of the views of the Brahmin class. Sedgwick was piqued by the notion of running a counterintuitive piece that might shock and astonish a New England gentry committed to Great Britain. He asked Mencken to write an essay linking Nietzsche's philosophy to German militarism.

Sedgwick reckoned that Mencken's thesis would be so offensive to the magazine's readers that it would have the effect of further convincing them that Kaiser Wilhelm was indeed an international menace.[18] "I write this," Sedgwick said, "in the full realization that you are (presumably) on the wrong side of this war and that the Munchnerbrau in your veins keeps you German, but the theory would hold regardless of the writer's personal prejudices." Mencken responded, "There can be no doubt that Nietzschism has been superimposed upon the old, unintelligent absolutism, and that it is largely responsible for the astounding efficiency now visible in peace and war."

Mencken titled his tribute "The Mailed Fist and the Prophet." In it, Mencken declared that the "philosophy of Nietzsche gave coherence and significance to the new German spirit and the new Germany gave a royal setting and splendor to Nietzsche." There was no cogent reason to be frightened by the Prussian war machine. Under Kaiser Wilhelm's leadership, he contended, the old Prussian aristocracy had been overtaken by a "new aristocracy of genuine skill and Germany has become a true democracy in the Greek sense. That is to say . . . the empire is now governed by an oligarchy of its best men."

Soon, Sedgwick commissioned an even more audacious piece from Mencken on why Germany's political system and culture outshone America's. Mencken promptly submitted what he called a "red-hot" essay that made the case for regime change in America itself. It explained that after Germany successfully conquered the United States, a new utopia would emerge. Alas, before Mencken's essay could see print, German U-boats, as part of their unrestricted submarine warfare against Great Britain, sank the Cunard ocean liner *Lusitania* on May 7, 1915. One hundred twenty-three Americans onboard the ship died and outrage over the attack was widespread in America. Sedgwick quickly decided discretion was the better part of valor. "Your reprehensible paper is damnably effective," he wrote to Mencken, but "I have no desire to foment treason."

For his part, Mencken didn't see anything remotely treasonous about exposing what he saw as American perfidy. On May 10 he coldly noted in his "Free Lance" column that the *Lusitania* "was a ship carrying munitions of war; the whole world was given fair warning that she would be sunk at sight; the Americans who sailed upon her knew that they were taking their lives in their own hands." Not only was Germany fighting "gallantly," but "surely no American who calls himself a fair man is going to defend the doctrine that the presence of our citizens on munitions bearing ships of the English naval reserve shall protect those ships against attack with the only means at Germany's present command."[19]

The real victims were Mencken and others who defied British and American propaganda about the war. Mencken's indignation at his own plight was unmistakable. In July 1915, for instance, he wrote: "The position of Americans of German blood is intensely uncomfortable, and the chances are all that it will grow even more uncomfortable anon. They can expect no allowance from their fellow Americans of English blood for yielding to the same quite human ties and sympathies which the latter make such a boast of: they must submit as best they may to the storm of hysterical denunciation and reviling, of villainous and filthy lying, of pecksniffian and abominable moralizing which now rages."[20] More than a few local students of the "Sage of Baltimore" saw through him. In September 1914, for example, one reader wrote to the paper's editors, "Do you conscientiously think you are living up to the neutrality of the United States in hiring a press agent for the propagation of the barbaric German Empire in the person of H. L. Mencken?"[21] Another tartly referred to him as "Herr Mencken."[22]

The sarcasm was not unmerited. In October 1915 Mencken disparaged a brave British nurse named Edith Cavell who had selflessly tried to assist the wounded, regardless of their nationality. A German firing squad in Brussels summarily executed the fortynine-year-old nurse. Mencken was unmoved. The British newspapers, he wrote, "wring tears from the boobs, and Dr. Wilson is dutifully protesting to Germany." In a classic instance of whataboutism, Mencken questioned why no one had mentioned the "20,000 Boer women and children done to death in English concentration camps in South Africa?"[23]

To be a political pilgrim often involves visiting the foreign country one so admires, particularly during wartime, when it can display its mettle in combat. Over the course of the twentieth century, Russia,

Italy, Spain, China, Vietnam, Cuba, and Chile all became destinations for western intellectuals on either the right or left. Mencken was something of an innovator in this regard, visiting wartime Germany in late 1915. He departed from Hoboken, New Jersey, to Copenhagen on December 28 as a war correspondent for the *Sun* papers on the Scandinavian American steamship *Oscar II*. The idea behind the voyage, as his editors rather defensively instructed readers, was that in this instance Mencken's pro-German bias was a plus: "His great admiration for everything German will help him get the 'inside story.'" After the intrepid traveler reached Germany by crossing the Baltic Sea on an unstable railroad barge, his first stop was Berlin, where he stayed at the posh Adlon hotel near the Brandenburg Gate. On January 27, 1916, Mencken traveled to the Eastern front along the Dvina River in Lithuania, where the temperature was forty degrees below zero. Mencken, who came under fire during his five days at the front, was most impressed by the hardiness of the German troops and the excellent quality of food for the officers, noting that he enjoyed a "capital Moselle" at the Officer's Home in Novo Aleksandrovsk.[24] A five-week trip to the Austrian front was supposed to be next, but Mencken's idyll was disrupted after German chancellor Theobald von Bethmann Hollweg appeared before the Reichstag on January 31 to announce that, in an effort to break the Allied naval blockade, unrestricted submarine warfare would resume in the Atlantic.

On February 3, Wilson severed official relations with Germany and handed German ambassador Count Johann Heinrich von Bernstorff his papers. An impatient Mencken pulled strings with General Erich Ludendorff to bypass a standard eight-week cooling-off period demanded by the German authorities, embarking upon a circuitous trip back to America, where his German American chums inquired whether Kaiser Wilhelm had offered him decorations in exchange for carrying out subversive activities in America.[25] In fact, Mencken's support for Germany was all out in the open. Americans failed to comprehend, as he put it in an essay for *The Atlantic* in November 1917 about his journey, that General Ludendorff (who would march with Hitler during the Munich Beer Hall Putsch in November 1923) was the country's "national messiah."

If Mencken confined his efforts to defending Germany to print, George Sylvester Viereck did not. Few American figures were closer to the Kaiser than the peripatetic Viereck, who worked closely with the German government during the First World War to promote its propaganda. Viereck, who enjoyed consorting with the great and powerful, had a taste for self-promotion—not to mention money (he was paid a great deal by Germany). His German sympathies quickly turned him into a notorious figure, earning him the sobriquet "George Swastika Viereck" by the 1930s. And in Rachel Maddow's popular 2022 podcast, *Ultra*, Viereck served as a central figure for his conspiratorial activities on behalf of the Third Reich.

As a journalist for the Hearst papers during the 1920s, his idols were Kaiser Wilhelm and Adolf Hitler. After serving a prison sentence during World War II for his activities as a German agent—Upton Sinclair wrote him that "if there is a Benedict Arnold of this war, you are he"—Viereck became a supporter of Senator Joseph McCarthy's anti-communist crusade before dying in relative obscurity in Holyoke, Massachusetts, where his son Peter (himself a Pulitzer Prize–winning poet who wrote a popular book illuminating Nazism's debt to nineteenth-century German Romantic thought) lived.

Like Mencken, Viereck thought of himself as a conservative aristocrat, alluding regularly to his putative Hohenzollern ancestry. And like Mencken, he grew up in a home that was suffused with German culture. Viereck's father, Louis, was born out of wedlock in Berlin in 1851 and became a naturalized American citizen in 1901. He was the editor of a socialist newspaper in Munich, where his American cousin and wife, Laura, bore him a child they named George Sylvester on December 31, 1881 (in German *Silvester* means New Year's Eve). In 1884, Louis became a member of the German Reichstag, but his socialist affinities landed him in jail. At his wife's urging, the family moved to America where an eleven-year-old George Sylvester published a poem in a German paper in Baltimore hailing the anti-socialist Bismarck.

As a youth, Sylvester was mentored by the playwright William Ellery Leonard and the literary critic Ludwig Lewisohn, both boarders at his home and admirers of German culture. Viereck fondly recalled that the two slightly older men "were to me, on the slippery slopes of a new Parnassus, what Virgil was to Dante."[26] Indeed, Leonard apparently saw Viereck as a new Goethe, while Lewisohn became his lover, writing a book in 1904 entitled *George Sylvester Viereck: An Appreciation*. By the time he graduated from the City College of New York in 1906, Viereck had published a collection of plays and two volumes of German poetry. In 1908, the *Saturday Evening Post* could state that he was "unanimously accused of being a genius." That year he published *Confessions of a Barbarian*, a book that lashed into America for its defects and saluted German cultural superiority.

In 1912, he assisted Theodore Roosevelt's third-party Bull Moose run for the presidency against Woodrow Wilson and Eugene Debs. After the election, Roosevelt helped him raise money for a new publication called *The International* that sought to highlight the latest trends in German literature. It was World War I—when Viereck led what amounted to a pro-German vanguard in the pages of his new publication *The Fatherland*, a weekly newspaper produced in New York and heavily subsidized by two German agents, Dr. Heinrich Albert, a lawyer, and Dr. Bernhard Dernburg, a banker—that completed his transformation into a political operator. In New York, Albert and Dernburg created what was known as a "propaganda cabinet" that included Viereck. Between 1914 and 1916 the Germans paid about $40,000 to Viereck himself as well as an additional $100,000 for the books and pamphlets that his Fatherland Corporation printed. The weekly, which had thirty employees, also sold photographs of German military heroes.

All along Viereck tried to sow doubt about American support for Great Britain in its battle against Germany, declaring that Americans were being lied to by elites about the true nature of the conflict. He suggested that a biased press was grossly exaggerating German atrocities and failing to report the remarkable progress of the Kaiser's army in battle. Viereck also intimated that there was an inherent German racial superiority over the Anglo-Saxons. Germany represented, he said, "the best in thought and action that has been attained among men." American Brahmins? Not so much. They had elected to "dissolve their racial characteristics and ideals in a solution of colorless New England Puritanism."[27]

Viereck could tap into a large German American community. By 1914, one in five Americans were of German origin, and there were over five hundred German-language newspapers. In the November 1896 issue of *The Atlantic*, the sociologist Josiah Flynt awarded German immigrants high marks, lauding their "respect for law and order, intelligence, thoroughness, perseverance, industry, honesty, and general good health." Pro-German sentiment flourished among American academics, many of whom had studied in Germany. The renowned scholar John Burgess, who taught at Columbia University, viewed Great Britain as susceptible to despotism and Germany as a bulwark of peace and liberty in Europe. Burgess's verdict was unequivocal: "It is full of the spirit of conservatism, and well regulated by law. . . . If it needs any reform, it is in the direction of more strength than less."[28]

In August 1914, when World War I began, German Americans rallied in numerous cities across the nation to support their former homeland. Wilson issued a Proclamation of Neutrality on August 19, declaring, "We must be impartial in thought as well as in action, must put a curb upon our sentiments as well as upon every transaction that might be construed as a preference of one party to the struggle before another." Viereck and Charles J. Hexamer, the head of the National German-American Alliance, who was awarded the Order of the Eagle, Fourth Class, by Kaiser Wilhelm that same year, called for an embargo on exporting war supplies, a measure that would have helped Germany. "Although the German-Americans described their proposal as the only genuinely neutral course," wrote the historian John Higham, "Americans interpreted the agitation as an attempt to undermine the nation's cherished neutrality in the interest of a foreign power."[29]

It's difficult to arrive at the conclusion that Viereck and Co. were in any way neutral. On the contrary, in a missive to Viereck's publication, *The Fatherland*, Hexamer assailed the alleged pro-British bias of the American press, stating that he was "nauseated by the lick-spittle policy of our country, which allows England to pull our nose, slap our face, and then licks the hand that smites us."[30] Nor was this all. In May 1915, after the sinking of the *Lusitania*, Viereck was suspected of having had advance knowledge about German designs upon it. He rejected the charge but his reputation was tarnished.[31]

Worse was to come. In July, a United States Secret Service agent tailed Viereck and Dr. Albert on the Sixth Avenue El in New York. After Viereck exited the train, Albert dozed off. When the train arrived at his station, he forgot his briefcase, which contained top secret documents. "A veritable box of Pandora," said Viereck. "Albert's portfolio unloosed every half-hatched plan of the Germans. The loss of the Albert portfolio was like the loss of the Marne."[32] American officials handed over photostats of the documents to Frank I. Cobb, the editor of the *New York World*, who ran them with the headline: "How Germany Has Worked in U.S. To Shape Opinion, Block the Allies and Get Munitions for Herself, Told in Secret Agents' Letters." The paper dwelled on the letters Albert and Viereck exchanged, including the latter's importunate requests for additional funds: "Will you please O.K. this and I shall then send my secretary for cash. I am sending this letter by boy as for obvious reasons I do not wish it to go through the mails."

With the 1916 election looming, Wilson presented himself as the peace candidate. Theodore Roosevelt, who attacked Wilson as a lily-livered coward for failing to confront Germany, lost the battle for the Republican nomination to former Supreme Court Associate Justice Charles Evan Hughes. Viereck was quick to take some of the credit for the defeat of the candidate he had supported four years earlier. "ROOSEVELT BEATEN, SAY PRO-GERMANS; Metz, Viereck, and Others Are Quoted as Saying That Propagandists Killed His Chances," blared a *New York Times* headline on June 7, 1916. "I am glad of it," Viereck declared. "The German-Americans set out to beat Roosevelt for the nomination, and I don't see how anyone can blame them," he said. "He had never said or written a word against England. It is all against Germany." Viereck predicted that German American support would ensure a victory by Hughes, and rumors circulated that Hughes and the German Americans had struck a secret pact to elect him.[33] Both Wilson and Hughes claimed to oppose war and to support America First. But it was Wilson who sailed to victory on the popular campaign slogan, "He kept us out of war."

That promise wouldn't hold. As American entry into war loomed, Viereck and his confederates became increasingly vociferous. Speaking in November 1916 to the Wisconsin branch of the National German-American Alliance, for example, Charles Hexamer blustered that Germany's superior culture meant that America should defer to it: "We will not permit our kultur of two thousand years to be trodden down in this land. We can give our German kultur only to America if we stand together and conquer that dark spirit of muckerdom and prohibition just as Siegfried once slew the dragon."[34] Such language inevitably fostered suspicions about German American loyalties. The lawyer and educator Gustavus Ohlinger, in an influential and overwrought book called *Their True Faith and Allegiance*, asked, "Is Germanism to be exalted over American citizenship? Are true faith and allegiance to be forgotten? Is the more perfect union to disintegrate? Is that sun that rose in glory at Philadelphia to be eclipsed by the policies of a foreign government, to sink finally in the murky exhalations of race prejudice?"[35]

On April 3, 1917, a day before war was declared by Congress, Baltimore erupted in anti-German violence. Almost a thousand pro-war protesters targeted the pacifist David Starr Jordan, chanting, "We'll hang Dave Jordan to a sour apple tree."[36] Mencken was alarmed. "All men with names like yours and mine will be jailed before September, 1918," he wrote to a friend. "Not wishing to leave anything to chance." He did not, burying a diary and other keepsakes from his recent trip to wartime Germany in his backyard.[37]

A few weeks later, Wilson signed Executive Order 2594 creating the Committee on Public Information—America's first official propaganda agency. Wilson appointed the former muckraking journalist George Creel to head it. His mandate was to make "public opinion willing to listen and then see to it that it listens to the right things."[38] Cities and states quickly followed the punitive example of the federal government, banning German music and firing radical teachers.[39] Fiction expressed the era's paranoia. In F. Scott Fitzgerald's second novel, *The Beautiful and Damned*, Anthony Patch's enigmatic Japanese servant Tana is jokingly described as Lieutenant Tannenbaum, "a German agent kept in this country to disseminate Teutonic propaganda through Westchester County." And in Katherine Anne Porter's novella, *Pale Horse, Pale Rider,* the twenty-four-year-old protagonist Miranda is harassed by professional patriots for declining to buy a Liberty Bond: "She was hardened to stories of personal disaster, of outrageous accusations and extraordinarily bitter penalties that had grown monstrously out of incidents little more important than her failure—her refusal—to buy a Bond."

There were many Americans who forthrightly opposed the wartime xenophobia and repression on democratic or civil libertarian grounds. By contrast, Mencken and Viereck aspired to substitute the Kaiser's willful and capricious authoritarianism for Wilson's. It did not appear to occur to them that they were complaining about what they wished to impose.

The Espionage Act of 1917 provided the basis for a government raid of his Manhattan offices, and his dubious dealings were scrutinized by Alfred L. Becker, the deputy attorney general of New York State. In July 1918, Becker announced that Viereck had been sending letters in quadruplicate using a secret code to Denmark and Sweden for retransmission to Germany.[40] Soon he became persona non grata: fortified by a message from its honorary vice chairman Theodore Roosevelt—"I will be glad to have you say for me that I cordially indorse [*sic*] the request for the expulsion of George Sylvester Viereck from league membership."—the Authors' League expelled Viereck from its ranks.[41] By August, Viereck, who was living in Mount Vernon, a suburb of New York, had to flee through the rear of his home after his wife successfully diverted a mob that gathered in front of

Chapter 2

MENCKENIZED HISTORY

The bilious and cantankerous H. L. Mencken, who revered German authoritarianism and scorned American intervention in World War I and World War II, in 1949.

One of the great ironies of the post–World War I era is that the insistence of the wartime allies on forcing Germany to accept official responsibility for the war in Article 231 of the Treaty of Versailles inadvertently abetted its attempt to escape culpability for the conflict. In America, many of the liberal intellectuals and journalists, including Walter Lippmann, who had urged Wilson to wage war for democracy now reproached him for agreeing to what they contended was a Carthaginian peace. Germany wasn't being welcomed into the family of nations, but punished with demands for enormous reparations that would cripple its economy and stoke nationalist fervor. Secret treaties agreed upon during the war were now unfairly carving up central and eastern Europe. Where was the crusade for democracy and peace? What happened to the claim that only open covenants openly arrived at would be honored?

"I am one of the millions who trusted implicitly in your leadership," wrote William C. Bullitt, a staff member at the Paris Peace Conference who resigned his position, in an emotional open letter to Wilson, "and believed you would take nothing less than 'a permanent peace based on unselfish, unbiased justice.'" This moralistic repudiation of the war immeasurably assisted Republican efforts to discredit Wilson's latest crusade.

That crusade was, of course, ensuring American entry into the League of Nations. In January 1918, Wilson had delivered his Fourteen Points speech to Congress (which Lippmann had drafted) and proposed the creation of an international league to preserve the postwar peace. When the time came, Wilson ensured that the Covenant of the League formed the first part of the Treaty of Versailles. But in September 1919, Bullitt, at the urging of Lippmann, delivered bombshell testimony before the Senate, denouncing the Treaty of Versailles as a dangerous sham and underscoring the reservations that Wilson's secretary of state, Robert Lansing, harbored about it. The Senate Foreign Relations Committee chairman, Henry Cabot Lodge, a blue-blooded Republican who despised Wilson and immigration to America in equal measure, was elated. The US Senate rejected entry into the League of Nations—on the specious grounds that it would subvert American sovereignty—in November 1919 and March 1920.

The verdict was unmistakable. America would not join a global organization to help preserve peace, but instead pursue its own interests first. Wilsonian internationalism was out. Isolationism was in. Nine months later Warren G. Harding won the presidency in a landslide, partly with the help of the German American vote. George Sylvester Viereck was overjoyed: "T. Woodrow Wilson is the most humiliated President in the history of the United States."[1]

At the heart of the isolationist movement was a powerful wave of revisionism about World War I that would shape American foreign policy for several decades. It rested on a farrago of myths— Wall Street was in cahoots with munitions manufacturers; elites were spreading fake news; East Coast bankers and diplomats were scheming to enmesh America needlessly in foreign wars—that were advanced and elaborated on in essays, books, and speeches by intellectuals and politicians. Yet if anyone was scheming to influence public perceptions of the war, it was the revisionists and their allies.

The debate over the war guilt question was initially stoked by the German Foreign Office and a cadre of perfervid German nationalists. As the Yale historian Samuel Flagg Bemis observed, "Never was a campaign of historical propaganda more successful than the *Kriegsschuldfrage*," or war guilt question.[2] In a stunning turnabout, Germany, the great power responsible for World War I, exploited Western unease over the terms of the Treaty of Versailles to embark upon a fresh round of militaristic expansion. For the Nazis, as the German historian Joachim Fest observed in his remarkable memoir *Not I* (2014), the war guilt clause played a potent part in allowing them to paint the West as intent on annihilating German nationhood. In 1919, consternation among Germans over the punitive treaty, it must be remembered, was well-nigh universal, including the novelist Thomas Mann, who warned that it "prepared the path for the Slavic Mongols."[3] Mann soon became a foe of the Nazis, but they exploited the widespread animus toward what Hitler deemed the Jewish-Marxist "poisoners of our people" who had supposedly betrayed Germany during World War I and at Versailles.

In America, as the historian Selig Adler noted, the "treaty fight of 1919 began a long-lasting affinity between German racial voting blocks and isolationist senators." Those senators included George Norris, Robert La Follette, and William Borah, all of whom were leading isolationists. At the same time, organizations such as the Steuben Society and the National Historical Society subsidized and promoted revisionist books and lectures that denounced Great Britain and the war. Soon enough, American nativists and German American nationalists—including William Randolph Hearst, the Steuben Society, the Knights of Columbus, the Ku Klux Klan, and the Daughters of the American Revolution—would join forces to "purify" American history.[4]

Historical revisionism would become, and remains to this day, central to the Right's romance with foreign dictators, the supposedly rational basis for its irrational love. American intellectuals and historians nurtured the idea that America was a weary titan that should avoid enmeshing itself in remote European affairs. Revisionism initially emerged from the ranks of disillusioned Progressives, including the historians Charles Beard and Harry Elmer Barnes, but more than a few migrated from left to right. Even if they stayed put, opponents of intervention on the Left often became heroes to the Old Right. They maintained that a German dictatorship was nothing to worry about and even had some admirable qualities that America should emulate. Historians such as Sidney B. Fay of Smith College questioned the conventional wisdom that Germany had been at fault, prompting one critic of the fashionable new revisionism to bemoan the rise of "Menckenized History."[5]

An early journalistic proponent was Mencken's close friend, Albert Jay Nock. A former Episcopalian priest who abandoned his wife and children, Nock became a writer for *The Nation*, then as now an organ of the Left, before moving to the reactionary Right and serving as a mentor to the young William F. Buckley Jr. Nock, who was born on October 13, 1870, in Scranton, Pennsylvania, revered small-town America. He lived until he was ten years old in Brooklyn before moving with his parents to the upper shore of Lake Huron to a house that was forty-five miles from the nearest railway. The only means of communication with the wider world were a steamboat in summer and a stagecoach in winter. Like Mencken, Nock venerated Germans. It was the Germans, Nock wrote, who "seemed strangely above their station; above it in education, breeding, culture, views of life."[6]

In 1915, Nock traveled to England at the behest of Wilson's secretary of state, William Jennings Bryan, a fierce opponent of intervention, to assess whether State Department officials were conniving with the British to undermine Wilson's official policy of neutrality. In Oxford, Nock met a British liberal parliamentarian named Francis Neilson who explained that he had recently completed a book about the origins of the conflict. Could Nock help him get it published in America?

He could indeed. Neilson's excoriation of Europe's road to war was published by the eponymous firm B. W. Huebsch, whose proprietor looked askance at the ascription of war guilt to Germany and who issued a steady stream of revisionist books about the war. Neilson's philippic, *How Diplomats Make War*, was the first, depicting the various Foreign Offices in Europe as a power unto themselves: "The diplomatic machine, stronger by far than any military organization, did its work night and day in the Chancelleries of Europe, no matter who was Foreign Minister."[7] He engaged in special pleading for Berlin, contending that it was the policy of the Entente nations to "isolate Germany by any means and at all costs." Once war broke out, none of the great powers had clean hands, especially because Great Britain, France, and others had concluded secret treaties that came to light once the new Bolshevik regime published confidential documents relating to the war. The recent cataclysm, as the revisionists depicted it, was the product of devious elites who had misled their populations and promoted militarism.

Their case relied on exaggerating the extent to which Wilson and his advisers could control events. In their zeal to blacken Wilson's reputation, the revisionists also skated over the fact that Germany had perpetrated widespread sabotage in America—including blowing up Black Tom Island, a munitions depot in New Jersey, in July 1916—that constituted a legitimate casus belli for war. After Germany resumed unrestricted submarine warfare and plotted in January 1917 to create a military alliance with Mexico that would allow it to recover Texas, Arizona, and Mexico, Wilson had little choice but to counter its imperial aspirations. Perhaps the surprising thing is not that Wilson entered the war, but that it took him as long as it did.

The revisionist arguments contained a virulent strain of Anglophobia. For Nock, it was England, not Germany, that was the troublemaker in Europe, always meddling in Continental affairs. During the war, Nock was a freelance writer for a variety of publications, including *The Nation*, where his radical opposition to the conflict had prompted the Wilson administration to suspend the magazine's mailing privileges temporarily. Now Nock aired his views in a publication that Francis Neilson and his heiress wife, Helen, founded in 1920 and modeled on the venerable *London Spectator*. It was called *The Freeman*, and boasted a number of prominent authors, including Thomas Mann, Charles A. Beard, and Suzanne La Follette. Mencken showered Nock with plaudits for his political writings, and *The Nation* and *The New Republic* also lauded them. Nock, though, rejected the praise from those two outlets. "We hain't liberal. We loathes liberalism and loathes it hard," he wrote.[8] Like Mencken, Nock was an intellectual extremist—a Social Darwinist intent on strangling state power in the cradle.

And like Mencken, Nock viewed with antipathy what he saw as a meretricious American patriotism. In *The Freeman*, Nock conducted his own retroactive battle against the war, bewailing the iniquities that were being inflicted upon Germany by the Western allies. The title of his slender book said it all: *The Myth of a Guilty Nation* (1922). He portrayed the Teutonic threat to Europe as a hoax, one that had been concocted by warmongers intent on crushing Berlin's wholly legitimate drive for recognition and status.

Nock's defense centered on the Treaty of Versailles. He didn't simply argue that the treaty constituted diplomatic malpractice by the victors, which it did, but that it perpetrated a falsehood, which it did not. Nock claimed that British propaganda had gulled

Americans, who were innocents at home and abroad. "Few had the information necessary," he wrote, "to discount the plain, easy, understandable story of a robber nation leaping upon an unprepared and defenceless Europe for no cause whatever except the ambition, as Mr. Joseph Choate said, 'to establish a world-empire upon the ruins of the British empire.'"[9] Germany's violation in 1914 of Belgian neutrality and perpetration of atrocities were treated as a figment of the imagination. Nock knew better. The reality was that "to picture Germany and Belgium as cat and mouse, to understand the position of Belgium otherwise than that she was one of four solid allies under definite agreement worked out in complete practical detail, is sheer absurdity."[10]

After the war, Mencken, too, defended Kaiser Wilhelm. In October 1922, Mencken conducted an interview with the waspish, spindle-legged crown prince, Friedrich Wilhelm, who had recently written a book that sought to refute German war guilt called *I Am Seeking the Truth*.[11] "In such days as these, I am, first of all, a German citizen and soldier," he told Mencken. A year later Friedrich Wilhelm returned to Germany where he soon became a prominent supporter of the Nazis.

One American outlet that sympathized with Germany was an elegant new magazine with a Paris green cover, *The American Mercury*, edited by Mencken and George Jean Nathan. Mencken said the publication would be the "gaudiest and damndest ever seen in the Republic." It featured a glittering array of authors from F. Scott Fitzgerald to W. E. B. Du Bois. Published by Alfred A. Knopf, it quickly became the most prominent political and cultural magazine in America, lampooning the "booboisie," condemning Prohibition, and promoting war revisionism.

In Saul Bellow's final novel, *Ravelstein*, the narrator Chick reminisces at the outset that "among the debunkers and spoofers who formed the tastes and minds of my generation H. L. Mencken was the most prominent." Walter Lippmann, in his column in *The Saturday Review of Literature*, deemed Mencken the "most powerful influence on this whole generation of educated people."[12] In part, Lippmann was referring to Mencken the verbal matador who impaled the pieties of the society he was condemned to live in. But Lippmann also discerned a contradiction that Mencken's fireworks tended to obscure. For all his worship of the Prussian aristocracy, Lippmann noted, Mencken appeared to believe that he could have it both ways. "He seems to think," Lippmann wrote, "that you can have a privileged, ordered, aristocratic society with complete liberty of speech. That is as thorough-going a piece of Utopian sentimentalism as anything could be."

In this regard, Mencken influenced the tone and substance of the American Right. A stubbornly utopian streak, and a quest for a past that never existed, are core doctrinal elements of it. Mencken was intent on more than entertaining his audience with rollicking tales about the ineptitude of the Harding and Coolidge administrations. Mencken didn't think that the problem was that Harding and Coolidge were too conservative. It was that they weren't conservative enough. He was an ideologue who relished tilting at the Republican establishment, the poohbahs who rigged democracy on behalf of big business and pretended to espouse small government. To an astonishing degree, the sense of victimhood and aggrievement that Mencken ventilated ad nauseam became constituent elements of the Old Right.

One of the authors that Mencken published in the maiden issue of the *The American Mercury* in 1924 was the revisionist historian Harry Elmer Barnes, who morphed from a liberal supporter of Wilson to a reactionary isolationist. Barnes had ardently supported American entry into the war, writing patriotic pamphlets for organizations such as the American Defense Society and the National Security League during the conflict. Then came the aftermath. Barnes, like not a few other liberals, was incensed by what he saw as his own naïveté about the treachery of Britain and France, not to mention Wilson's ineptitude and hypocrisy. Barnes would end his career as a proponent of Holocaust denial, claiming that Allied atrocities in the Second World War vastly exceeded those of the Nazis and that Hitler was the "most reasonable" of the prewar statesmen, but it is important to remember that he was a highly influential historian through the 1930s.[13]

After traveling to Berlin in 1921, Barnes was feted by various nationalist aristocratic organizations that voiced their fury over the Treaty of Versailles. His interviews with German politicians and soldiers left him convinced that a grave injustice had been perpetrated against Germany by England, France, and America. A born controversialist, Barnes played a key role in helping to topple the standard narrative that America had been on the side of the angels during the war.

Barnes wrote a column for the Scripps-Howard newspapers, lectured around the country, and joined the executive committee of the American Civil Liberties Union. Born near Auburn, New York, on June 15, 1889, Barnes earned his Ph.D. at Columbia

University in 1918. Barnes, who visited Kaiser Wilhelm in exile in 1926, was part of the mainstream historical establishment. And he wrote several books in the 1920s that depicted Germany as the victim of allied aggression, including *The Genesis of the World War* and *In Quest of Truth and Justice*.

For Barnes, as he later explained in his atrabilious essay "Revisionism and the Historical Blackout," World War I was the turning point, the moment when America was expelled from the Garden of Eden. Before it, there had been no income tax. The national debt was trivial. The federal budget in 1913 was a mere $724,512,000—at the time he wrote his essay, it was almost $100 billion. There was no "police state." The Supreme Court interpreted the Constitution strictly. Nor was the situation that much different in Europe. England was run by the laissez-faire Liberal Party. France had created a stable Third Republic. Hohenzollern Germany had civil liberties, constitutional restraints, and a parliamentary government. Even imperial Russia was on the path to a constitutional monarchy. What was not to like? The golden age came to an end in August 1914. Barnes traced almost every contemporary affliction to the conflict: "The rise and influence of Communism, military state capitalism, the police state, and the impending doom of civilization, have been the penalty exacted for our meddling abroad in situations which did not materially affect either our security or our prestige."[14]

Barnes was hardly an isolated figure. The author of a book that Barnes hailed in 1926 as "trenchant, timely, and courageous" offers a vivid example of the popularity that revisionism enjoyed in America. Frederick Bausman, who was born on March 23, 1861, in Pittsburgh, Pennsylvania, attended Harvard Law School and served as a justice of the Supreme Court of the State of Washington. Incensed by the measures that Wilson had adopted to suppress dissent during World War I, Bausman wrote a revisionist book titled *Let France Explain* (1922). Four years later, he indited an influential and conspiratorial critique of American intervention, *Facing Europe*. Bausman also wrote on the war and American foreign policy for the Hearst press after he retired from the bench. Convinced that the wartime allies had deceived a credulous and naïve Wilson into joining their side, Bausman fell all over himself to paint Kaiser Wilhelm's Germany as an almost uniquely virtuous nation. A conservative nationalist who viewed Great Britain as a malevolent power, Bausman advanced a variety of arguments that pointed the way forward for the Right in the 1930s, including its admiration for Germany and its hostility to the liberal Eastern establishment and Wall Street bankers. Bausman may have studied law at Harvard, but he viewed the pro-war Anglophile elite in America with suspicion.

Like Nock, Bausman argued that Germany, a model of thrift, sobriety, and industry, had been encircled by a rapacious England that sought to quash it. The Prussian aristocracy, in contrast to England's, was an admirable one. Unlike the British grandees, the Prussian nobility could not afford to idle its time away on the links or indulge in "delightful weekend parties." Its stern moral code meant that Germany was "the best governed of modern states," indeed the "most dazzling state of modern times."[15]

In Bausman's view, the claim that Germany was obsessed with imperial expansion could not withstand serious scrutiny. It was, rather, a peaceful society that had annexed no territories in Europe since unification in 1870. "Let Germany desire ever so little expansion," Bausman wrote, "and the greedy, the dangerous Teuton was prowling again!" Bausman suggested that, far from being an aggressive power, Germany was a fearful one. "Vast German populations," he wrote, "can be invaded in a few hours by either France or Russia, who were known to be united by a written though unpublished alliance."[16] How much better it would have been to conciliate German fears rather than to stoke them!

Another theme that Bausman propounded was straight out of a Henry James novel: Americans were gullible romantics who had been duped by the crafty Europeans.[17] With British supremacy on the high seas posing the true threat to America, he wrote, "it is time our people have their minds recalled to the truth as to how we were beguiled into the war, how much our Allies appropriated to themselves, how they deceived us, and how they at last have become dangerous to this country which befriended them."[18] Germany had valiantly held back the Slavic hordes during the war.

Cleansing, if not purging, school textbooks of nefarious British influences became an obsession of the Right during the 1920s, one stirred up by the atrabilious newspaper mogul William Randolph Hearst, who had demanded that the US Senate reject entry into the League of Nations and placed the slogan "America First" on the front page of the *San Francisco Examiner* in 1919.[19] In 1922, Hearst editor Charles Grant Miller published a book called *Treason to the American Tradition* upbraiding American historians for colluding with the British to recolonize America intellectually. Miller complained that American history books reflected the "international mind," which was "always the British mind."[20] In 1923, he gloated that "as a result of exposures made in the Hearst newspapers there has been a clean sweep of Anglicized histories from the public that if America gets to know England was a guilty party in the causes of the World War, America no longer will fawn at her feet, as some do." In his concluding testimony, Bausman went even further. The British lion menaced America itself: "England has chosen the easiest way to conquer a country. It is not by cannon, but by propaganda. It is the first instance I have known in which a nation was so insidiously attacked."

That same month, Bausman published an essay in Mencken's *The American Mercury* portraying American elites as globalist sellouts. He condemned them for failing to pursue America's interests first. America, he wrote, was being mulcted by the very countries that entertained predatory designs upon it. "Has there ever been one in all history," he asked, "in which the class most powerful in controlling government and public opinion was determinedly bent on giving away enormous sums of the country's money to nations already heavily armed and expressing contempt for a sacrifice which they would accept only as their due?"[25] American bankers, lawyers, and journalists, he concluded, were in thrall to Great Britain, subordinating America's national interests to a foreign power. At a moment when Italy and Germany were succumbing to fascism, his doctrinaire denunciations of Great Britain as the real threat to America could hardly have been more blinkered. This jurist, who died in 1931, buttressed the arguments on behalf of Germany for an American Right that felt an instinctual kinship with a new crop of European autocrats.

As the revisionists whittled away at myths about the First World War, America's formerly self-confident claim to stand for democratic values was further sabotaged by a new sympathy for eugenics on both the left and right. Progressives and Fabian socialists had

Chapter 3

MUSSOLINI'S VICARS

Mussolini and Hitler celebrating in January 1940. Both dictators regularly wrote essays extolling the virtues of fascism for press baron William Randolph Hearst's publications.

During the early 1920s, America experienced a backlash to the massive immigration from eastern and central Europe that had occurred in recent decades. A push to restrict, if not halt, the influx of what were seen as inferior races that could dilute the American bloodstock coincided with the rise of the Ku Klux Klan, an economic recession, and the rise of fascist movements abroad, which were often seen as representing a necessary and desirable bulwark against Russian Bolshevism. Indeed, after 1919, the Red Scare morphed into a permanent campaign on the Right to ferret out domestic traitors beholden to Moscow.

As the conviction hardened that Jews and Bolsheviks were one and the same, fears of the subversion of traditional American values by immigrants from eastern and central Europe, over a million of them Jewish, became ubiquitous. "Throughout the United States," the historian Leonard Dinnerstein wrote, "there was near universal concern about Jews infiltrating cherished organizations and abodes."[1] Henry Ford published the *Protocols of the Elders of Zion* in his *Dearborn Independent* and claimed that a vast Jewish conspiracy aimed to overthrow American government. Woodrow Wilson was not only a virulent racist who resegregated the federal government, but he also expelled a number of Jewish radicals, including the anarchists Emma Goldman and Alexander Berkman, to Russia during the 1919 Red Scare on the USS *Buford*, which the press dubbed a "Soviet ark." Wilson was followed in the presidency by Warren G. Harding, a dullard who campaigned on "America First" and backed restrictions on immigration. During Harding's brief presidency (he died of a heart attack in San Francisco in 1923), Congress passed the Johnson Immigration Quota Act in May 1921, which favored northern European countries over eastern and southern Europe and established the first numerical limit on immigration in American history.

In October 1921, Harding tackled the contentious issue of race relations in America in a speech marking the semicentennial of the founding of Birmingham, Alabama.[2] After watching a parade from the balcony of the Tutwiler Hotel, Harding traveled to Woodrow Wilson Park, where he spoke at length about the "fundamental, eternal, and inescapable differences" between the races as well as the possibility of more educational opportunities for Black Americans. During his speech, Harding made a point of alluding to a new book about race that the *New York Times* editorial page said deserved "respectful consideration" and that captured the attention of many Americans, especially those who were apprehensive about immigration from eastern and central Europe. "Whoever will take the time to read and ponder Mr. Lothrop Stoddard's book on The Rising Tide of Color," Harding said, "must realize that our race problem here in the United States is a phase of a race issue that the whole world confronts."

That Harding would cite Stoddard's new book—which the Black scholar W. E. B. Du Bois dismissed as a work of "pseudo-science" in December 1921—about the dangers that foreign populations posed to the white race was one sign of the extent to which fears about what we would today call a "Great Replacement" were coming to the fore in America. Another arrived when F. Scott Fitzgerald depicted Stoddard as "Goddard" in *The Great Gatsby*, published in 1925. In part Fitzgerald was taking a swipe at his publisher, Charles Scribner. Scribner had a soft spot for white nationalist books and published Italian leader Benito Mussolini's memoir in 1928. In *The Great Gatsby*, Tom Buchanan—a former gridiron star at Yale and an inheritor of old money—announces that he's been unmoored by a new book about the decline and fall of the West. His fear of displacement from his position at the top of the WASP hierarchy could scarcely be more palpable: "Civilization's going to pieces. . . . I've gotten to be a terrible pessimist about things. Have you read 'The Rise of the Colored Empires' by this man Goddard?"

Who indeed was Goddard—that is, Stoddard? Why did both Harding and his successor, Calvin Coolidge, so admire him? A pivotal figure in mainstreaming ideas about eugenics and fascism, Theodore Lothrop Stoddard, who was born on June 29, 1883, in Brookline, Massachusetts, came from a wealthy New England family that could trace its lineage back to the seventeenth century, when the Puritans emigrated to America. His father, John Lawson Stoddard, a graduate of Williams College and Yale Divinity School, was an educator who amassed a fortune by delivering popular lectures about his journeys around the world. Indeed, in contrast to his son, John Lawson is referred to approvingly in *The Great Gatsby*; at one of Gatsby's lavish parties, Nick Carraway and Jordan Baker steal away from the festivities and enter the estate's Gothic library, where they discover a "stout middle-aged man, with enormous owl-eyed spectacles," who excitedly brandishes volume one of *John L. Stoddard's Lectures* to demonstrate that Gatsby had ensured that the shelves contained books of real substance whose pages he never cut.

A fervent admirer of German culture and Kaiser Wilhelm, Stoddard was living in Europe when the First World War erupted and he related his impressions in a missive in 1914 to the German-American Defense Committee, *The Truth About Germany and the War in Europe*. In it, he tried to awaken his countrymen to the origins of the war, lambasting Great Britain and praising Kaiser Wilhelm and the German military caste. No nation could have been more virtuous than Germany, a cultural, economic, and military powerhouse that deserved laurels for its sterling conduct rather than international odium: "If people were not blinded by envy, dazed by fear and hypnotized by the expression, 'German War Lord,' they would feel both sympathy and admiration for this magnificently disciplined and cultured nation, facing north, south, east and west, to conquer and repel its foes on land and sea!" Great Britain, he declared, may have professed high motives about freedom and liberty, but it was an imperialistic power that had gone to war for the most sordid of reasons—to crush Germany's economic prowess and to preserve its own trade supremacy. To add insult to injury, France and Great Britain were enabling a despotic, semi-barbaric Russia to enact its "cherished plan of making a Slavic onslaught on the Teuton." In his 1916 pamphlet, *A Letter to a Wilsonite*, he observed that much immigration into America in recent years had been Latin or Slav in origin, but that "the Teutonic race constitutes one of the most valuable elements in the population of our country."

Lothrop gave Papa's enthusiasm for all things Teutonic a much darker twist. He embraced eugenics and the Nazi regime, while warning against the West's "race suicide." It was imperative to elevate birth over merit to preserve and protect America's natural racial aristocracy.[3] In 1914, Stoddard earned a Ph.D. in history at Harvard, whose president emeritus, Charles William Eliot, had declared two years earlier at a meeting of the Harvard Club in San Francisco that "each nation should keep its stock pure. There should be no mixing of the races."[4] Stoddard fit right in. He studied under the supervision of another New Englander, Archibald Cary Coolidge, who was the first editor of *Foreign Affairs*. Stoddard became convinced that he was making great discoveries about the importance of race to the future of Western civilization. A fellow graduate student, Dexter Perkins, recalled in his memoirs that Stoddard was "the most conceited man I ever knew." Perkins recounted that Stoddard was dumbfounded when anyone dared contradict him at Harvard and that when they met up in Paris, where both were working on their respective dissertations, Stoddard would read out sections after dinner aloud and periodically proclaim, "Isn't that wonderful? Isn't it perfect?"[5]

Stoddard's patrician arrogance fueled his white supremacism. With his illustrious family background and degrees from Harvard, he thought of himself as belonging to a superior Nordic caste. An energetic publicist, he quickly turned his dissertation into a book called *The French Revolution in San Domingo*. It examined the battle between the Haitian slaves, who revolted in the 1790s, and their French overlords. This historical episode led directly to what Stoddard called "the extermination of the white race" in Haiti.[6] Stoddard's point was clear: a successful and sanguinary Black uprising against white dominance had occurred—and it could occur again.

Stoddard was influenced by the racial theories of the nineteenth-century French aristocrat Arthur de Gobineau, who claimed that the Nordic and Aryan races were inherently superior to any others, and of the British German philosopher Houston Stewart Chamberlain, whose murky writings helped shape Hitler's thinking. A member of the American Historical Association and president of the Boston Loyal Coalition, Stoddard was part of a wider group of establishment figures that propounded eugenics theory, including Henry Fairfield Osborn, the president of the American Museum of Natural History, and Ellsworth Huntington, a geographer at Yale and author of *The Character of the Races*. Stoddard wrote numerous books explicating his belief in a racial competition between whites and the rest of the world. After *Hearst's International* revealed in 1923 that he also served as a secret adviser to the Ku Klux Klan, Stoddard responded that the magazine was a "radical-Jew outfit."[7]

The introduction to Stoddard's *Rising Tide* was written by a chilly New York patrician named Madison Grant. Grant was the author of a formative book on race and eugenics that appeared in 1916, *The Passing of the Great Race; Or, the Racial Basis of European History*. Grant resided in a palatial Fifth Avenue mansion and breathed contempt for inferior breeds. A graduate of Yale, a member of Theodore Roosevelt's Boone and Crockett Club, a founder of the Bronx Zoo, a director of the American Eugenics Society, and a vice-president of the Immigration Restriction League, he had imbibed the race theories of European thinkers such as Gustave Le Bon and Gobineau. Grant believed that the notion that America should be a multiethnic democracy was bunk. He observed that "it would be in a democracy, a virtual impossibility to limit by law the right to breed to a privileged and chosen few." His studies led him to conclude that geography was destiny—new immigrants from southern Europe could not be successfully assimilated into American society, a conclusion that was shared by politicians such as Senator Henry Cabot Lodge, who had contended in an 1896 essay called "The Problem of Immigration" that a flood of "low, unskilled, ignorant foreign labor" was suppressing wages for the average workingman. But what this Boston Brahmin really objected to was an increase in "races most alien to the body of the American people from the lowest and most illiterate classes among those races."

Grant's big revelation was that no less than three distinct groups of Europeans existed: Nordics, Alpines, and Mediterraneans. He viewed Nordics as "the Master Race," reviled Jews, and endorsed sterilizing "weaklings" and "worthless race types." In a new edition of his book published in 1918, he went out of his way to exempt Nordics from culpability for Germany's bellicose conduct during the Great War. Instead, it was "an expression of a population that was not Nordic at all or even Teutonic, but 'very largely Alpine.' "[8] His findings were frequently cited in congressional committee hearings during the early 1920s on immigration restrictions.[9] Hitler called it "my bible." When Ostara Publications, a white nationalist publishing house, exhumed Grant's lucubrations a century later, it hailed them as a "call to American whites to counter the dangers from both non-white and non-north Western European immigration."

Stoddard captured public attention with his claim that the fratricidal strife the Nordic countries engaged in during World War I had opened the door to a revolt against the white West. "White solidarity was riven and shattered," Stoddard wrote. "And fear of white power and respect for white civilization together dropped away like garments outworn." The worst thing about the war was that it had consumed the best and brightest white men. The flower of Western civilization could not be easily replaced, if ever. According to Stoddard, "the war bore heavily on all white race-stocks, but it was the Nordics—the best of all human breeds—who suffered far and away the greatest losses."[10]

Stoddard viewed global affairs through a racial prism. On May 30, 1920, the *Washington Times* ran a full-page excerpt of Stoddard's book under the headline, "Japan's Aim a Race Control to Rule World, Says High Authority; U.S. First Mark." For good measure, the paper included a map prepared by Stoddard illustrating the "Yellow, Brown, Black, and Red races" as a stain spreading across the globe. Stoddard's message attracted attention abroad, too. "The moral of such a book as that Mr. Lothrop Stoddard has written," the *London Daily Telegraph* wrote, "is that, so far from making things easy for the brown and yellow races, we should, on the contrary, protect ourselves against possible incursion."[11] Stoddard's book was a standard text for officers at the US Army War College into the 1930s.[12]

In *The Revolt Against Civilization* (1922) Stoddard explained just how Americans could protect themselves against the "Under-man." His book received a rave review from Harvard psychologist William McDougall, whose bigoted *The Group Mind* (1920) had stated that the "negro" race was incapable of producing "any individuals of really high mental and moral endowments." A year later, McDougall published *Is America Safe for Democracy?*, in which he depicted America as headed for precipitous decline unless it adopted a eugenics program, an idea Stoddard drew upon for *The Revolt Against Civilization*.[13] In it, Stoddard depicted Bolshevism (synonymous with Jews) as representing the threat of a racially inferior Slavic invasion and called for the creation of a "neo-aristocracy" that could keep the "Under-man" in check. Stoddard broached "a system of hardened segregation, the banning of mixed marriages, limited communal rights in political matters, and the separate development for blacks in the south" in a 1922 interview.[14] The idea of an *Untermensch*, or Under-man, was picked up by Hitler and became a mainstay of Nazi racial doctrine.

Grant and Stoddard's proselytizing about inferior races and immigration restrictions played a key role in preparing the ground for the passage in 1924 by Congress of the racist and discriminatory Johnson-Reed Act, which included the Asian Exclusion Act and

National Origins Act. It targeted immigration from southeastern Europe as well as from Asia. "America must remain American," President Coolidge declared when he signed it into law. Republican senator David A. Reed said that the act would ensure that the "racial composition of America at the present is made permanent." The *Los Angeles Times* stated on April 13, 1924, that a "Nordic Victory Is Seen in Drastic Reduction."

Stoddard battled the German Jewish immigrant and Columbia University professor Franz Boas, the founder of modern anthropology. A brilliant scholar who was featured on the cover of *Time* in 1936 for his pioneering work and opposition to Nazi Germany's bogus racial science, Boas had nothing but contempt for Stoddard's piffle about a Nordic race, debunking his book, *The Rising Tide of Color*, when it appeared in 1920. Boas scoffed at the term "race" as a modern invention that bore no relation to reality, dismissed the pertinence of IQ tests, and argued that environment and experience were key in determining an individual's prospects. Appearing before the House Committee on Immigration and Naturalization in 1924, Stoddard asserted that Boas's denials of profound racial differences between immigrants and old-stock Americans represented the "desperate attempt of a Jew to pass himself off as 'white.'"[15]

Others also attacked Stoddard. "NORDIC SUPERIORITY IS CALLED A MYTH," ran a *New York Times* headline on January 11, 1926. The *Times* reported that Stoddard's views, which had been "warmly controverted" at a meeting of the Foreign Policy Association at the Hotel Astor, came under fire at another event in Manhattan that featured John Langdon-Davies, a journalist and member of the British Labour party, who had written a book a year earlier, *The New Age of Faith*, condemning Grant and Stoddard as "race fiends." He stressed, like Boas, the significance of environmental factors as opposed to biological ones. "All the superiorities or inferiorities which some people, such as Mr. Stoddard, attribute to race are really attributable to a good or bad education or environment," he said. "If Lothrop Stoddard had been adopted by a negro at 2 years of age he would not be able to drive a car, wear a tuxedo or talk about the new scientific realism." That "scientific realism" was neither scientific nor realistic; rather, it offered a spurious biological cloak to legitimize nasty prejudices against immigrants. Perhaps Stoddard's greatest setback came when he debated the Black educator and writer W. E. B. Du Bois in March 1929 in Chicago on the topic "Shall the Negro Be Encouraged to Seek Cultural Equality?" Du Bois wiped the floor with him—and Stoddard refused to debate him again.[16]

If Fitzgerald, Du Bois, and Boas viewed Stoddard as a huckster, another writer from New England, H. P. Lovecraft, more than shared his views about the merits of Nordicism and the dangers immigration posed to the Anglo-Saxon stock. In 1915, Lovecraft began publishing a little magazine called *The Conservative* that espoused monarchy over modern democracy, among other things. An anti-Semite and a racist, Lovecraft loathed southern and east European immigrants, whom he described as "squat yellow Mongoloids."[17] For Lovecraft, Stoddard, and other intellectuals, Benito Mussolini—the first European fascist leader to seize power—emerged as an object of admiration and even a standard-bearer.

Mussolini, who began his career as a left-wing journalist,

founded the National Fascist Party in 1921, capitalizing on Italy's internal political turmoil and sense of aggrievement over the Treaty of Versailles to lead a revolution that he claimed would liberate his nation from the great powers.[18] In October 1922, Mussolini led his infamous March on Rome and the Italian King Victor Emmanuel II appointed him prime minister. Three years later, after his *squadristi* murdered the Socialist opposition leader Giacomo Matteotti, Mussolini consolidated power, promulgating the new Laws for the Defense of the State that turned him into a full-fledged dictator. J. P. Morgan partner Thomas Lamont arranged for a $100 million loan from the American government to Mussolini's regime. "Implicitly sanctioning Mussolini's power grab," wrote the historian Ruth Ben-Ghiat, "the act started a century of US support for right-wing authoritarian leaders."[19]

Initially, Mussolini's apparent dynamism appealed to a wide swath of Americans. But the greatest and most lasting fervor for Mussolini emanated from the American Right, which lauded him for dispensing with democracy to defend traditional religion and family values. In their hearts, they knew he was right.

Mussolini may not have been entirely welcome on American shores had he failed to present himself as a defender of whites: "In the propaganda it disseminated abroad, Italy presented the global public with a bundle of measures aimed at saving not only Italians, but the entire 'white race,' as Mussolini confidently proclaimed."[20] Mussolini and his followers were intent on creating an *uomo nuovo*, or "New Man," that would result in a racially pure and hierarchical society. Slavs, homosexuals, criminals, and Jews were to be extruded from it. The popular belief that Mussolini was largely free of the racial fanaticism of the Nazis is a fable. Instead,

Mussolini's early efforts to establish a new warrior society were eagerly followed by Hitler and his camarilla.

Mussolini's bombast elicited a good deal of admiration in America, too. The American Legion, a veterans' organization founded in 1919 that strictly limited membership of Black veterans, viewed the Italian war veterans who backed Mussolini's March on Rome in October 1922 as ideological brethren. To those on the Right who longed for decisive measures rooted in mass action, Mussolini's Fascist movement seemed to demonstrate that a traditional nation-state could indeed be defended against the globalists. One such figure was American Legion National Commander Alvin Owsley who portrayed Italy as a role model for America and invited Il Duce to attend the San Francisco Legionnaire convention. Owsley declared, "If ever needed, the American Legion stands ready to protect our country's institutions and ideals as the Fascisti dealt with the destructionists who menaced Italy."[21]

Another group of Mussolini idolators, as the historian John Patrick Diggins noted, was more highbrow. It consisted of intellectuals and politicians who admired his readiness to crack down on Communists, including the Harvard scholar of French literature Irving Babbitt, who, together with Paul Elmer More, founded the intellectual movement known as the New Humanism. An admirer of the English politician and philosopher Edmund Burke and a mentor to T. S. Eliot, Babbitt influenced conservative thought in the interwar era through his calls for an ethical elite, an aristocracy of "intelligence and character" that would distinguish his disciples from the merchant class. The New Humanists blanched at the notion of equality among men, which they believed would only produce an equality of mediocrity rather than merit. It was imperative to exercise moral self-restraint, to emphasize the Apollonian, not the Dionysian, side of human nature. Along with this credo ran a deep skepticism about democracy for its leveling tendencies. In some ways, it appealed to Old Right figures, including Albert Jay Nock. Nock and the Humanists were dismayed by what they saw as "contemporary society's lowly acquisitive aspirations and by an educational system bent on training at the expense of knowledge."[22] Decades later, the conservative political theorist Russell Kirk mourned that Babbitt's hard truths were being ignored and that whether "some humane restoration can be worked may depend upon the existence of a remnant which can understand Babbitt's sentences and endeavor to clothe them with flesh."[23] But it was also the case that Babbitt and others exhibited what the literary critic Allen Tate termed "a kind of moral fascism" in their emphasis on a powerful external authority.[24]

In *Democracy and Leadership* (1924), a classic text on the Right, Babbitt stated that eventually "the growth of a false liberalism" might mean that "a predominant element of our population, having grown more and more impatient of the ballot box and representative government, will display a growing eagerness for 'direct action.' "[25] Babbitt abandoned scholarly detachment to float what amounted to a no-enemies-to-the-right doctrine: "Circumstances may arrive when we may esteem ourselves fortunate if we get the American equivalent of a Mussolini; he may be needed to save us from the American equivalent of a Lenin."[26] What those "circumstances" might be and how they reflected a humanistic spirit he did not specify.

Exceeding Babbitt in his sympathy for fascism was the poet Ezra Pound. Pound moved from populist nostalgia to endorsing fascism, leaving America in 1924 for Italy, where he indulged in abstruse meditations about usury. He saw democracy as a hoax, writing "It's so much waste of time to speak of this or that 'democracy.' The real government was, and is, to be found behind the scenes."[27] Like not a few American fascists, he was an anti-Semite, condemning "Jewspapers" in the notorious World War II radio broadcasts that ended up getting him convicted for treason.

Perhaps the most effective promoter of Mussolini in America was the Republican operative and diplomat Richard Washburn Child. Many of the themes that Child advanced would be sounded by conservative admirers of Hitler in the 1930s. Like Stoddard, Lodge, and others, he was a New Englander who abhorred the social transformation of America. Child, who was born in 1881 in Worcester, Massachusetts, earned an undergraduate degree from Harvard in 1903 and a law degree from the same institution three years later. He established a law office in Boston, but his true passions lay elsewhere. In 1912, he began writing for Collier's and working for the Progressive Party in Massachusetts. He became friendly with Theodore Roosevelt and was drawn to his advocacy of the strenuous life. Child's next hero was Mussolini, whom he also viewed as personifying virile masculinity.

In 1921, after Child served on his presidential campaign as a speechwriter, Harding appointed him ambassador to Italy, where he witnessed the March on Rome. An elated Child drove around the city in search of violent battles between Blackshirts and Communists, deeming Mussolini's fighters the new Spartans. He made it clear to Mussolini that the US government would not impede his power grab and ascension to the post of prime minister. "His analysis of the fascist movement," wrote the historian Katy Hull, "and the new Italian prime minister contributed to Washington's positive reception of Mussolini."[28]

In September 1923 the Italo-American Association held a banquet in Rome for Child, which Mussolini himself attended. Child thanked him for providing "an example of courageous national organization founded upon the disciplined responsibility of the individual to the State." Mussolini, in turn, was pleased by Child's efforts to buff his image in America. Indeed, Mussolini, a former journalist, was a careful steward of his public reputation, granting numerous interviews to businessmen, reporters, and statesmen.

After his tour as ambassador ended in 1924, Child wrote numerous articles about Fascist Italy for the *Saturday Evening Post*, a redoubt of conservative family values. His essays about the decline of those values in America during the Roaring Twenties emphasized Italy's attempts to promote the family and religion.[29] In 1925, in his memoir, *A Diplomat Looks at Europe*, Child extolled Mussolini for disposing of Italy's "flabby democracy."[30] The *Philadelphia Inquirer*'s review of it was titled "Richard Child's Good Opinion of Mussolini."[31] In 1928, he also wrote the foreword to the American edition of Mussolini's autobiography. His likening of Mussolini to Napoleon and Tolstoy prompted an acerbic reviewer in the *Des Moines Register* to refer to Child as "Mussolini's vicar in America."[32]

In his hymns to Mussolini, the vicar presented the dictator not only as an administrative whiz but also as a deeply spiritual person. Mussolini, he wrote, was an "unparalleled leader," an "unselfish and loyal priest" urging his nation to embrace the higher cause of fascism, a valiant effort that could only be undone by an unfaithful laity.[33] The editors of the *Saturday Evening Post*, too, depicted

Signor Benito as an admirable fellow—"Old-Fashioned and Eternal."[34] Mussolini's Italy was a model of hard-working efficiency that, in stark contrast to hedonistic America, cherished manliness.

As part of his push for "family values," Mussolini sought to raise Italy's birthrate. Il Duce was following the example of the Roman emperor Augustus who in 18 B.C. introduced the *lex Julia maritandis ordinibus*—a law that senators had to be married and seek to produce three or more children. In a speech on May 28, 1927, in the Chamber of Deputies that attracted international attention, Mussolini announced that "the fact remains that the fate of nations is intimately bound up with their powers of reproduction."[35] Italy's imperial aspirations, he said, hinged on increasing its population size from forty million to sixty million by 1950. He told the assembled deputies that he had introduced a special tax on bachelors to "give the nation the demographic lash of the whip." He concluded by asserting that "this State is composed of a concentrated, organized, authoritative democracy." Mussolini, who had hollowed out Italian democracy, claimed to embody it, the first in a line of authoritarians who would allege that they, not the defenders of liberalism, were the true democrats as they represented the will of the people.

Lothrop Stoddard saw it the same way. That fall he published an essay in *Harper's Magazine* called "Realism: The True Challenge of Fascism."[36] To flip through the issue today is to recognize the stature Stoddard had attained as an authority on current affairs. Other contributors included James Rowland Angell, the president of Yale University, and Lewis Mumford, the renowned sociologist and literary critic.

Stoddard's essay was pitched perfectly—written in bland and soothing tones, as though the author were a detached observer who was merely explicating rather than endorsing the phenomenon of fascism. Stoddard acknowledged that many Americans might labor under the misapprehension that the Italian Fascisti and Mussolini were uncouth roughnecks, or worse. But there was more to it than that. Fascism, he said, posed a legitimate intellectual challenge to American democracy that should be confronted rather than wished away.

One virtue of Fascist thought, after all, was that it dispensed from the outset with much of the sentimentality and worship of empty phrases that tended to permeate discussions of domestic and foreign affairs in America. Terms such as democracy, liberty, equality, inalienable rights, and parliamentary government might sound lofty and important and worthy, but upon closer inspection they amounted to very little indeed. "Yet there they sit," wrote Stoddard, "like Gods in a heathen temple, paralyzing the creative thought and energy of mankind! Before them we meekly lay our problems." Popular government had come to be seen as a panacea for political woes, when it was in fact the cause of them.

Exporting the Anglo-Saxon model of government to the rest of the world, Stoddard suggested, was no solution. Exhibit A was Italy. Its parliamentary government had been hijacked by a political caste that did nothing but temporize and enrich itself. It was the Fascists who had established order and progress by overthrowing the old regime. Every nation faced a Darwinian struggle for survival. In Stoddard's view of Italy, "their dictatorship must continue, not only in order to imbue the Italian people with the Fascist philosophy but also because the post-war world is such a dangerous place and Italy is so badly situated therein that only a strong, patriotic regime can put Italy where she belongs or even save her from disaster."

Stoddard was careful to stipulate that he was not trying to determine "whether the Fascists are right or wrong in their particular diagnosis of Italian politics," but he did state that the contention that the remedy for the shortcomings of any democracy was more democracy was preposterous. He aired several arguments that would become favorite talking points for the Right in succeeding decades.

"Why should we assume that what is politically good for us," he asked, "is necessarily good for everyone else? May not the truth be that the world is big enough for several distinct types of government, suited to the respective temperaments and capacities of the various human groups?" He retreated to his racial diagnosis. It was only the peoples of northern European stock who demonstrated an instinctive tendency toward democratic self-government. Other countries required a more hierarchical state. The blunt fact was that as modern science had demonstrated, "men are not created equal" and can only rise according to their inherited abilities. In the end, fascism, however nasty it might appear, had a "distinct tonic value."

With the crash of the stock market and the beginning of the Great Depression in October 1929, democracy in America came into disrepute. If the Left could look to the Soviet Union as a beacon, the Western Right looked to Italy, Nazi Germany, and fascist Spain. In England, Oswald Mosley's British Union of Fascists sought to replicate Mussolini's rise to power. In the US, Senator David A. Reed, the co-sponsor of the 1924 Immigration Act and a member of the advisory council of the American Liberty League, declared on the Senate floor on July 1, 1932, "I do not often envy other countries and their governments, but I say that if this country ever needed a Mussolini, it needs one now."

Chapter 4

AN INTELLIGENT FASCISM

The popular conspiracy theorist Elizabeth Dilling,
hailed in Germany as the "female Führer," appears before
Congress in January 1939 to accuse Franklin and Eleanor
Roosevelt of abetting communism in America.

In America, the political Right was aghast at the election of
Franklin D. Roosevelt to the presidency in 1932. In their quest
to restore the old order, conservative elites embarked upon what
amounted to a war against Roosevelt, one that included books with
titles like *The Menace of Roosevelt and His Policies* by Howard E.
Kershner, as well as a Business Plot by industrialists and bankers
who founded the American Liberty League to plan a coup attempt
in 1933.[1] Many of Roosevelt's foes attacked him as an American
Caesar when it came to domestic affairs, either likening him to

Hitler or professing to their own attraction to fascist strongmen abroad.

It was H. L. Mencken who fired the first salvos. When Mencken attended the 1932 Democratic National Convention, he hoped that his close friend Albert C. Ritchie, the governor of Maryland, would win the nomination. "It would be hard to find a delegate," he wrote, "who believes seriously that Roosevelt can carry New York in November, or Massachusetts, or New Jersey, or even Illinois."[2] After Roosevelt secured the nomination, Mencken reluctantly voted for him; he viewed the incumbent, Republican Herbert Hoover, as a statist who stood for high tariffs and a government alliance with big business. Mencken was a radical libertarian at a time before the parties had sorted themselves ideologically. Despite his hatred of the mob, he was, as far as he had any political home, a Democrat who felt closest to the southern Bourbon wing of the party, which was represented by reactionaries such as Ritchie.[3] Ritchie decried the New Deal, declaring that "American self-government is being destroyed before our eyes."[4]

On December 8, 1934, when he attended the semiannual stag dinner at the Gridiron Club in the grand banquet room of Washington's Willard Hotel, Mencken met Roosevelt, who bathed him with what Mencken referred to as his "Christian Science smile." Mencken delivered the opening "loyal opposition" speech but pulled his punch. Roosevelt did not. He began by praising Mencken for the "temperateness of his remarks and criticisms" before excoriating him and the assembled press corps for their pathetic ignorance—by drawing on quotations from Mencken's own column a decade earlier, "Journalism in America," that described the "stupidity, cowardice and Philistinism of the working newspapermen." As he listened, it began to dawn upon Mencken that Roosevelt represented a far more cunning adversary than he had realized. "I'll get the son of a bitch. I'll dig the skeletons out of his closet" he said to Ritchie. By the end of 1935, Mencken was regularly lacing into "Dr. Roosevelt," much as he had "Dr. Wilson." With his vituperative tone and scorn for democracy, Mencken helped stoke the simmering hatred of Roosevelt on the Right.

Mencken, in fact, had already been noodling around with Nazi and Fascist doctrine, which he thought had some appealing features, at least when contrasted with Roosevelt's New Deal. "The more he reflected upon the Fascist experiment," wrote his biographer Edgar Kemler, "the more he believed that Fascism, for better or for worse, had a promising future in the Western world, and that an 'intelligent Fascism' operated by incorruptible naval officers might be just the thing for America."[5] He wasn't the only one to view that future as a promising one.

Enter Lawrence Dennis. Dennis was a former State Department official and Wall Street analyst, a contributor to *The American Mercury*, an adviser to Charles Lindbergh and the America First Committee, and a foe of Franklin Roosevelt. Hitler, he once said, was "not only the greatest political genius since Napoleon but also the most rational."[6]

In 1939, Ezra Pound urged Americans to read Dennis's works. In 1941, he was dubbed "America's No. 1 intellectual fascist" by *Life* magazine, which had previously run a photo of Dennis standing next to a uniformed Nazi in Nuremberg. The British historian E. H. Carr called Dennis "that rare phenomenon—an American critic of democracy." Less benign was the assessment of Roosevelt's secretary of the interior, Harold Ickes, who termed him the "brains" of American fascism. The brains of American fascism also happened to be something else—a man of mixed-race background who as a teenager began passing as white.

Lonnie Lawrence Dennis, who was born in Atlanta, Georgia, on December 25, 1893, earned fame for his eloquence as a child, preaching the gospel not only in America, but also in Europe.[7] "Already displaying the disdain for the masses that during his adulthood caused him to dismiss legions as being simply 'dumb,'" his biographer Gerald Horne wrote, "he referred to those assembled as 'goats' and 'hellhounds.'"[8] As a youth Dennis reinvented himself. He attended Phillips Exeter Academy, which seems not to have realized that he was Black, then entered Harvard in 1915. He volunteered for military service in 1917 and served in France, commanding a company of military police. There he became acquainted with a variety of prominent members of the Eastern establishment, including Archibald Roosevelt (Theodore Roosevelt's fifth son), Hamilton "Ham" Coolidge (the great-great-grandson of Thomas Jefferson), and Joseph P. Kennedy (future father of John F. Kennedy). Upon graduating in 1920, Dennis entered the US diplomatic service. He wanted a taste of action, and got it in 1925 in Honduras, where he was chargé d'affaires at Tegucigalpa and called in the US Marines to install Miguel Paz Barahona as Honduras's new president. "The Honduran house has now been swept, dusted, tidied," *Time* reported.[9] His next posting was Nicaragua, where Dennis pushed General Emiliano Chamorro Vargas to yield power to a provisional government.[10] As Dennis put it, the conservative Adolfo Díaz, who became president, "represents the strong man, the man of character and solid experience that Nicaragua needs for the execution of its patriotic ends."[11] Dennis never lost his admiration for the strongman.

But Dennis did harbor doubts about the efficacy of American intervention in the region and he created a furor with a fusillade of charges about the inner workings of the State Department. "Wealth and politics," he said, were key to promotion in the diplomatic service, not to mention "English mannerisms" and "supercilious affectations."[12] In 1927 he resigned from the State Department. In an essay in *Foreign Affairs* titled "Recognition, Revolution and Intervention," Dennis questioned Washington's propensity for embarking upon regime change in Latin America. He suggested that it was misusing international law to act imperialistically along the practiced lines of Great Britain. "Whenever the American representative mentions to the head of a de facto government," he wrote, "a number of things which the United States government desires, and intimates that compliance with these wishes might help along recognition, the United States is using *Machtpolitik* or economic imperialism in a very overt manner."[13] In its eagerness to install new regimes, he wrote, Washington was chasing a will-o'-the-wisp of constitutionalism and order. How much wiser it would be to refrain from attempting to supervise free and fair elections at the point of a gun! The truth was that nations did not require democracy to flourish economically. So why bother to try and assume the white man's burden in Central and Latin America?

He provided a paradigmatic statement of the political Right's indifference to liberal democracy in countries that were, in his estimation, transparently unsuited for it. The language was more abstract than Lothrop Stoddard's about Italy, but the sentiments were not dissimilar: "It is no criticism of our gallant missionaries of order and fair elections to reiterate that self-government, like every other art, must be learned by practice, by trial and error— not absorbed from foreigners in control of certain vital government functions."[14] The United States was wasting its resources in Central America. Unlike England, it had no surplus population to export and was economically self-sufficient. "We may well stop and consider," he wrote, "whether our highest destiny lies in assimilating the Mediterranean, Negro and Indian races and cultures found in the republics immediately to the south of us."[15]

During the 1920s and 1930s, as during World War I, many Americans leveled critiques of intervention abroad on democratic or pacificist grounds. But in another echo of wartime, others censured American intervention out of an antipathy toward democracy. In Dennis's case, disillusionment didn't prompt him to move to the radical left but to the fascist right. With his acute social and political antennae, he sensed that the Right offered the more exciting opportunities. And with his contrarian instincts, he found a home on the Right, or at least as far as someone referred to by the New York Times as "deeply bronzed" with "bristly hair" could.

In 1933, the year Hitler came to power, Dennis joined a fortnightly journal called The Awakener („Deutschland, erwache!" or "Germany, awake!" was a Nazi party slogan) as an associate editor. It was Dennis's first ceremonial step into the ranks of the American fascists. His fellow associate editor was Allen A. Zoll, who founded American Patriots, Inc., and organized the picketing in 1939 of the New York radio station WMCA after it banished the fascist Father Charles Coughlin from the air. The journal, which was regularly praised several times by the Nazi propaganda outlet World Service, saw itself as "a national organ of uncensored opinion." It was founded by one Harold Lord Varney, the managing director of the Italian Historical Society, a front group for Mussolini's Fascist regime. Varney, who would later write for the John Birch Society's magazine *American Opinion*, installed Joseph P. Kamp as executive editor. Kamp, whose parents had emigrated from Germany to America, was one of the leading anti-Semitic agitators on the Right; his pamphlets for the Constitutional Educational League were distributed at the German Bund's Madison Square Garden rally in 1939.[16]

Dennis's oratorical prowess rendered him a potent antagonist of the American Communist Party. On March 4, 1934, before an audience of 3,000 at the Mecca Temple in Manhattan, Dennis debated Clarence A. Hathaway, editor of the party's newspaper the *Daily Worker*, about whether communism or fascism should supplant capitalism. Each agreed that capitalism was doomed. But Dennis argued that Americans were "conditioned" against communism and that only fascism would create a state ruled for "the greatest good of the greatest number."[17] His enthusiasm for fascism reached a much larger audience a year later when Dennis participated in a debate, "Which Way America: Fascism, Communism, Socialism or Democracy?," at Manhattan's Town Hall that was broadcast by NBC in May 1935 for its new radio show *America's Town Meeting of the Air*. Dennis didn't speak obliquely or euphemistically about his enthusiasm for fascism. "I consider Senator [Huey] Long, Father Coughlin and other champions of the discontent of people as precursors of fascism," he said. "I salute Senator Long, Father Coughlin and a great many other honest leaders."[18]

In 1936 Dennis published a new book, *The Coming American Fascism*. In it, he dismissed capitalism as a failed relic of the past and condemned liberalism, asserting that fascism reflected the popular will better "than a weak liberal State, because the powerful State can do more than the weak State to shape social events of importance, and also chiefly because the powerful State can make the people genuinely like or assent to what it does."[19] Perhaps it should come as no surprise, then, that he lauded Mussolini and Hitler for addressing the economic problems that assailed capitalism in a responsible and effective manner that America should duplicate. As a reviewer of Dennis's book in the *New York Times* put it: "What it really implies is irresponsible power, exercised by those who now exercise power but with no checks and balances to restrain their insolence."[20]

His status as the leading fascist intellectual in America earned him an effusive welcome in the summer of 1936 in Italy and Nazi Germany. Dennis met Mussolini in Rome, where he enjoyed the use of an official car. He was also treated like a dignitary when he next traveled to Berlin, where he stayed at the Central Hotel and spoke with a variety of Nazi officials, including propaganda minister Joseph Goebbels ("something of an intellectual") and deputy Führer Rudolf Hess ("a man of considerable learning"). After attending the Nuremberg Nazi Party rally in September, he returned to America, where he met with George Sylvester Viereck and Heribert von Strempel to discuss future activities on behalf of Nazi Germany, including lectures and publications. To all intents and purposes, he was functioning as a Nazi agent.[21]

Dennis's movements attracted the attention of the FBI. A former fiancée reported that when she accompanied Dennis to a movie theater and a newsreel flashed a picture of the Führer, he would stand up and salute, "Heil Hitler."[22] His worship of strongmen was also evident in his book *The Dynamics of War and Revolution* (1940). He contended that "the people can rule with rationality and success only through a single leader, party and governing agency."[23] It would require a fascist elite—presumably with him as its intellectual guru—to rescue America from the Roosevelt administration and its headlong rush to war.

———

Dennis may have been America's premier intellectual fascist, but its leading anti-communist was a religious zealot from Chicago named Elizabeth Dilling. Like Dennis, Dilling was an enthusiastic collaborator of the anti-Semitic activist Joseph Kamp, recounting in May 1940 that "I enjoyed a data collecting, gabfesting expedition with my friend Joseph Kamp, head of the Constitutional Educational League. He constantly puts out fiery releases and has written the finest, most telling pamphlets."[24] In his dystopian 1935 novel *It Can't Happen Here*, Sinclair Lewis based Adelaide Tarr Gimmitch, a conservative activist who opposes women's suffrage and supports dictatorship, on Dilling. After Dilling self-published a book titled *The Red Network: A '"Who's Who" and Handbook of Radicalism for Patriots* in 1934—it was dedicated to "those sincere fighters for American liberty and Christian principles"—she barnstormed around the country, delivering lectures about the New Deal and communist subversion (which she viewed as one and the same) and compiled thousands of file cards on individuals she suspected of treachery to America. She established a wide variety of contacts with Far-Right figures, spoke at German American Bund rallies, and headed a nationwide Mothers' movement to stymie military and economic aid to Great Britain. In 2017, the *Daily Beast* aptly described her as "The 1930s' Steve Bannon."[25]

Dilling, who was born on April 19, 1894, in Chicago into a prosperous family, briefly studied the harp and foreign languages at the University of Chicago. During a trip to the Soviet Union in 1931 with her husband Albert Wallwick Dilling, she was shocked by the widespread misery and squalor that they encountered. The crowded breadlines, rationing cards, begging children, desecrated churches, denunciations of Christianity, boasts of world revolution—all left an indelible impression upon her. After returning to America, Dilling later recounted that she was stunned by the refusal of her fashionable suburban "intellectual" friends to credit her accounts of Soviet depravity. Their insouciance instilled in her the conviction that "Good Christian women," as she put it, had to alert America to the Soviet threat. She became a devout disciple of Iris McCord, a Moody Bible Institute teacher who broadcast religious programs on the institute's radio station.[26] Soon Dilling was herself conducting extensive research for her own radio broadcasts, examining the anti-communist files amassed by such figures as Harry A. Jung, the founder of the American Vigilant Intelligence Federation and the filmmaker of *The Protocols of Zion*. In her public appearances, Dilling would often imitate Eleanor Roosevelt, titillating her audiences by adding a Yiddish accent.

Like other members of the Far Right during the New Deal era, including William D. Pelley, who based his Silver Shirts movement on Heinrich Himmler's SS, Dilling viewed communism as a threat to the American way—and Hitler's Third Reich as a bastion against Bolshevism. During a trip to Germany in July 1938, she attended the Nuremberg Nazi Party rally and praised the "great improvement of conditions there over 1931. Personally I thank God for the opposition Germany is making against communism." On her next visit, which was paid for by the Nazis, she announced that Germans were "contented and happy" under Hitler.[27]

Dilling was repeating Nazi propaganda about Hitler's vital role in preventing Bolshevism, the ideology of a barbaric Slavic civilization, from conquering the West. This was a persistent theme both before World War II and afterwards; the Right always saw Hitler, not Stalin, as America's natural ally. The Führer crushed labor unions, supported big business, and espoused martial values. To American businessmen such as Fred Koch (father of Charles and David) Hitler seemed like an enlightened statesman. Koch wrote to a friend in 1938 that "Although nobody agrees with me, I am of the opinion that the only sound countries in the world are Germany, Italy, and Japan, simply because they are all working and working hard."[28] Hitler's sins were regarded as venial; Stalin's, mortal.

In contrast to Nazi Germany, America was far too lax when it came to the communist threat. Dilling claimed, among other things, that the YMCA and the League of Women Voters were communist front organizations. She attacked universities as hotbeds of radicalism, embarking on a campaign with the Illinois drugstore magnate Charles Walgreen to purge the University of Chicago of so-called radical professors.[29] Dilling conceded that Roosevelt himself may not have been a card-carrying communist, but she blamed him for appointing numerous "Red revolutionaries" to his administration. Indeed, Dilling declared that she would prefer Hitler to Roosevelt as America's president.[30]

Her book *The Jewish Religion: Its Influence Today* was originally titled *The Plot Against Christianity*.[31] What she termed "Talmudic Judaism" was the progenitor of modern communism. According to Dilling, the hundreds of thousands of Jews who had fled Nazi Germany for New York City were not persecuted refugees, but hardened subversives who intended to launch a Marxist revolution in America. In 1938, Dilling spoke at a pro-American rally at the Hotel Commodore, where two thousand people listened to her praise the Third Reich and watched propaganda films featuring Hitler and Mussolini.[32] Two years later, she published another exposé, *The Octopus*. It singled out the Anti-Defamation League of B'nai B'rith as the power behind a communist conspiracy in America.[33] So mephitic was the book that she felt compelled to use a pseudonym, the Reverend Frank Woodruff Johnson. In Germany itself Dilling was dubbed "the female Führer."[34]

For all the excitement that Mussolini and Hitler generated on the Right, there was another dictator in Europe that many conservatives admired. On June 17, 1936, Spanish Nationalists carried out a military coup against the democratically elected Second Republic, triggering a civil war. The war between the Loyalists and Nationalists became a cause célèbre for the American Left and Right. The conflict, which served in some ways as a dress rehearsal for World War II, drew in both Nazi Germany and the Soviet Union. Hitler and Mussolini aided the Nationalist leader, General Francisco Franco, as did Pope Pius XI. The Pope, an implacable foe of liberalism, depicted Franco as a freedom fighter against god-less communism, prompting many American Catholics to follow suit. The key aim of Franco's American supporters was to pressure Roosevelt to maintain the Neutrality Acts he signed in 1935 and 1936, thereby ensuring that the Loyalist forces could not receive arms from the US even as left-wing volunteers joined what was popularly known as the Abraham Lincoln Brigade to fight along-side the Loyalists.

For Catholics, who had long been demonized in a largely Prot-estant America as disloyal to the country and loyal to the Vati-can, Franco was something of a deliverance. His militancy in the face of the Red Menace allowed them to flaunt their loyalty to American values by denouncing communism and the domestic Left, much of which supported, or at least tolerated, Roosevelt and the New Deal. "To American Francoites," wrote Austin J. Clements, "the truth was the Spanish Civil war was not a con-flict between communism and fascism as most Americans main-tained, nor between democracy and fascism as the Republicans insisted; rather, it was a struggle between godless communism and Western Christendom."[35]

Franco worship was fostered by variety of Catholic organi-zations and publications as well as demagogues such as Charles E. Coughlin, an anti-Semitic Catholic priest who was based in Royal Oak, Michigan, and was the host of a popular weekly radio show. After Franco defeated the Loyalists, the radio priest, as he was known, took to the airwaves on July 30, 1939, to crow about the earthly savior's triumph and to warn his own detractors in no uncertain terms that he would not take their attacks lying down: "You panderers of Communism, you cringing, cowardly advocates of press-muzzling, we will fight you in Franco's way. Call this inflammatory if you will. It is inflammatory. Christianity is the peaceful way until there is left no other way than self-defense—the Franco way." Others who enlisted in Franco's cause included Dilling, who traveled to the Nationalist zone in Spain and deemed Franco a "brave Christian."

Thomas F. Woodcock, a contributing editor to the *Wall Street Journal*, agreed. He saw events in Spain as an "open war upon faith as faith—a war in fact upon the Almighty Himself." The Boston banker and diplomat Cameron Forbes visited Nationalist Spain and delivered lectures in America emphasizing Franco's restoration of law and order. Then there was H. L. Mencken, who viewed Franco as almost as American as apple pie. He even compared him, in a way, to George Washington: "Franco was no more an agent of Mussolini and Hitler than Washington was agent of Louis XVI. If he takes whatever help he can get from the non-democratic Italians, then Washington took whatever help he could get from the still less democratic French."[36]

Perhaps no one was a more effective promoter of Franco than the New York businessman Merwin Kimball Hart. "FRANCO THANKS AMERICANS; Merwin K. Hart Gets Message of Gratitude From Spain," a *New York Times* headline noted on February 21, 1939, a month before the Republicans surrendered in Madrid. Whether El Caudillo was a proponent of the free market wasn't a real issue for Hart; he was a fascist foe of communist collectivism, and that sufficed.

A corporate lawyer and president of the New York Economic Council, Hart steadily fanned isolationist and pro-fascist sentiment. After the Second World War, he became a Holocaust denier as well as the head of the New York chapter of the John Birch Society until his death in November 1962. In 1950 the congressional Buchanan committee accused Hart's National Economic Council of "an ill-concealed anti-Semitism." Well before then, Hart blamed Jews for spreading communism in the United States and hired the likes of Albert Jay Nock to write for his National Economic Council weekly, *Review of Books*. Far from being a marginal figure, far from being seen as a crank, he received generous donations from corporations such as Standard Oil, Armco Steel, Gulf Oil, and Bethlehem Steel to propagate his free-market orthodoxy.[37] In his postwar study of Protestant extremists, *Apostles of Discord*, Ralph Lord Roy judged Hart "a favorite of all the antidemocratic forces in the United States."[38]

Hart was born in 1881 in Utica, New York, and like so many other leading figures on the radical Right, attended an elite university. A member of Franklin Delano Roosevelt's Harvard graduating class, he formed the Utica Mutual Workmen's Compensation Insurance Company in 1914 before joining the US Army as a captain in 1917. Hart served on an Industrial Survey Commission during Roosevelt's tenure as governor of New York, but opposed unions and higher taxes. In 1931, he founded the New York State Economic Council, whose offices were located in the Empire State Building. When the Great Depression began, he blamed government overregulation for causing it. Only businessmen possessed the right prescription to cure the nation's ills. After Hart met President Herbert Hoover in May 1932, he exhorted him to slash the federal budget to get the economy moving again. "URGES ECONOMY ON HOOVER," read the *New York Times* headline.[39] In 1936, Hart proposed that any American receiving government aid should be stripped of the right to vote. A year later, he made public a letter he had sent to the followers of the New York State Economic Council and the Committee of American Private Enterprise urging them to "rise in revolt" against the "forces of destruction of the Roosevelt Administration." Roosevelt, Hart said, was a dangerous radical trying to overthrow venerable American institutions. It was time to counter "excessive Government spending, radical influences in Washington, hostile legislation and Government persecution."[40]

By the mid-1930s, the historian David Austin Walsh noted, Hart "increasingly viewed the struggle against organized labor and the New Deal in the United States as but one front of a global war against international communism."[41] Another front was Spain. Hart worked closely with a variety of Franco enthusiasts, including the famous art deco muralist Hildreth Meière, the lobbyist Clare Singer Dawes, and former ambassador to Spain Ogden Hammond, to promote the Nationalist cause.[42] They created an organization called the American Union for Nationalist Spain that held rallies, raised funds for Franco, and helped promote the propaganda film *Spain in Arms* that was aired before large crowds in Boston and Manhattan in February 1939 to coincide with George Washington's birthday.[43]

Hart himself was eager to follow in the footsteps of his new chums, many of whom had already visited Spain. When he finally traveled to Spain in September and October in 1938, it was as though he had arrived in the promised land. He delivered a talk on Radio Málaga, asserting that Spain "was the main battle-front of the world against one of the greatest threats to civilization in all human history." In 1939 he published a book based on his impressions that he called *America—Look at Spain*. (How long before a Newsmax host writes *America—Look at Hungary?*) In it, Hart attempted to portray the communist menace as omnipresent. He warned Americans about a Spanish scenario taking place in their homeland. The communist strategy, he wrote, had been to deprive Spaniards of the right to own or carry arms in order to subdue them more easily. It was worth recalling that, in America itself, numerous laws had been passed to limit the right to bear arms. "In view of the fact that active communism in the United States dates from the end of the World War and that many of these anti-gun laws have been passed since that time," Hart asked, "is it entirely unlikely that the passage of these laws is due to Communist influence?"[44] The message was clear: if Americans wanted to defend themselves adequately against communism, it was necessary to pack heat—especially considering the number of Jewish radicals who had congregated in Manhattan to overthrow capitalism.

In linking America and Spain, Hart embraced the familiar line on the Right about the dangerous gullibility of American liberals. He highlighted the naïveté of Spanish liberals who had been forced to flee their country to avoid liquidation at the hands of the communists. He suggested that American liberals might end up similarly disillusioned (or even similarly dead), fantasizing about whether the president of his alma mater, James B. Conant, might someday regret naming "an avowed Communist to a fellowship?"[45] Moreover, when it came to economic matters, Nationalist Spain had much to recommend it. Hart touted the Spanish work ethic as superior to the American one. Spain had no prevailing wage rate, the 'democratic processes' and all that sort of thing, he is perhaps unconsciously carrying out a plan inaugurated for just such as he during the Seventh World Congress of the Communist International."[47] In equating communism and democracy, Hart revealed himself as an enemy of both.

His antipathy was widely shared. Major General George Van Horn Moseley, who had retired from the armed services in 1938, was an admirer of Lothrop Stoddard and a leading exponent of fascism in America. In March 1939 Moseley spoke to an audience of over one thousand at a Women's National Defense Committee meeting in Philadelphia in the Bellevue-Stratford Hotel, where he revealed that Jews were seeking world hegemony and financing communism. He further explained that Spanish Francoism and German Nazism were "only anti-toxins and will disappear when the disease of communism is cured," adding that "in fact, the finest type of Americanism can breed under their protection, as they neutralize the effects of Communism."[48] Appearing before the House Committee on Un-American Activities on May 31, he stated that the nettlesome problem of communists in America could be "handled in 5 minutes from the White House" by unleashing the US Army and described the German-American Bund as a fine patriotic organization.[49] The following day, he told the committee that American Jews who "affiliate themselves" with "world Jewry" should be forbidden to vote or hold public office.[50] His first day of testimony was featured on the front page of the New York Times, which noted that he had "many admirers among the audience of a hundred or so." A few months later Moseley, like Hart, equated democracy itself with communism. The last thing either wanted was for America to support freedom abroad.

On November 29, 1939, Hart held a rally called "Mass Meeting for America" at Madison Square Garden, where Texas congressman Martin Dies was the principal speaker. His speech was titled "The Insidious Wiles of Foreign Influence," an allusion to George Washington's Farewell Address in 1796.[51] In it, Dies denounced the idea of intervention abroad, declaring that "we in America are not now in danger of any invasion of foreign armies, despite the lies of warmongers and propagandists." Rather, the "insidious wiles" of foreign influence from Germany, Italy, and Soviet Union were threatening to undermine red-blooded "Americanism." Dies's appearance at Hart's rally prompted the journalist and novelist Vincent Sheean to send a sharp letter to *Time*. Did Dies, in condemning foreign wiles, realize that the chairman of the meeting was himself "a conspicuous exponent of such foreign points of view as that of General Franco's Fascism?"[52] Sheean added, "When Mr. Dies appears under such auspices, he gives us cause to wonder where his own loyalties lie."

As usual, Hart took nothing lying down. Responding with his own letter to *Time*, he stated, "Mr. Dies' patriotism needs no defense. His words speak louder than any words his friend could utter."[53] But Hart himself had more than a mild predilection for fascism. In February 1940 he resumed his attack on American democracy in a speech at the Nassau Club in Princeton, New Jersey, where he asserted that "Democracy is the rallying cry under which the American system is being prepared for despotism."[54] In September 1940, Hart delivered a speech inaugurating a luncheon series about "true Americanism" at the Union League Club in New York City. Its title was "The Alien Influence in Our Midst."

Hart said that it was "time to brush aside this word 'democracy' with its connotations" and banish the specter of "Marxism" from America.[55] Hart went on to suggest that it was refugees from Nazi Germany who were the source of the problem. Their presence, he said, meant that "we have our international liberals, too. They want to involve us with other nations—they want to draw us into their wars." He echoed Judge Frederick Bausman and the Hearst press in the years immediately after the First World War, claiming that American school textbooks had been transformed into tools of indoctrination. They were crammed full of Marxist ideas to "help in the overthrow of the American system." Unless a great revival of Americanism took place—and unless America stayed out of World War II—"the Republic is doomed."

In one of its habitually timorous editorials, the *New York Times* took issue with Hart's remarks, suggesting that "we do think he ought to have been more careful of his words, which might well give comfort to foes who despise both the forms and the realities of freedom."[56] More careful? Giving comfort was exactly what Hart wanted to accomplish. Freda Kirchwey, who was the editor and publisher of *The Nation*, wrote that "the *Times* has no excuse to soft-pedal the activities of Merwin K. Hart. He is as consistent a fascist as American reaction has developed."

Hart's antagonists in the Roosevelt administration were keenly aware of the stakes. Roosevelt's lieutenants realized—and publicly declared—that the battle between the American supporters and foes of intervening to support Great Britain against Nazi Germany wasn't simply over American neutrality. It wasn't over isolationism. It was about whether America should remain a democracy—or align itself with fascism.

Chapter 5

DEMOCRACY UNDER FIRE

Senator Burton K. Wheeler and Charles Lindbergh
delivering the Bellamy salute at an America First
Committee rally in Madison Square Garden in May
1941. Lindbergh declared that Americans had no
more opportunity to vote on war or peace in the
1940 presidential election than "if we had been in a
totalitarian state ourselves."

On October 16, 1940, Attorney General Robert H. Jackson delivered a speech at the Boston City Club to the Law Society of Massachusetts. It was called "Democracy under Fire."[1] That year Hitler's *Wehrmacht* had already conquered Norway, Denmark, the Netherlands, Belgium, Luxembourg, and France. The Battle of Britain continued to rage. But Jackson did not speak about foreign affairs. Instead, he focused on the domestic threat of fascism, observing that a school of thought had arisen that made a specious distinction between an American republic and democracy. Its members were pleased with democracy only as long as it coincided with their own interests. Making short shrift of Hart's recent claim at the Union League Club that it was time to "brush aside this word 'democracy,'" Jackson noted that he and others were opposed to popular government. "We are witnessing the most ominous gathering of forces against freedom and democracy," Jackson concluded, "that has been seen in my time."

Two months later, Harold L. Ickes, secretary of the interior, amplified Jackson's warning. From the outset, Ickes, a former Chicago lawyer, publicly assailed America's appeasers. In December 1938 he rebuked Henry Ford and Charles Lindbergh for accepting medals from the Third Reich, declaring that any American who accepted a decoration from it "automatically foreswears his American birthright."[2] Rather than use his name, he referred to Lindbergh as the "No. 1 Nazi fellow traveler" or "the Knight of the German Eagle." The stakes could not have been higher. When Hitler delivered a speech on January 30, 1939, to the Reichstag to celebrate the sixth anniversary of his ascension to power, he declared that a new war in Europe would lead to "the annihilation of the Jewish race in Europe"—and attacked Ickes by name.

Ickes was unrelenting. "ICKES DENOUNCES 'APPEASERS' HERE; Lists Lindbergh, Merwin Hart and Lawrence Dennis as in 'Dangerous Group,'" exclaimed a *New York Times* headline on December 18, 1940. In a December 1940 speech at Columbia University titled "The Threat of Fascism," Ickes said that the American appeasers of Hitler could unravel the nation. He was careful to acknowledge that freedom of the press and the Bill of

Rights should be scrupulously observed. But he denounced isolationists, Nazi sympathizers, and "soft sentimentalists," for conniving with the Nazi regime. He complained that they enjoyed
many protections. "They are native-born—often of old lineage,"
he said, "they have wealth and position and many bear honored
names; they confuse the sincere patriot by a casuistic expostula-
tion of their devotion to American institutions and the ideal of
peace; their subtle arguments and their pretended willingness to
sacrifice themselves for the common good are calculated to bring
about divided councils until the harm they do is irreparable." Ickes
divided them into four different groups—native fascists, the German American Bund, the Italian Fascisti, and the communists and
their fellow travelers. He described Lindbergh as a "a peripatetic
appeaser who would abjectly surrender his sword even before it is
demanded," Dennis as "the brains" of American fascism, and Hart
as someone who missed few chances to "sneer at democracy."

Dennis responded with a long letter to the *New York Times*
that, far from expressing outrage, struck a tone of lofty bemuse-
ment. The closest thing to fascism in America, he said, was Ickes
himself and "Mr. Roosevelt's third term." Hart, by contrast, was
livid. He demanded a retraction for what he claimed was slander.[3]
Ickes ignored him.

Some historians have likened the efforts of the Roosevelt
administration to target native American fascists as representing
a "Brown Scare" along the lines of the original "Red Scare."[4] The
problem with this interpretation is that there really was something
to be scared about. The notion that Nazism in America was mythical was itself a myth. "This was truly a nationwide 'Plot against

America,'" the historian Bradley W. Hart wrote, "rather than a regional flash in the pan."[5]

At the center of that plot was a disaffected German American whose efforts during the First World War to help the Fatherland had failed. Now it was round two for George Sylvester Viereck. But first he had to dodge Martin Dies—a tall, cigar-chomping, tow-headed Texas congressman with a proclivity for hyperbolic allegations—who wanted to battle what he saw as subversives running riot in America. Dies was a conservative Democrat, a foe of labor unions, and a sympathizer of the Ku Klux Klan.

Dies was the first chairman of the House Special Committee on Un-American Activities, a temporary body that was renewed five times before it was turned into a standing committee in 1945. In 1938, the year that Dies set off on his hunt for subversives, Franklin Delano Roosevelt condemned his committee as "flagrantly unfair and un-American."[6] Dies, who had begun his career in 1931 in the House by proposing a bill to suspend all immigration to America for five years, made sure to declare that he was every bit as concerned about Nazi Bundists as he was about communists. "DIES OPENS WAR ON PROPAGANDISTS; G. S. Viereck, Author, Friend of Ex-Kaiser, Subpoenaed, Cancels Passage to Europe," read the *New York Times* front-page headline on August 4, 1938. Dies had what he wanted, a prominent headline with his name in it. It turned out not to be a battle, much less a war. A week later, he lost interest in the case and Viereck sailed off to Europe to visit Kaiser Wilhelm and Adolf Hitler.[7]

Dies might have looked more closely at Viereck. The latter's propaganda efforts had never ceased. Viereck first met Hitler in Munich in October 1923 in a private home belonging to a former admiral of the German Navy. A few weeks later, Hitler staged his abortive Beer Hall Putsch. But Viereck caught little trace of Hitler the agitator. Over tea, they discussed the fate of Germany. "No milder mannered reformer," Viereck wrote, "ever scuttled ship of state or cut political throat." It was necessary to ensure, Hitler said, that there "will be no room for the alien, no use for the wastrel, for the usurer or speculator, or anyone incapable of productive work."[8] Viereck was "dazzled" by Hitler, a "widely read, thoughtful, and self-made man."[9]

Viereck claimed to regard it as a "consecration" to interpret the land of his fathers. He consecrated himself to drawing a direct line between the former German monarchy and Hitler's impressive new work to rebuild the nation. After returning from a trip to Germany in September 1933, he reported that "The former Kaiser is very sorry that he cannot be in Germany of late, in order to take part in the rejuvenation of his people. He feels that Hitler has completed the work which Bismarck began. Hitler has saved Germany and the world from Bolshevism."[10] While Hitler was pleased to enjoy Wilhelm's support, the last thing he wanted was for him to return to Germany, where the Kaiser, in another of his fantasies, hoped to be restored as monarch.

Viereck had more than an emotional interest in Germany's fate. He also had a pecuniary one. He quickly established extensive and lucrative ties to the new Nazi regime, including the German Foreign Ministry. He filed reports to the ministry about political developments in America.[11] In 1934 he admitted to a congressional committee that he was receiving a monthly stipend of $1,750 from an American publicity agency that was being funded by Joseph Goebbels's Ministry of Propaganda. The German consul general in New York also disbursed funds to Viereck for services "concerning the general aspects of public relations."

Viereck was having a lively time defending Germany's national honor. In 1937 Viereck published a work of fiction, *The Kaiser on Trial*, which defended the former emperor and blamed propagandists and "money lenders" for the war. Viereck also floated a no-fault account of the origins of World War I, comparing America and Germany to explain "how William II was drawn into the war as was Woodrow Wilson, by masters of intrigue at home and abroad, by accidents, blunders and misunderstandings, by madmen parading as statesmen, by lying friends and hypocritical foes."[12] In April 1937, he warned in the isolationist magazine *Liberty* that diplomatic elites—everyone except Hitler—in London and France were conspiring to plunge the continent once again into conflict.

In 1938, Viereck's German paymasters tasked him with disseminating anti-British propaganda in America, under the auspices of the German Library of Information. The indefatigable Viereck became the associate editor of a new magazine called *Today's Challenge*. The editor, and Viereck's boss, was Dr. Friedrich Ernst Auhagen, a former second lieutenant in the Kaiser's Army, a Columbia University professor—and a Nazi agent. Auhagen's publication featured essays by Lawrence J. Dennis, Representative Hamilton Fish III, and Senators William E. Borah and Ernest Lundeen. At the first public meeting, on April 19, 1939, of the American Forum, Dennis delivered a speech with the title "America and

Germany—Contrasts Without Conflicts." There was no need, in other words, for Germany and America to entertain any real disputes, let alone embark upon war. It was the very message that Viereck—and his Nazi associates—sought to spread.

Viereck liked to claim that he was simply a consultant for the German government, but his involvement obviously went beyond that. Once the Nazis launched their war in September 1939, Viereck stepped up his activities. He purchased a shoestring German American publishing operation in Scotch Plains, New Jersey, called Flanders Hall. It operated out of a small office in the Scotch Plains Bank Building. Founded in September 1939 by Siegfried and Adolf Hauck Jr. and Siegfried's wife, Mary, it published such classics as *The 100 Families That Rule The Empire* by Giselher Wirsing, a captain in the SS and the editor of the *Münchner Neueste Nachrichten*.[13] (Viereck also served as a well-paid correspondent for the Munich daily.) Viereck himself ghostwrote the isolationist book *We Must Save the Republic* (1941) for Illinois Republican congressman Stephen A. Day, which was published by Flanders Hall.

Above all, Viereck lobbied American lawmakers on behalf of the Third Reich. In carrying out this mission, his principal minder was Baron Heribert von Strempel, the first secretary of the German embassy in Washington.[14] Strempel, who had large sums at his disposal, ran an extensive propaganda network that included supporting Viereck's activities and funding the isolationist journal *Scribner's Commentator*.[15]

Viereck worked closely with Lundeen, who had voted against American entry into World War I in 1917, earning him the epithet of "shadow Hun" from Theodore Roosevelt during a speech in Lundeen's home state of Minnesota. A local club voted to expel him for harboring "a disloyal and seditious spirit."[16] After the war, Lundeen opposed American entry into the League of Nations. In Lundeen, Viereck discovered an eager disciple. Viereck bombarded him with his books and tattered copies of *The Fatherland*. Soon enough Viereck was ghostwriting pieces for Lundeen that portrayed Roosevelt as a warmonger. Viereck told Lundeen, "I think in the long run you will find collaboration with me, especially if we can regularize it, more profitable both political and financially than anything that you yourself can do, loaded down as you are with work."[17] Viereck teamed up with a gallimaufry of isolationist lawmakers, including New York's Hamilton Stuyvesant Fish III and Montana's Burton K. Wheeler. Sometimes Viereck worked from Lundeen's office—"dictating German propaganda directly onto the floor of the Senate."[18]

Viereck exploited the franking privilege of Congress—the ability to send free official mail en masse to constituents—on behalf of the Third Reich. Key to his scheme were Lundeen and Fish. Fish, a foe of the New Deal, was the ranking member of the House Foreign Affairs Committee and a Nazi sympathizer. Fish addressed a German Day meeting at Madison Square Garden on October 2, 1938. The idea was to have a rally that would be what might be called Nazi-adjacent—demonstrate support for the Third Reich but not go as far as Fritz Kuhn's German Bund. But at the meeting about one-third of the audience delivered a Nazi salute during the playing of the Horst Wessel Lied.[19] Fish joined the America First Committee and relied on a Nazi white paper in 1939 to urge that Roosevelt be impeached for concluding secret alliances with

Poland and France, declaring "I cannot conceive of the German Foreign Office fabricating or forging documents." During a visit to Nazi Germany in August 1939, he told American newsmen that "Germany's claims are just." He had tea with the German foreign minister, Joachim von Ribbentrop, at a castle near Salzburg, Austria, and flew to Oslo on a German government airplane.[20] A long-standing anti-communist, his hope was that Nazi Germany would defeat the Soviet Union.

Viereck, who was in contact with dozens of legislators, arranged not only to send copies of their isolationist speeches to constituents but also to disseminate outright Nazi propaganda in unaddressed franked envelopes that he managed to procure.[21] In particular, Viereck hired an isolationist publicist named Prescott Freese Dennett to relay propaganda items to an assistant of Fish named George Hill whom *Time* later branded "Not Fish, But Foul."[22] After inserting extracts of them into the *Congressional Record*, Hill reprinted and sent them to a Washington-based front organization that Viereck had established—the Islands for War Debts Committee. From there, "Viereck's material emerged bearing the Great Seal of the United States as a headpiece and with a Congressman's frank to take it through the mails postage-free to hundreds of thousands of American citizens."[23] The chairman of the war debts committee was none other than Lundeen.

In March 1940, as the Nazis were preparing to invade France, Lundeen was a speaker at a white-tie dinner in New York at the Waldorf-Astoria Hotel held by the Board of Trade for German-American Commerce. A Nazi flag hung prominently on the wall next to an American one, and numerous Nazis were at the head table with Lundeen, including the Duke of Saxe-Coburg and

Consul General Dr. Hans Borchers. "It is our duty to cultivate friendly, cordial relations with the great German Reich and its people," Lundeen declared. In August, Lundeen was scheduled to deliver a major address in Minnesota praising German culture and Hitler that Viereck had drafted for him, but he was a passenger on a Douglas DC-3 that crashed on a trip from Washington to Pittsburgh, killing him and the other passengers. Viereck was unfazed. He handed a similar speech to Theodore H. Hoffmann, the head of the Steuben Society, and it was inserted into the *Congressional Record*. Another isolationist senator, Gerald P. Nye, used his franking privilege to mail it around America.

———

Even as Viereck conspired on behalf of the Third Reich from his apartment on Riverside Drive in New York, which was adorned with photographs of Kaiser Wilhelm and Hitler, a welter of other organizations emerged to oppose the war with names such as Citizen's Keep America Out of War, War Debts Defense Committee, and the Make Europe Pay War Debts Committee. The financial backer behind many isolationist groups was William Randolph Hearst.

Known as "Hitler's Man in America," Hearst not only admired the Führer, but commissioned him and Mussolini to write for his newspapers for handsome fees. Hitler informed American readers of the "enslavement of an entire nation" at Versailles and the "forced transfusion of their own lifeblood from Germany to France, England, and America."[24] In August 1934, Hearst traveled to Germany, where he endorsed the recent Nazi plebiscite merging the posts of chancellor and president following the death of President

Paul von Hindenburg, ignoring the fact that the plebiscite turned Hitler into an absolute tyrant. "The results," Hearst said, "represent a unanimous expression of the popular will."[25]

After attending the Nuremberg Nazi Party rally in early September, the Chief, as Hearst was known, conducted a one-hour interview with Hitler in Berlin. During his visit, he concluded a secret arrangement to air Nazi propaganda in Hearst newsreels in America in exchange for the ability to run news footage in German theaters. In 1935, Nazi ideologist Alfred Rosenberg bragged to Hitler that Hearst was enamored of his (Rosenberg's) essays: "Since these articles, as Hearst personally informed me, presented well-founded arguments, he begged me to write further articles for his papers."[26] The alliance between Hearst and Hitler meant that "the journalist who began his long career as a champion of progressive policies found himself, near the end, labeled an American fascist."[27]

One notable move Hearst made in 1939 was to back the "Mothers' Movement" against intervention, which attracted 5 to 6 million members to a new organization called the National Legion of Mothers of America.[28] Hearst's *Los Angeles Herald-Express* declared that the organization was "motivated solely by patriotism" and consisted of mothers "grimly determined to fight any attempt to send their sons to fight on foreign soil."[29] Elizabeth Dilling supported the movement. So did her friend Cathrine Curtis. A former Hollywood actress, Curtis moved to New York to host a radio show for WMCA called "Women and Money" in 1934.[30] Curtis, who was a staunch believer in free-market economics, condemned the New Deal and hailed the Supreme Court for overturning FDR's National Industrial Recovery Act; and she collaborated with Merwin K. Hart and Joseph Kamp to impede American intervention in World War II. Curtis lectured in dozens of states, distributed numerous pamphlets and books, and maintained a "Jewry file."

In September 1939, Curtis founded the Women's National Committee to Keep the U.S. Out of War in twenty-five states to pressure Congress.[31] The aviatrix Laura Ingalls pitched in by flying in restricted space over the National Mall to Capitol Hill on September 26, 1939, to drop isolationist pamphlets that declared, "American women do not intend to again have their men sent to die on foreign soil."[32] Ingalls went on a speaking tour for the America First movement in July 1941, delivering straight-armed Nazi salutes and condemning America's "lousy democracy."[33] Her husband, Clayton Ingalls, had ties to Manfred von Killinger, the German consul in San Francisco, and established a group called the American Nationalist Confederation that was supposed to lead an armed uprising. In 1941 she was arrested and convicted in Washington by the Justice Department as a paid Nazi agent. Her lawyer said the government was engaged in a "witch hunt."[34]

But it was another aviator who truly drove the national debate over intervention. In late October 1940, a conference was held in Washington, DC, by representatives of no less than fifty peace organizations to form a No Foreign War Committee. Lindbergh addressed it. The chief backer of the supercommittee was the oil tycoon William Rhodes Davis, whom a British judge deemed "an unscrupulous and ruthless financier" for his efforts to divert Mexican oil to Germany, Italy, and Sweden and who worked together with the industrialist Fred Koch.[35] But after a brief burst of publicity, the committee faltered in its effort to promote isolationism and Lindbergh gravitated to another organization based in Chicago, Illinois: this one called, simply enough, America First.

In his 2004 novel *The Plot Against America*, Philip Roth imagined an alternate history in which Lindbergh captures the Republican nomination at a stalemated convention and goes on to win a surprise victory against Roosevelt in 1940. "The terror of the unforeseen," Roth wrote, "is what the science of history hides, turning a disaster into an epic." Lindbergh allies the US with the Axis powers, contemplates war with Canada, and severs the rights of American Jews. The "what if" novel succeeds in part because the scenario Roth presented wasn't that iffy.

In late June 1940, when the Republican party held its convention in Philadelphia, Hitler was at the zenith of his power. France was prostrate. Great Britain was forced to rescue its forces from Dunkirk. Most of the Republican candidates were isolationists, including Senator Robert A. Taft and former president Herbert Hoover. Indeed, on March 8, 1938, shortly before Nazi Germany's Anschluss with Austria, Hoover had met with Hitler and Hermann Goering. The agreeable meeting in the Reich Chancellery with Hitler had left Hoover convinced that the Nazis posed no threat to Western Europe and indeed that German rule over parts of Czechoslovakia, Romania, and Hungary would provide superior governance in those regions.[36] At the 1940 Republican convention, Hoover attacked Roosevelt for disparaging Hitler and Mussolini. He said that "if we are to keep cool and not stimulate war there must be an end to provocative speech by our officials."[37] Hoover also proclaimed that totalitarian liberals in the Roosevelt administration were supporting economic policies that would lead to communism, fascism, and Nazism in America.

As secret documents released by the State Department in 1956 indicated, Hamilton Fish III collaborated with Nazi propagandists to get the 1940 Republican National Convention to adopt an isolationist platform.[38] He failed. After a tumultuous floor fight between the interventionist and isolationist factions, the forty-eight-year-old Wall Street lawyer Wendell Willkie ended up being nominated. To the despair of mossback Republicans, the Eastern establishment had prevailed over the small businessmen of the American heartland.

Willkie argued for "one world," but isolationism did not go away when he captured the nomination. Instead, Lindbergh became its avatar. He presented himself as espousing peace but what he represented was sympathy for authoritarianism. Lindbergh styled his opposition to aiding Great Britain as foreign policy realism rather than the result of a romantic attachment to Nazi Germany. He claimed that the Third Reich's military prowess meant that any attempt by America to counter it was foredoomed. But there was more to it than that. Lindbergh, who was awarded the Service Cross of the German Eagle by Hermann Göring during a trip to Germany in October 1938, had much in common with the Nazis, particularly in his obsession with Nordic racial myths. Writing in *Reader's Digest*, for instance, Lindbergh contended that it was imperative to hold back "the infiltration of inferior blood" from Asia. Lindbergh was also disturbed by the influx of Jews from Europe, noting in his journals, "we are getting too many."

Such concerns were common. Lothrop Stoddard, who traveled to Europe as a special correspondent for the North American Newspaper Alliance from October 1939 to January 1940, wrote a book about his stay called *Into the Darkness* (a reference to the blackouts in Berlin, not the nature of the regime). He began his trip with a display of filial piety, visiting his stepmother Ida at her villa in Merano, Italy (which Mussolini by special edict had spared from becoming a troop headquarters).[39] Special highlights included a meeting with Hitler, an honor that the Führer rarely conferred to foreigners at that late date. Stoddard was most impressed by Hitler's approach to German racial stock and eugenics, or "race-betterment." He noted that the Jewish problem was regarded as "a passing phenomenon" and that it was soon to be "settled in fact by the physical elimination of the Jews themselves from the Third Reich."[40] Stoddard also attended the hearings of a sterilization court in Berlin that administered the "Law for Prevention of Hereditary Diseases," which had come into effect in July 1933. Its aim was to ensure the sterilization of the mentally retarded, epileptics, chronic alcoholics, and others the Nazis deemed "asocial." Stoddard came away from these sinister hearings "convinced that the law was being administered with strict regard for its provisions and that, if anything, judgments were almost too conservative."[41]

Nor was the America First Committee, which Lindbergh joined in April 1941, exempt from enthusiasm for the Third Reich. It was founded as an idealistic bipartisan group on September 4, 1940, and its members ranged from the Socialist Norman Thomas to Sears, Roebuck executive General John Wood. But it was rapidly hijacked by the Right, particularly after Wood named two notorious anti-Semites, Avery Brundage, the president of the US Olympic Committee, and Henry Ford, to its national committee. Brundage was in cahoots with Nazi Germany; after the conclusion of the 1936 Berlin Olympics, he received a lucrative contract to construct a new

Air Force Reserve. The clash between him and the administration only intensified. Roosevelt was feeling emboldened: at the end of December, he called for transforming America into an "Arsenal of Democracy."

On May 18, 1941, Ickes spoke at an "I am an American Day" gathering in Manhattan's Central Park and dismissed the "carefully pickled tripe" espoused by isolationists that democracy was a relic of the past. Next, in a Bastille Day speech before the France Forever organization, he launched what the *New York Times* called "one of the most bitter attacks ever made on Mr. Lindbergh by any member of the Roosevelt Administration." Referring to "Nazi scuttlefish" who "pour ink on the truth to blacken out the light of freedom," Ickes stated that Lindbergh had initially remained silent about the June 22 German invasion of the Soviet Union until he received his talking points from Berlin. "I have never heard Lindbergh say a word for democracy itself," Ickes concluded. "Has any one of you?"[46]

Lindbergh was infuriated. He made public a letter to Roosevelt disavowing any link to the Axis powers and demanding an apology from Ickes.[47] For his part, Ickes was delighted that Lindbergh had been foolish enough to display his ire publicly. Lindbergh's more consequential misstep arrived on September 11, 1941, when he delivered his incendiary speech "Who Are the War Agitators?" in Des Moines, Iowa. He singled out the three "powerful elements"— the British, the Roosevelt administration, and Jews—intent on entangling America in World War II. He expressed his dismay that the majority of Jews were not opposed to intervention and stressed that "their greatest danger to this country lies in their large ownership and influence in our motion pictures, our press, our radio and our government." The *Chicago Tribune* lamented that Lindbergh's comments tarnished an otherwise noble cause.

Who were the true warmongers? The Roosevelt administration, which stood by Great Britain and against Nazi tyranny? Or those who wanted to propitiate Hitler? Many who denounced Roosevelt presented themselves as isolationists. In fact, more than a few were pro-fascist. They were preaching preemptive surrender in the guise of foreign policy realism. In a speech on October 8, 1941, on the CBS radio network, Rear Admiral Richard E. Byrd, speaking under the auspices of the Council for Democracy, got it right. "Whenever a man stands before you and tells you to bow down before the mythical invincibility of the Nazi tyranny," he said, "that man is a warmonger." He added, "Whenever he tells you that democracy is done for, that we must not have the faith in the eternal strength of our democratic institutions, that man is a warmonger."[48] Ickes, too, weighed in. In an October 20 speech at Chicago's Sinai Temple, he scoffed at the "appeasers and defeatists" ranging from Lindbergh to Senator Burton K. Wheeler to the *New York Daily News*.[49]

When Japan bombed Pearl Harbor on December 7, 1941, an America First rally was taking place in Pittsburgh's Soldiers & Sailors Memorial Hall. After an incensed Enrique Urrutia, a colonel in civilian clothing, declared, "I wonder if the audience knows that Japan has attacked us and that Manila and Pearl Harbor have been bombed," he was escorted out by police and jeered as a mouthpiece for Roosevelt. And after a reporter passed him a note that Japan was at war with America, Senator Gerald P. Nye addressed the meeting for fifteen minutes before informing the audience of the attack. He stated, "I can't somehow believe this. But I suppose I must."[50] It took him awhile. After Pearl Harbor, Nye claimed that the attack was "just what Britain planned for us!" Senator Robert Rice Reynolds, who was the chairman of the Senate Military Affairs Committee, sent the fascist Gerald L. K. Smith, who published a magazine called *The Cross and the Flag* that decried the war, a congratulatory note.[51] In her novel *Manhattan Beach*, Jennifer Egan captured the lingering animosity toward Roosevelt and the war: Aunt Brianne tells her patriotic niece Anna Kerrigan, "They've bewitched you, dearie. It wasn't even our war. The Japs played right into Roosevelt's hands—I'd not be surprised if he paid them to do it, the weasel."

With American entry into the war, however, its opponents were reduced to a querulous rump faction. Roosevelt wanted payback.[52] George Sylvester Viereck's work with Congress—specifically, with Representative Hamilton Fish—had already prompted the Justice Department to convene a Washington grand jury that approved a five-count indictment in October 1941 against him for violating the 1938 Foreign Agents Registration Act. His world was collapsing. Viereck had registered as a German agent, but there were numerous omissions in his original filing and in November Viereck's publishing house was dissolved.[53]

The lawmakers who had consorted with Viereck now scrambled to disassociate themselves from him. When Fish testified at Viereck's trial, he erupted when the Justice Department prosecutor, William P. Maloney, asked, "Is it a coincidence that the views on Nazi propaganda in his [Viereck's] book are similar to those you have held as a Congressman?" Fish leaned forward in his chair and yelled, "The man that makes that statement lies!" Maloney replied, "Are you referring to Mr. Viereck?" "No," Fish said, "I'm referring to you." But

Fish's former assistant George Hill, who was convicted for perjuring himself before the grand jury investigating Viereck, made it clear in his testimony that he had been introduced to Viereck by Fish in July 1940 and had been instructed to distribute pamphlets at Fish's behest.[54] Fish claimed to have no memory of the encounter. After the jury returned a guilty verdict, *Time* magazine gloated that the "thick-lipped, bespectacled" Viereck faced up to six years in prison.[55]

Viereck may have been arrested, but during wartime Franklin Roosevelt wanted a mass trial of the fascists and Nazis who had been plaguing him for years. Attorney General Francis Biddle resisted the idea. To prove that they had engaged in a broader conspiracy would be a heavy lift. But in July 1942, Biddle yielded to Roosevelt's demands, arraigning American fascists—ranging from Elizbeth Dilling to Gerald B. Winrod to, again, Viereck—under the provisions of the Smith Act of 1940. The act had originally been introduced by Representative Howard W. Smith to counter communist subversion and forbade efforts to "advocate, abet, advise, or teach" the violent overthrow of the American government. The government kept adding new conspirators to the indictment, including Lawrence Dennis, who was included in the final round.

When the trial finally began in April 1944, it turned into a debacle. Some of the defendants were plainly unhinged—Lois de Lafayette Washburn, who claimed that Jews were trying to sell her into "white slavery," gave the Nazi salute as she left the courtroom on the first day. Elizabeth Dilling proclaimed that it was "the New Deal and Communism," not the defendants, that were on trial and Lawrence J. Dennis maligned federal prosecutor O. John Rogge as "Vishinsky," the perfervid prosecutor during the Moscow show trials.[56] The *Chicago Defender* wondered what Dennis was doing among the rabble-rousers, but noted that he had "appointed himself to put the entire hateful philosophy of Nazism into elegant and palatable literary form."[57] After the presiding judge Edward C. Eicher died of a heart attack in November, a mistrial was declared.

In 1946, Dennis, in a book called *A Trial on Trial* that he co-wrote with Maximilian St. George, stated that the Roosevelt administration, relying upon smears and innuendo, intent upon stifling dissent and promoting left-wing orthodoxy, had conducted its own version of the Moscow show trials. The true fascists weren't the defendants but their persecutors. "Fascist-baiting," Dennis and St. George wrote, "is in every way identical with red-baiting."[58] The trial set the stage for the Right to pursue its own—and far more virulent—politically motivated attacks on the Roosevelt administration as a hotbed of communist traitors after World War II.

In short, the 1944 trial, not to mention the popularity of the Roosevelt administration as it oversaw the Second World War, intensified the sentiment among conservatives that they needed to fight back against liberal encroachments, whenever and wherever possible. Once the war ended in Allied victory, they claimed the conflict was an unnecessary one and trivialized Nazi war crimes. A war that is often viewed in retrospect as a moment of unanimity in the United States in fact saw the flowering of a movement that pandered to authoritarianism. The Right was not chastened by the Second World War. It was emboldened.

Chapter 6

AMERICA FIRST, LAST, AND ALL THE TIME

Joseph McCarthy relishes his defeat of Robert La Follette Jr. in the 1946 Republican senatorial primary in Wisconsin. As a first-term senator, he whitewashed Nazi war crimes in Malmedy, Belgium, against American soldiers.

In William Wyler's ironically titled 1946 film, *The Best Years of Our Lives*, three soldiers return from World War II on a B-17 Flying Fortress to their hometown of Boone City. They bond with each other during the trip back, but experience difficulties readjusting to civilian life. In one scene, former bombardier captain Fred Derry, who is frustrated at having to work as a drugstore soda jerk, watches from behind the counter as former Navy petty officer Homer Parrish, who has mechanical hooks for hands, is accosted by an older customer—dressed to the nines in a double-breasted chalk-stripe suit, pocket handkerchief, and fedora—who exclaims, "You got plenty of guts. It's terrible when you see a guy like you that had to sacrifice himself. And for what?" Homer is befuddled. "And for what? I don't get ya, Mister." He replies, "We let ourselves get sold down the river. We were pushed into war." After Homer declares that it was the Japanese and Nazis who did the pushing, his customer responds that America had been "deceived" into the war by a "bunch of radicals" in Washington. "We fought the wrong people, that's all," he says. "I'm not selling anything but plain old-fashioned Americanism." As an enraged Homer grapples with the America Firster, ripping off his American flag pin, Fred Derry leaps over the counter to administer the coup de grâce, a roundhouse punch that sends him sprawling.

In reality, it wasn't quite that easy to deliver a knockout blow to what the isolationist lout presented as plain, old-fashioned Americanism. For one thing, congressional Republicans were unbowed. On May 16, 1945, barely a week after the Second World War had ended, Wisconsin congressman Frank Bateman Keefe attacked his Illinois colleague Adolph J. Sabath for lamenting that figures such as Merwin K. Hart, George Van Horn Moseley, and others were free to continue their activities to subvert American democracy. In expressing his apprehensions, Sabath had referenced an "Orientation Fact Sheet 64" that the US Army issued in March 1945 explaining that it wasn't always easy to identify fascism, that it was best to combat it "by making our democracy work" and that "an American fascist seeking power would not proclaim that he is a fascist." Conservatives denounced the fact sheet as a dangerous document. "I am fearful," Keefe said, "that a new political gangsterism has been developed in this country which seeks to include as

Fascists all individuals or organizations who dare to express dissent from the existing New Deal order." It was the New Deal liberals, he said, who supported "true fascism."[1]

A bevy of prewar isolationists chimed in to decry Truman. They said that joining the United Nations after the war jeopardized American sovereignty. They said that the allies in Western Europe, including the British, were socialist moochers. And they said that it was time for the Europeans to fend for themselves. Take Hart. In an appearance before the Free Enterprise Society at Harvard on February 4, 1948, Hart praised Franco's Spain, lambasted the Marshall Plan, and decried "the international Jewish group which controls our foreign policy."[2] (Something about Harvard seemed to bring out the worst in the Hart family: Hart's son, Merwin, had created a poster in 1939 as a student at Harvard that requested two minutes of silence in memory of the Spanish "Reds" and included names such as "Felix Finkleberger," a derogatory reference to the Jewish Supreme Court justice Felix Frankfurter.)[3] Hart's venom toward Jews became increasingly pronounced after World War II: he asserted both the Roosevelt and Truman administrations were "infested" with Jewish appointees.[4] In a December 15, 1949, *Economic Council Letter* titled "Is Christianity To Die?," Hart, who regularly met with Republican congressmen and senators in Washington, observed that "a wealth of evidence can be adduced to show that the Zionists have Mr. Truman's Administration in the hollow of their hand. The Socialist program is their program, as it is in Britain."

Indeed, the old Anglophobia persisted as well. After 1945, North Dakota senator William A. "Wild Bill" Langer remained a staunch proponent of isolationism, opposing the Marshall Plan and the establishment of the North Atlantic Treaty Organization

(NATO). He deemed England the "enemy of the people" and backed a second "revolutionary war to regain our independence from Great Britain." In 1951, he sent a telegram to the pastor of the Old North Church in Boston urging him to hang two lanterns from the belfry to warn Americans that Winston Churchill was coming to America.[5]

Then there was the newspaper baron Colonel Robert R. McCormick. McCormick, who published the *Chicago Tribune*, his sister Eleanor "Cissy" Patterson, who owned the *Washington Times-Herald*, and his cousin Joseph Medill Patterson, who founded the *New York Daily News*, were dubbed the "Three Furies of the Isolationist Press" by *Time*. Known as the "greatest mind of the fourteenth century," McCormick was a graduate of Groton and Yale who moved to the Right during the 1930s. He saw Roosevelt's New Deal as exemplifying "the spirit of the big red square in Moscow" and as a sinister effort to abolish the Constitution. He also despised England, claiming, among other things, that Rhodes Scholarships were a plot to subvert the loyalty of America's elites and turn them into British spies. As war with Nazi Germany loomed, he scoffed at the dangers posed by Hitler. After entry, he indicated that the real danger was that Roosevelt would exploit World War II to seize totalitarian power for himself and create a "superstate." In October 1944, McCormick inaugurated a revisionist wave about World War II when the *Chicago Tribune* featured a twenty-five-page essay by John T. Flynn, a former Roosevelt supporter who had moved right, accusing the president of deliberately provoking a Japanese attack in December 1941.[6] A year later, Flynn once more appeared in the *Tribune* to reveal "The Final Secret of Pearl Harbor."

In an interview in 1946 at his high paneled office in Tribune

Tower with a *New York Times* reporter, the rumbustious McCormick made it clear that his views about American foreign policy had not changed one iota. He complained about the snobbery he experienced from Eastern elites when he was a student at Groton and attacked the pro-British "international Bankers in New York who have been in charge of the Republican party."[7] The British and the continental Europeans, he complained, were simply a bunch of deadbeat socialists, while the Democratic Party consisted of "Russian-loving communists." In the Midwest, he said, "we are for America first, last and all the time." McCormick ended the interview after his secretary announced that he had a visitor—Judge Joseph R. McCarthy, the Republican candidate for US senator from Wisconsin.

To drum up support for the Right, McCormick had attended a meeting in October 1944 hosted by the former president of America First, Robert E. Wood, in Chicago that also included Charles Lindbergh and William H. Regnery. The mission of these conservative worthies was to create a newsletter called *Human Events*, a reference to the opening of the Declaration of Independence: "When, in the course of human events . . ." It would be edited by William Chamberlain, Frank C. Hanighen, and Felix Morley. A former member of America First, Hanighen had co-authored the influential book *Merchants of Death* with H. C. Engelbrecht in 1934, blaming the avarice of arms manufacturers for propelling America into World War I. Morley, a former editor of the *Washington Post* and president of Haverford College, believed that the American government practiced a form of subtle censorship of independent journalistic views that came close to rivaling the propaganda measures of Joseph Goebbels. To expand the publication's reach, the editors turned to Henry Regnery, a former admirer of Franklin Roosevelt who had gone hard right. But they ended up bridling at Regnery's ambitious proposals to increase readership, fearing that they would dilute the quality of the publication. The result was that in 1947 Regnery and the editors decided to create a book publication wing that would be separate from the newsletter.[8] Regnery's publishing operation was born—and it soon launched a fusillade of revisionist books about World War II and Nazi Germany.

Regnery, who was born in Hinsdale, Illinois, in 1912, the year Woodrow Wilson was first elected president, exercised a good deal of influence on the postwar conservative movement, both in domestic and foreign affairs. His father, William Henry Regnery, was a staunch Catholic and wealthy textile manufacturer whose own father, Wilhelm, had emigrated to America from Ensch, Germany, in the nineteenth century. In his memoirs, Henry Regnery recalled that his father was skeptical of accounts of German atrocities during World War I, regarding them as British propaganda, and was incensed by the Treaty of Versailles.

As a college student at MIT, Henry read widely in German literature, including Thomas Mann's novel *The Magic Mountain*, and he went on to study in Bonn for two years, traveling to Nazi Germany in August 1934, a month after Hitler staged the Night of the Long Knives, his bloody purge of the SA. Regnery recalled that he saw nothing to disturb him that summer and, in fact, relished his stay in the fatherland, where he continued his study of the cello. He also visited churches, castles, and old East Prussian estates; as he later recalled, "it all seemed incredibly beautiful and romantic."[9]

In October, he registered to study German and economics at Bonn University. He seems to have had an idyllic time, visiting with Silesian nobility, listening to Mozart and Strauss operas, and playing the Brandenburg concertos.

Nazism, he wrote, "seemed far removed from us and the university, so far as we could tell, intact and largely unaffected." Anti-Semitism was "not particularly evident" and "the cities were clean and orderly."[10] Yet during Regnery's stay the Nazis introduced, in September 1935, the Nuremberg Race Laws. Jews were stripped of their citizenship. Marriages between German Jews and non-German Jews were forbidden. Jewish officers were expelled from the army and Jewish students banned from sitting for doctoral examinations.

Regnery, though, never saw much difference between Hitler and Roosevelt. Quite the contrary. He drew a moral equivalence between the two leaders. In his judgment, "Both Hitler and Roosevelt—each in his own way—were masters of the art of manipulating the masses, and by a strange quirk of fate they died within a few weeks of each other."[11]

With the end of the Second World War, Regnery attempted to propagate a sense of disillusionment not dissimilar to the one that took hold after the First World War. He was encouraged in his efforts by Harry Elmer Barnes who, as the historian Deborah Lipstadt has noted, provided "the most direct link between the two generations of American revisionists and the Holocaust deniers."[12] Regnery incited a fresh wave of revisionism that ranged from alleging that Roosevelt had known about the attack on Pearl Harbor ahead of time to maintaining that the Nuremberg war crimes trials amounted to victor's justice. Just as secret agreements had existed during First World War that made a mockery of the idea that the allies were fighting for democracy, so the Yalta and Potsdam accords clearly contradicted the professed idealistic aims of America and Great Britain. The Right suggested that the real accomplishment of the war wasn't to liberate Europe from Nazi tyranny. Instead, it was to debilitate Germany and open the door for the Soviet Union to conquer Eastern Europe.

Regnery's new publishing house devoted itself to such topics, as did a rival conservative press, Devin-Adair Publishing Company, which was headed by Devin Garrity.[13] In 1947 Garrity published George Morgenstern's *Pearl Harbor: The Story of the Secret War*, a conspiratorial work that maintained that Roosevelt, far from being ignorant of Tokyo's plans, was fully aware that Japan would attack: "For years afterward the story was carefully cultivated that the Japanese attack was a treacherous surprise, launched when there was no remotest reason for expecting it, and therefore a great shock to the leaders of government."[14] Soon Regnery Publishing, too, took up the revisionist cudgels. It was World War I all over again, except that this time the revisionism was aimed at rehabilitating a genocidal regime.

During the 1930s, the Right had argued that FDR was a budding tyrant. Now, as Henry Regnery saw it, there was scant difference between Hitler and Roosevelt not only in their rhetorical prowess, but also when it came to fighting the war. In a spasm of absurdity, Regnery presented Hitler as obsessed with fighting to the last gasp—and Roosevelt as "on the same level of irresponsibility," for insisting on a policy of unconditional surrender.

Then there were the aerial bombings of German cities, which had destroyed major cities such as Dresden and Hamburg, and the 1944 Morgenthau Plan, which had proposed turning Germany into a pastoral country. Sympathy for Nazi Germany became a frequent theme in the Right's postwar revisionism, which aimed to present America as intent on a Carthaginian peace when, in fact, the Morgenthau Plan was only briefly considered and dismissed. According to the Right, however, the greatest betrayal had already taken place when Winston Churchill and Roosevelt met with Joseph Stalin at the 1943 Tehran and 1945 Yalta conferences to carve up Europe into spheres of influence. Yalta became the rallying cry for the Right, the moment when traitorous liberals had supposedly handed over Eastern Europe to Stalin. The truth was that Stalin's armies were already marching through Eastern Europe, and the Yalta accords simply bowed to the inevitable. As leading figures on the American Right saw it, however, World War II had been something of a hoax. The so-called crusade for democracy had simply emboldened Communist Russia, transforming it into a great power rivaling the United States.

It was a consistent theme, and one often tinged with racial anxiety. In the introduction to his wartime journals (published in 1970), Lindbergh wrote that "we won the war in a military sense; but in a broader sense it seems to me that we lost it, for our Western civilization is less respected and secure than it was before. In order to defeat Germany and Japan, we supported the still greater menaces of Russia and China—which now confront us in a nuclear-weapon era. . . . Much of our Western culture was destroyed. We lost the genetic heredity formed through eons of many million lives."[15]

This theme, that America had lost out by fighting for freedom against Nazism, was a pervasive one on the Right. In 1950,

Regnery Publishing launched its initial revisionist work, *America's Second Crusade*, by the well-known journalist and historian William Henry Chamberlain. After his work was rejected by a variety of New York publishers, Chamberlain, at the urging of Harry Elmer Barnes, turned to Regnery.[16] Barnes was in regular contact with a variety of historians and journalists, encouraging them to send their works to Regnery and other conservative publishers.

According to Chamberlain, "A negative, destructionist attitude toward Germany was closely, if unconsciously, bound up with approval of, or acquiescence in, Soviet ambitions for domination of Europe. These attitudes were two sides of the same coin."[17] In waging war against Nazi Germany, America had inadvertently helped to create a new and far more dangerous power in the form of the Soviet Union. The notion that America could eliminate the totalitarian threat to freedom while aiding the USSR had proven to be "a humbug, a hoax, and a pitiful delusion."[18]

Similarly sweeping claims were advanced in another Regnery book, this one by the historian and former adviser to the Senate Foreign Relations Committee, Charles C. Tansill. A right-wing Catholic, Tansill entered the lists on behalf of Germany whenever and wherever he could. After the First World War, Tansill claimed that Woodrow Wilson had conspired to commit America to war even as he ran for reelection on a peace platform in 1916.[19] In October 1936, he delivered a radio broadcast that was transmitted from Berlin to the United States, declaring that "without the buoyant optimism of the Führer Germany would have lapsed into Bolshevism."[20] As a guest of the Carl Schurz Association and the Nazi government, he was one of fourteen Americans vouchsafed an official invitation to the Nuremberg Nazi Party rally. Upon his return to America, in a talk to the Presbyterian Ministers' Association, he stated that the Wehrmacht formed "a kind of peace insurance in Europe" against communist aggression. He added, "I consider Hitler one of the ablest orators of the modern age. He has a fine, resonant voice and a compelling personality. His power as a convincing public speaker has done much to strengthen his position in the country which under his leadership has regained law, order, hope and self-respect that were completely shattered by the Treaty of Versailles."[21]

On March 9, 1937, the *Washington Post* reported that Tansill—"outspoken defender of Adolf Hitler and the Nazi regime"—had been fired by American University for his pro-Nazi views. Tansill told the *Post* that "at present there is strong, hysterical opposition to the principles of Der Fuehrer."[22] Tansill, who landed a position at Fordham University before ending his career at Georgetown University, did not deviate from his support for Germany or racist policies in America. In *America Goes to War* he defended Germany's role during the First World War.[23] In June 1947, he delivered a talk in the National Capitol's Statuary Hall on the 139th anniversary of Jefferson Davis's birthday in which he castigated Abraham Lincoln as a "do-nothing soldier" who was "invincible in peace and invisible in war."[24] Just as FDR had lured the Japanese into attacking at Pearl Harbor, so Lincoln, Tansill charged, had tricked the South into bombarding Fort Sumter. In *The Back Door to War*, Tansill contended that Hitler's true aim was to combat Bolshevism and that FDR—"a master of mendacity"—had heedlessly involved America in the conflict. He saw conspiracies everywhere. Several decades later, in a piece for the John Birch Society's *American Opinion*, Tansill contended that President

John F. Kennedy should be impeached for his illegal activities in foreign affairs.[25]

Perhaps the most outlandish revisionist work was produced by Southern Methodist University English professor John Beaty, whose *The Iron Curtain over America* first appeared in 1951 and was reprinted eight times by 1952.[26] It was touted by Merwin K. Hart's *Review of Books* in February 1952, which reprinted a radio address by the former National Commander of the American Legion, Colonel Alvin M. Owsley, hailing Beaty's effusions as "one of the great documents of our time." Senator Pat McCarran said it was a "fine book" and Senator William Langer stated it should be "compulsory reading in every public school."[27]

Beaty concocted an elaborate conspiracy theory centering on "Khazar Jews" who had supposedly inveigled American into World War I and toppled Tsar Nicholas II. After emigrating to America between 1919 and 1924, they seized control of the Democratic Party, infiltrating the Roosevelt administration to push for a new global conflict and for the US to accede to Stalin's postwar demands.[28] An unnecessary war, Beaty wrote, had been conducted "in foul obeisance before the altar of anti-Christian power in America."[29] Only after Roosevelt had treated Germany's diplomatic approaches with "contemptuous rejection" did Hitler betray "his own conscience" by signing an accord with the Soviet Union—the Molotov-Ribbentrop Pact of 1939—to carve up Poland. Whether Hitler had a conscience to betray may be wondered. But as Beaty saw it, America was compounding its original mistakes by treating Germany harshly after World War II—a policy that "weakens us immensely to the advantage of Soviet Communism."[30] In fact, American policy was to integrate Germany into the West as quickly as possible and it made the *Wirtschaftswunder*, or economic miracle, that took place during the 1950s possible.

Beaty's work complemented the books published by Regnery and Devin-Adair. In his memoirs, Regnery conceded that it might have been imprudent to launch his enterprise with revisionist works about the Third Reich, but he felt a moral obligation to publish them. In palliating the crimes of Nazism, Regnery seems to have believed that he was a brave dissident upholding the values and standards "on which civilization rests."[31] He thus published a variety of other works, including Montgomery Belgion's *Victors' Justice* and two by the left-wing British publisher Victor Gollancz. (Regnery felt a sense of communion with Gollancz over the latter's crusade for Arabs who had been dispossessed by the establishment of Israel. Regnery would publish three books in the 1950s attacking the Jewish state, including the venomous *What Price Israel?*) Then there was Freda Utley's *The High Cost of Vengeance*.

Utley offered what was likely the locus classicus of revisionism about Nazi Germany. Her intellectual journey from socialism to anti-communism turned Utley into an anti-communist heroine to American conservatives, including Russell Kirk and Ronald Reagan. In the *New York Times*, Kirk called her a "keen polemicist, a gadfly (or perhaps a wasp), and a woman of principle."[32]

Utley, who was born on January 23, 1898, in London, grew up in a socialist milieu. Her father, Willie Herbert Utley, was a journalist and the acting secretary of the Fabian Society. She graduated from the London School of Economics, where she became friends with the philosopher Bertrand Russell. As a member of the "1917 Club" in London, she became acquainted with leading left-wing intellectuals, poets, artists, and academics, traveling to the Soviet Union in 1927 in the conviction that "the Communists were in the process of creating the best economic and social system which the world had ever known."[33] After marrying a Russian economist named Arcadi Berdichevsky in 1928, she lived in Moscow and grew increasingly disillusioned with real, existing socialism. Her husband was arrested and exiled to Siberia by Stalin's secret police in 1936, and Utley never saw him again, only learning in 1963 that he had perished at Komi in the Arctic North in March 1938, one of Stalin's countless victims. Utley flew to England in July 1936 with her son Jon Basil (who became publisher of *The American Conservative* toward the end of his career).

In December 1939 they boarded a Dutch ship together with Jewish refugees from Austria and Germany bound for America. Utley dedicated herself, as she put it, to "alerting America to the Communist menace."[34] Warning America about communism meant questioning the need to confront Nazism. Utley became a member of the America First movement and published a memoir in September 1940 called *The Dream We Lost*, which explained that Stalin's Soviet Union was more evil than Hitler's Germany.[35] She also wrote for an isolationist publication called *Common Sense*, which displayed little of it. She admired the fact that, far from endorsing Roosevelt and Churchill's Atlantic Charter of 1941, the magazine recognized that "the Roosevelt-Churchill commitment to the total defeat and disarmament of Germany must lead to a second Versailles with even worse consequences."

After the Second World War, *Reader's Digest* and the isolationist Foundation for Foreign Affairs sent Utley to Germany. The result was *The High Cost of Vengeance*, which Harry Elmer Barnes helped her to draft. She assailed the Western allies for replicating the mistakes that they had committed after World War I. History, she said, was repeating itself. It wasn't that the Germans were incapable of democracy. Instead, the victorious armies of the West were blighting Germany's prospects. While Stalin's Russia had gobbled up Eastern Europe with the connivance of Roosevelt, the Western allies' benighted occupation policies had "reduced the defeated enemy country to the status of an African colony."[36] Utley dismissed the idea that Nazi Germany was guilty of unique crimes. "Were the German gas chambers really a greater crime against humanity," she asked, "than our attacks on such nonmilitary objectives as Dresden?"

In her telling, Supreme Allied Commander Dwight D. Eisenhower had flown in journalists, photographers, and politicians to visit German concentration camps to obscure American war crimes. According to Utley, "There was no crime the Nazis had committed, which we or our allies had also not committed."[37] Delbert Clark, the former Berlin bureau chief for the *New York Times*, reviewed her book. "It is astonishing," he wrote, "how much misinformation the author has been able to pack into a few pages in support of the hypothesis armed with which she invaded Germany last year."[38]

There was no topic on which Utley packed in more misinformation than the issue of German war crimes at Malmedy, Belgium, on December 17, 1944, during Hitler's final military offensive, the

Battle of the Bulge. Utley maintained that Malmedy was a flagitious case of what she called "the Nuremberg dictum"—the idea that America could behave as it pleased, which it did nowhere more so than in the Malmedy trial, held from May to July 1946 by the United States Army Tribunals. Interrogations were conducted in Schwäbisch Hall near Stuttgart, and the trial itself in Dachau concentration camp. There, seventy-three members of the 1st SS Panzer Regiment "Adolph Hitler" division that had been led by Lieutenant Colonel Joachim Peiper, who was former adjutant to the head of the SS, Heinrich Himmler, stood trial for murdering dozens of American POWs. The army judges found the accused guilty.

Colonel Willis M. Everett, the leader of the defense team, felt humiliated by the verdict. In the hope of undermining it, he set about collecting dubious affidavits from the defendants in which they alleged that they had been subjected to brutal torture methods while confined at Schwäbisch Hall. The US Supreme Court declined to hear an appeal.[39] The secretary of the army, Kenneth C. Royall, created a three-man commission to review the sentences that included Edward L. Van Roden, a judge at the Orphans' Court in Pennsylvania. After he returned to America, Van Roden, who had previously "endorsed a pro-Nazi and anti-Semitic book, which accused FDR of being surrounded by Jews," rode his service on the commission to relative public prominence.[40] He claimed that a terrible miscarriage of justice had taken place. Utley agreed. She maintained that the "methods employed by the investigators and prosecutors in these cases were worthy of the GPU, the Gestapo and the SS."[41]

Utley's political comrade, Senator Joseph R. McCarthy, who was a foe of intervention in the Second World War before Pearl Harbor, seized on the Malmedy case. In 1949, the Wisconsin senator was casting about for an issue that could earn him some publicity. In November 1945, as a warm-up for his Senate campaign and on the eve of the Nuremberg war crimes trials, McCarthy had adopted pro-German positions, including a radio talk in which he condemned the American military for "using the soldiers of our former enemy as slave labor." In a note to a friend, he bemoaned the mistreatment of the "clearly innocent GI Joes of the German army."[42] McCarthy, who was for a time the most powerful and feared politician on the Right, cut his political teeth defending Nazis who had massacred American soldiers.

One of McCarthy's main backers was a wealthy Wisconsin businessman named Walter Harnischfeger, who was enjoined during World War II by Roosevelt's Fair Employment Practices Committee for refusing to hire anyone other than white Protestants and who said that the Nuremberg trials were "worse than anything Hitler did. It beats Dachau."[43] Harnischfeger's nephew, Frederick von Schleinitz, apparently enjoyed exhibiting a copy of *Mein Kampf* that Hitler had autographed for him.[44] Harnischfeger was also a supporter of Merwin K. Hart, who hired Freda Utley to work for him in 1951 and who noted, "It cannot be overlooked that a large number of the Communists in the United States are Jews."[45] Harnischfeger's counsel, Thomas W. Korb, helped McCarthy get up to speed on the Malmedy case.

Maryland senator Millard E. Tydings, the chairman of the Armed Services Committee, convened a subcommittee on the Army's handling of Malmedy in March 1949. Tydings, who invited McCarthy to attend the hearings led by Senators Raymond E. Baldwin, Estes Kefauver, and Lester Hunt, got more than he bargained for. "The hearings," his biographer Ted Morgan noted, "provided a revealing glimpse of what McCarthy would later become in his anti-Red crusade."[46]

McCarthy harangued the American interrogators, alleging that they had engaged in violent tactics—kicking the defendants in the groin and crippling them for life. Another tack he adopted was to insinuate that the interrogators—"refugees from Hitlerism," or "39ers"—were Jews out for revenge. These "non-Aryan refugees," he suggested, "intensely hated the German people as a race."[47] He asked one witness, "If you were a German would you feel that you would be willing to have a matter of life and death decided by this man Rosenfeld?"[48] He attacked the committee, declaring that he was "very much disturbed" by what he saw as an attempt on its part "to want to whitewash the Army."[49] Despite McCarthy's outbursts, the subcommittee exonerated the Army. McCarthy claimed the subcommittee report was a "whitewash" and accused his Republican colleague, Senator Baldwin, of being "criminally responsible."[50]

Utley praised McCarthy. "Senator McCarthy," she wrote, "showed his fundamentally liberal convictions when in 1949 he insisted upon a reexamination of the German accused of complicity in the Malmedy massacre, whose 'confessions' had been extorted by torture. He took the position that due process of law must be upheld." In Utley's view, it was "totalitarian liberals" who refused to accept the truth about American misdeeds that rivaled, or even eclipsed, the crimes of the Nazis themselves. For all the national publicity it created, however, Malmedy proved to be a mere blip. McCarthy and his allies were after bigger game. The debate over "Who lost China?" provided it.

Chapter 7

MONSTERS ABROAD

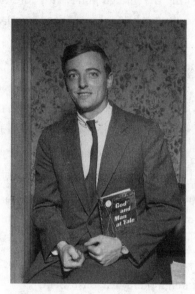

The proud author: William F. Buckley Jr. in 1951, a skeptic of democracy who would praise various autocrats, including South Africa's Hendrik Verwoerd and Chile's Augusto Pinochet.

When Harry S. Truman succeeded Franklin Roosevelt to the presidency in April 1945, he not only had to finish the battle against Nazi Germany and Japan, but also prepare for the postwar era. As Stalin carved up Eastern Europe, Truman decided to defend Western Europe against Soviet aggression by championing the Marshall Plan and NATO. In Asia, he began the transformation of Japan into a democracy and successfully resisted communist aggression against South Korea. With his approval of NSC-68 in 1950, the policy document that called for a massive military buildup to deter the Soviet Union, he further established the basis for America's victory in the Cold War.

Yet the Right depicted Truman not simply as a serial bungler, but an active benefactor of communist traitors in the federal government. It went from castigating the foreign policy elite for doing too much before the Second World War to counter Nazism to declaring that it wasn't doing enough to roll back communism. A rear guard of Republican legislators, led by Ohio senator Robert A. Taft, a long-standing foe of American militarism and an opponent of the Nuremberg war crimes trials as victor's justice, condemned NATO and the Marshall Plan as antithetical to a proud American tradition of avoiding entangling alliances. But the Right began to push for a more aggressive stance beyond the nation's borders after the fall of China in May 1949 to Mao Zedong's People's Liberation Army and Stalin's explosion of an atomic bomb in August of that year, maintaining that Truman was dangerously compromising American national security. These events, it argued, were not accidental. They were the product of a nefarious American foreign policy establishment.

Few figures played a more central role in prompting the Right to alter its approach to foreign affairs than Generalissimo Chiang Kai-shek, whom *Time* magazine hailed as "Christendom's most famed living convert." Formerly isolationist Republicans now adopted a new approach—Asia First.[1] "The demands for unilateralism in foreign affairs, selective military intervention, and strident anticommunism," wrote the historian Joyce Mao, "all owed a great deal to overseas conflicts with Asian communism."[2] In short, the fall of China offered the GOP a prime opportunity to rebrand itself.

Was Chiang an Asian Franco, a brave and worthy Christian leader battling atheistic communist hordes? He wasn't, but then, Franco wasn't the Franco of the Right's imagination, either. A corrupt authoritarian whose refusal to carry out land reform doomed his rule over China, Chiang opened the door to a communist takeover. But a phalanx of American politicians and activists—what was known as the "China lobby"—claimed that he was a valorous leader who could easily expel the communists from the mainland with sufficient American aid.

In her memoirs *Odyssey of a Liberal*, for example, Freda Utley stated that the problem with Chiang was that he did not enjoy totalitarian powers. Authoritarianism, she wrote, was the necessary precursor to any kind of representative government.[3] She, like many other conservatives, blamed his downfall on a State Department teeming with pro-communist officials. As the influential Republican congressman Walter Judd, a former missionary to China, put it, "Since 1945, our policy in Asia, in fact if not in words, has been one of abandonment of the Chinese government."[4] Indeed, the belief in a liberal conspiracy to abandon America's friends and allies to its enemies—Stalin, Mao, Fidel Castro, Ho Chi Minh, the Ayatollah Khomeini, the Taliban—became a staple of right-wing thinking.

The romanticization of Chiang was promoted by Henry Luce, whose parents had been missionaries in China, and by his wife Clare Boothe Luce, who was close to Madame Chiang Kai-shek. Henry, who was born in China on April 3, 1898, always harbored warm feelings for the country of his youth. He embarked upon his own mission to lionize Chiang, featuring him and his wife on the cover of *Time* in 1937 as "Man and Wife of the Year." As the head of the publishing empire of *Time*, *Fortune*, and *Life*, Luce was one of the most powerful media potentates in America. It was Luce who in 1941 coined the term "The American Century." He believed that the Pacific, not the Atlantic, was where America's true destiny lay.

Luce and his wife first met the Chiangs in 1941 and declared that they would be remembered for "centuries and centuries." Henry and Clare were convinced that the United States had a moral obligation to join forces with the Nationalists against the communists. Chiang made it clear to Luce that he opposed political or land reform and that he intended to crush the communist insurgency militarily. Four years later, when Luce traveled to China again, Chiang put on an extravagant welcome. Luce was greeted by ebullient schoolchildren and various newspaper editors and deans of Christian colleges, but he "was unaware that the citizens and children who cheered him in October 1945 were really actors playing roles in Chiang's version of Potemkin's village."[5] After Mao's forces captured Beijing, Luce was disconsolate, blaming Truman and moving even further to the right. It was *Time* that first asked, "Who Lost China?"

The battle over China propelled Joseph McCarthy's war against the Eastern foreign policy establishment. In ushering in an age of anxiety about communist traitors, McCarthy helped to jolt the GOP out of its old isolationism. In his history of the Old Right, Murray N. Rothbard shrewdly observed that McCarthy persuaded urban Catholics from the Eastern Seaboard to end their allegiance to the Democratic Party and vote Republican. The urban Catholic constituency, he wrote, was opposed to libertarian doctrines on the Right, and its "main political interest was in stamping out blasphemy and pornography at home and in killing Communists at home and abroad."[6]

The debates about communism and patriotism were inflamed by a sublimely arrogant former State Department official who checked all the establishment boxes—Harvard Law School graduate, law clerk to Supreme Court Justice Oliver Wendell Holmes, and president of the Carnegie Endowment for Peace. In August 1948, *Time* senior editor Whittaker Chambers, appearing before the House Un-American Activities Committee, fingered Alger Hiss as a fellow communist during the 1930s who had handed over secret documents to Soviet officials. Hiss, it transpired, *was* an actual traitor and he became synonymous, at least on the Right, with a maleficent liberal managerial elite. Hiss's detractors grossly inflated his significance, pretending that he had almost single-handedly influenced the outcome of the Yalta Conference. Chambers, who was vilified by the liberal Left for his apostasy, became a hero to William F. Buckley Jr., Ronald Reagan, and a host of other conservatives who saw him as a prophet, a genuine witness who had emerged from the communist crucible intact to warn his countrymen about the Kremlin's perfidious intentions. But they did not heed Chambers's warnings against associating too closely with McCarthy.

In February 1950, two weeks after Hiss was convicted of perjury and sentenced to two years in prison, McCarthy delivered a speech in Wheeling, West Virginia, accusing the State Department of harboring numerous traitors. Overnight, he created a national uproar as "McCarthyism" became a byword for a demagogic witch-hunt. In essence, McCarthy announced a culture (or, if you prefer, class) war on the Eastern establishment, decrying the "bright young men who are born with silver spoons in their mouths." As he denounced "appeasement" and "treason," McCarthy became the main threat to American democracy—"the first American," as the *New Yorker*'s Washington correspondent Richard Rovere wrote, "ever to be discussed and described as being himself a menace to the comity of nations and the strength of alliances."[7]

McCarthy always needed coaching, and he was educated in his militancy by Alfred Kohlberg, a New York millionaire and textile importer who regularly backed conservative causes (including Merwin K. Hart's organization) and revered Chiang. In 1946, Kohlberg, who was born in San Francisco in 1887, founded the innocuous-sounding American China Policy Association. He employed it to sully the reputations of State Department officials working on Asian affairs. As the *New York Times* reported, Kohlberg supplied McCarthy with what he claimed was damning information on China hands such as Owen Lattimore, an adviser to Chiang Kai-shek, and Ambassador-at-Large Philip C. Jessup.[8] Another source was William J. Goodwin, a lobbyist for Chiang and a former member of Father Coughlin's Christian Front. Goodwin acknowledged to the *Times* that he had "laid the groundwork" for McCarthy's feverish accusations.[9] If there was a conspiracy, then, it was the one spearheaded by McCarthy and his associates to besmirch the State Department.

―――

Chambers may have regarded McCarthy with disquiet, but Buckley worshiped him. He saw that McCarthy had tapped into something more than hostility toward the New Deal and the regulatory state. He represented something new—the rise of a revanchist

Right that could topple the liberal order. More than anyone else, Buckley forged the hatreds unleashed by McCarthyism into a lasting political weapon. Trolling the libs, denouncing political correctness, and overthrowing the deep state—all had their sources in Buckley's early efforts.

In the early 1950s, American liberals believed that they had triumphed, that a new consensus around liberalism reigned and that any sharp ideological disagreements were a thing of the past. Buckley would have none of it. At a moment when conservatism was in the doldrums, bereft of fresh ideas and energy, represented by an elderly war hero, Eisenhower, who could have run for the presidency as a Republican or Democrat, Buckley became its golden boy, writing dozens of books and thousands of newspaper columns, serving as editor of *The National Review* for decades, and running for mayor of New York in 1965. He was the animating force of the conservative movement, an impresario of outrage and impudence who, as Dwight Macdonald observed in *Commentary*, "would rather argue than eat." Arthur Schlesinger Jr. called him "the scourge of American liberalism."

Buckley's political views were shaped by his father, by Albert Jay Nock, and by the Yale political theorist Willmoore Kendall. In different ways, each instilled in him the belief that only a kind of conservative praetorian guard could maintain order. For much of his life, Buckley was on active service for the conservative cause, deploying his immense charisma and wit to win it fresh followers. He brought conservatism into the modern age, without ever wholly severing his ties to his youthful dalliance with isolationism and America First.

He derived his much of his affection for authoritarian leaders from his Irish Catholic father William Sr., a successful lawyer and businessman. William Sr. deeply admired Mexico's ironfisted ruler Porfirio Díaz, an anti-communist, a foe of organized labor, and a devout Catholic. William Sr., who was born on July 11, 1881, grew up in San Diego, Texas, on the border with Mexico. He spoke Spanish fluently and earned a law degree at the University of Texas.

After graduating in 1907, he opened an office in Mexico City before moving to Tampico, where he defended American and British oil interests. In 1909 he met Díaz, who gave free rein to American oil companies to drill along the Gulf of Mexico. After Díaz was ousted in 1911, Buckley backed the military strongman Victoriano Huerta, who overthrew the democratically elected government of Francisco I. Madero in 1913. Buckley urged President Woodrow Wilson to support Huerta's provisional government, but Wilson refused. In fact, the president wanted to depose Huerta. Wilson engaged in gunboat diplomacy, sending in the Marines to occupy the port of Veracruz in April 1914. The result was a fiasco as anti-American protests erupted across Mexico. Buckley was horrified. In a spasm of liberal moralism, America was seeking to impose democracy on a country that was unfit for it. Mexico City fell into anarchy. Widespread attacks against the Catholic Church took place, and the new Constitution of 1917 explicitly targeted it as well as foreign oil interests.[10] Buckley testified about the Mexican civil war before Congress, aided Catholic priests in Mexico, and helped an unsuccessful insurrection. In November 1921, after Álvaro Obregón came to power, Buckley was summarily deported.

The experience left an indelible mark upon him and his family. He bought a forty-acre eighteenth-century estate called "Great Elm" in Sharon, Connecticut, and a summer home in Camden,

South Carolina, known as Kamschatka (built in the 1850s by Confederate general James Chesnut and his wife Mary, the famed Civil War diarist). Buckley raised his ten children as rebels on behalf of tradition, regaling them with tales of his derring-do on behalf of the Catholic Church in Mexico. All his life he saw communist plots and left-wing revolution lurking everywhere. An anti-Semite and America Firster, William Sr. proclaimed that Hitler and Stalin should be left to fight it out between themselves. Preferably the former would dispose of the latter. Anti-Semitism as well as isolationist sentiment was rife in the Buckley clan: When four of his siblings burned a cross outside a Jewish resort in 1937, William Jr. recalled that he "wept tears of frustration" at having been excluded from the revelry because of his youth.[11] As a freshman at Millbrook, a Protestant preparatory school, William Jr., who graduated in 1943, was a proud America First advocate, attending several of the movement's rallies and faithfully reading *Scribner's Commentator*, which devoted itself to puffing Lindbergh and other isolationist figures. When tasked to deliver a five-minute speech before the school body, Buckley chose the topic "In Defense of Lindbergh."

Another influence on Buckley Jr. was more esoteric—an American journalist and political philosopher whom his father had befriended. At his father's urging, Buckley, then in his senior year at Millbrook, read Albert Jay Nock's sardonically titled book, *Memoirs of a Superfluous Man* (1943), which he cited for the rest of his life.[12] Nock, who wore a cape, carried a walking stick, and referred to himself as "a senile Tory," regularly visited the Buckleys, *père et fils*, at the family compound in Great Elm. Nock was himself influenced by the German sociologist's Franz Oppenheimer's 1915 book *Der Staat* ("The State"), which depicted its subject as an instrument of constant economic predation. The American state was also controlled, as Nock saw it, by what the Spanish philosopher Ortega y Gassett had dubbed a mediocre "mass man" in *The Revolt of the Masses*.

Only an elite—one that Nock, drawing on the Victorian cultural critic Matthew Arnold's concept of the "saving Remnant," shortened to "the Remnant"—could preserve Western civilization from mob rule. Democracy itself was the problem. It fostered mediocrity, hollow men who, once ensconced in the halls of power, were almost impossible to dislodge. Like H. L. Mencken, Nock viewed democracy as "an ochlocracy of mass-men led by a sagacious knave."[13] Nock's contempt for the masses, disdain for government, and skepticism of democracy would become the leitmotifs of Buckley's career as he enlisted in the Remnant.

Buckley's studies with the Yale political theorist Willmoore Kendall were also formative. Kendall, who was a Trotskyist in the 1930s, admired Franco, endorsed Joseph McCarthy and defended South Africa's apartheid system. Like McCarthy, Kendall loathed liberal elites. And like McCarthy, he wanted to counter them by rallying populist forces. A gifted scholar and slashing orator, Kendall championed the fusion of elite conservatism with populism, maintaining that liberals possessed an "instinctive dislike for the American way of life and for the basic political and social principles presupposed in it." He became a frequent correspondent with the University of Chicago political theorist Leo Strauss, who also emphasized the need for an intellectual elite to advise the philosopher-king.

In 1947, during his sophomore year at Yale, Buckley became a protégé of Kendall's. It eventually became a fraught relationship as disciple surpassed mentor, at least in terms of public acclaim and notoriety, but Buckley, who imitated Kendall's elaborate syntax, never lost his admiration for him. A tribute of sorts appeared in Buckley's 1999 novel *The Redhunter*. Buckley, whom Kendall recruited into the CIA in 1950, portrayed his old professor as Willmoore Sherrill of Columbia University, a curmudgeon who extols Joseph McCarthy and chides his colleagues for their complacent liberalism.

Kendall, who was born on March 5, 1909, grew up in Oklahoma. His Sooner origins instilled in him a lifelong suspicion of an Eastern establishment that he viewed as inimical to the virtues incarnated by the American heartland. At age seventeen, Kendall, who was fluent in Spanish and French, graduated from the University of Oklahoma with a degree in Romance languages. In 1931, he won a Rhodes Scholarship to study at Pembroke College, where he became the proud convert of his own scholarship, embracing Trotskyism after perusing Marx's *Das Kapital*.

After graduating from Oxford, Kendall worked as a journalist for United Press International in Spain. His sympathy for the Left began to diminish as Spain lurched into civil war and anarchy, instilling in Kendall a permanent fear of the violent consequences of sudden social collapse. He returned to America to take a position as an instructor at Louisiana State University and to earn a Ph.D. in political theory at the University of Illinois. Amid what he dubbed a "comfortable pluralism," Kendall shucked off his Trotskyist views. His early scholarly essays hailed the wisdom of the common man, attacked judicial review, and castigated efforts to "equate democracy with a particular set of 'natural rights.'" At bottom, the Bill of Rights, he stated, functioned as a mechanism to perpetuate liberal elite power.

In 1942 he began working for the government. "Intelligence work," his biographer Christopher Owen wrote, "pushed him away from the Left, for it was as an intelligence officer that Kendall made his rightward turn."[14] Kendall despised the liberals in the CIA and State Department, presaging the Right's hatred of both as redoubts of the deep state. In his short story based on Kendall's life, "Mosby's Memoirs," Saul Bellow voices Kendall's contempt for the foreign policy mandarins: "He said that the Foreign Service was staffed by rejects of the power structure. Young gentleman from good Eastern colleges who couldn't make it as Wall Street lawyers were allowed to interpret the alleged interests of their class in the State Department bureaucracy."

Yale served as Kendall's staging ground for successive assaults on liberal orthodoxies. In 1950, for example, he publicly supported the Mundt-Ferguson Communist Registration Act that would have forced communists to register with the Attorney General of the United States. The bill failed in the Senate. Kendall stated that communists were "incapable of participating in democratic government."[15] He was a proponent of what he called "absolute majoritarianism" to enforce public orthodoxy. It was time to get with his anti-communist program or to get out.

Buckley and his close friend L. Brent Bozell Jr. adopted Kendall's views with a vengeance. On campus, Gaddis Smith, a Yale graduate and historian, recalled, Buckley was "almost a God-like figure." In February 1950, when the *Yale Daily News* held a banquet dinner for the university's retiring president, Charles Seymour, Buckley, who was the paper's chairman, silenced the room after he rose to announce that Yale should promote "active Christianity" and free enterprise.[16]

Kendall and Buckley needed a political horse to ride. McCarthy was it. In 1951, in an essay in *The Freeman*, "Senator McCarthy's Model?," Buckley likened McCarthy to FDR. Buckley stated that the Right—condemned by Roosevelt in 1936 as representing "forces of selfishness and of lust for power"—now had its own populist demagogue. The moment to arraign the New Deal elites had arrived.

Buckley's best-selling 1951 book *God and Man at Yale* reflected the hostility of Kendall and Merwin K. Hart to democracy itself. In December 1951, Hart's National Economic Council held a dinner in Buckley's honor to celebrate his book.[17] Buckley argued that the duty of the university was to preach Christianity and free enterprise rather than relativistic doctrines that might well subvert the anti-communist struggle, as communism was the greatest threat to liberty that mankind had ever faced. To Buckley, academic freedom was merely a smokescreen for tenured radicals to suborn their young charges by propagating anti-American, even totalitarian, doctrines under the guise of independent inquiry. Put bluntly, Buckley wanted to replace his imagined left-wing academic community with a right-wing one.

In 1952, Buckley and Bozell created the Independent Committee Against Communism to help defeat Connecticut Democratic senator William Burnett Benton, who had called in 1951 for McCarthy's expulsion from the Senate.[18] "Senator Benton," charged a radio spot they wrote, "has pampered and coddled loyalty and security risks in his own office. Senator Benton energetically leads the Administration's efforts to cover up Communist treachery in government."[19]

Buckley was intent on reshaping the GOP. The advent of the Cold War, he argued, meant that the Right not only needed to raise doubts about liberals but also to abandon, or at least attenuate, its antipathy toward big government if it hoped to wage battle against communism. In an essay in *Commonweal*, Buckley maintained that new thinking about the federal government was overdue in conservative ranks. He propounded what amounted to doctrinal heresy— "we have got to accept Big Government for the duration" in order to overcome Moscow's global communist conspiracy.[20]

None other than Robert "Mr. Republican" Taft adapted to the perestroika taking shape in his party. Taft had entered Congress in 1938, the low ebb of conservative fortunes, when the Right depicted the New Deal as a totalitarian collectivist program and championed isolationism. Now, as part of his quest for the Republican presidential nomination in 1952, Taft, in his book *A Foreign Policy for All Americans*, argued for confronting China and for pushing the Europeans to provide more for their own defense. Writing in the May 1952 *The Atlantic*, Arthur Schlesinger Jr. observed that "Senator Taft, indeed, is a man in transition, an Old Isolationist trying hard to come to terms with the modern world." In his new incarnation as cold warrior, Taft warned that America should focus on protecting Taiwan from further communist aggression. The new dogma on the Right was that Washington should "untie Chiang's hands."[21]

But Dwight D. Eisenhower, not Taft, was the Republican nominee in 1952. Once more, the GOP establishment had spurned Taft and the populist forces he represented. An aggrieved Right began to pressure the GOP more than ever.[22] The moderate Eisenhower became its bête noire, condemned for failing to roll back communism. The young guns of this new revanchism, Bozell and Buckley, were both close to McCarthy. Bozell worked for McCarthy and Buckley wrote a speech for him denouncing James B. Conant, which McCarthy converted into a letter to Eisenhower.

McCarthy had backed Eisenhower during the 1952 race, but a rift with him began to develop over Conant's nomination. Recently retired as president of Harvard, Conant was slated to replace the Wall Street lawyer and former assistant secretary of war John McCloy as high commissioner for Germany. McCarthy professed to harbor grave doubts about Conant's fidelity to the anti-communist cause. He singled out a 1944 speech by Conant, which had been drafted by Harry Dexter White, a pro-communist Treasury Department official, praising the abortive Morgenthau Plan to pastoralize Germany as indicating that the former Harvard president had "played into the hands of our enemy."[23] Once again, this anti-communist ogre illustrated the Right's penchant for going soft on the Third Reich in the service of hyping the Soviet threat.

In 1954, on the eve of the televised Army-McCarthy hearings—which ended up leading to McCarthy's censure by the Senate in December of that year—Buckley and Bozell published *McCarthy and His Enemies*. Once again, liberals were defined as the great enemy of America for their complacency in the face of the communist threat. Buckley and Bozell stated that McCarthy's great challenge was "how to get by our disintegrated ruling elite, which had no stomach for battle, and get down to the business of fighting the enemy in our midst."[24] McCarthy himself couldn't follow their explication of McCarthyism, observing "It's too intellectual for me."

Yet the thrust was clear enough. They saw in McCarthy a welcome rabble-rouser who could bypass the gatekeepers of the 1950s consensus society—the Ivy League intellectuals, the Wall Street bankers, the liberal media. Buckley and Bozell's praise for him amounted to a popularization of Kendall's teachings about majoritarian rule and social consensus. At the heart of Kendall's sallies was a sweeping claim: John Stuart Mill had it wrong. The rights of the minority need not be respected. Instead, majority rule meant that Americans should excise the social "cancer" of communism from the body politic—just as McCarthy was doing.

In his zeal to promote the rollback, not just the containment, of communism, McCarthy accused Eisenhower of a "shrinking show of weakness" toward Communist China and demanded a naval blockade of it.[25] He also suggested that the administration should unleash Chiang to attack the "soft underbelly" of Mao's regime. Meanwhile, the businessman Robert Welch, the founder of the John Birch Society, published a book, *May God Forgive Us*, with Regnery Publishing that ascribed Truman's firing of General Douglas MacArthur to communist influence. After visiting Taiwan in 1955, Welch was enraptured, writing a pamphlet upon his return that depicted Chiang as a Jeffersonian republican. Chiang, he wrote, had grown up on a farm and embodied Western spiritual values.[26]

In targeting liberals as subversives, McCarthy and his ilk maintained that they were employing the same playbook that the Roosevelt administration had employed during the early 1940s, when it put Viereck and other Nazi agents on trial. The emphasis on loyalty and anti-communism was the most flagrant example of a long-standing trend of foreign policy informing conservative views of what was happening in—what was wrong with—America. And it underscored how the Right's addled version of history revealed its disdain for anyone who didn't share its animosities and hatreds. The Right was still loyal; liberals and the Left were still undermining American freedoms.

In August 1955, Joseph McCarthy wrote a letter to fellow conservatives about a new magazine that a young activist named William Buckley Jr. wanted to establish. He said that it would make an important contribution—"I am myself investing a token amount as a sign of my faith in it"—and referred to Brent Bozell, who was slated to become the magazine's Capitol Hill correspondent, as his "top assistant here in Washington."[27] The magazine's editorial staff included William S. Schlamm, a former editor at *Fortune*; James Burnham; and Willmoore Kendall—all ex-communists who warmed to McCarthy. Their counter-revolutionary spirit was unmistakable. In a letter to Frank S. Meyer, an editor at *The National Review*, Dwight Macdonald observed that it was "not a conservative magazine precisely because it doesn't stick to tradition, to conservative principles, but simply expresses the viewpoint of the Buckley type of anti-liberals, which are much too close to McCarthy for my comfort."[28]

Put otherwise, Buckley's associates were extremists, whether they called themselves conservatives or libertarians or fusionists. Once they had assailed liberals from the left. Now they assailed them from the right. In either case, their mantra remained unwavering—illiberalism and hostility to democracy. The magazine's inaugural editorial was warmed-over McCarthyism, expostulating about a vast left-wing conspiracy "engaged in a major, sustained assault upon the sanity, and upon the prudence and the morality of the American people." In 1956, a little over a year after the Senate censured McCarthy for his own incessant assaults upon the sanity, prudence, and morality of the American people, Buckley appeared with him at a rally at Carnegie Hall, where the Wisconsin senator engaged in his habitual bluff and bombast, condemning Eisenhower's armistice agreement with North Korea and praising General Douglas MacArthur—an American Caesar if there ever was one—as "the contemporary George Washington."[29] Later that year, McCarthy wrote an essay deriding former Secretary of State Dean Acheson's book, *A Democrat Looks at His Party*, for *The National Review*. After McCarthy's death at the Bethesda Naval Hospital of liver failure on May 2, 1957, Buckley, Bozell, and Schlamm wrote columns for the magazine competing with one other to fawn all over him. The reverence that the magazine's editors displayed toward Tailgunner Joe was also directed toward a host of strongmen abroad.

One such figure was Portugal's António de Oliveira Salazar. In 1956, the magazine invited him to publish an essay called "Be Resolved to Fight." In it, the Portuguese dictator declared that he was fighting for Western civilization and Christian values: "I do not doubt the spiritual and human inspiration which has enabled it to extend its radiations outward toward the universal brotherhood of souls, races and peoples."[30] Two years later, despite these professions of brotherhood, Salazar had his PIDE secret police exile and murder the opposition leader, Humberto Delgado. Salazar relied on torture, forced confessions, election fraud, and concentration camps to remain in power.

Another dictator that the magazine defended was Rafael Trujillo of the Dominican Republic. Kendall served as an adviser to
Trujillo and told the political philosopher Leo Strauss in a 1957
letter that the strongman had been treated unfairly in the Western press. El Jefe's bloody and corrupt rule over the Dominican
Republic, Kendall wrote, exemplified "Hobbes' 'public-spirited
philosophy,' in your own phrase, translated into palpitating reality;
wherefore to call it, as men commonly do, a dictatorship based on
something called force, is to miss all in it that is most interesting."[31]
Another fan of Trujillo was a co-founder of The National Review,
Revilo P. Oliver. In a 1959 speech to the Daughters of the American Revolution, Oliver, who was a classicist at the University of Illinois and a fervent anti-Semite, reprobated Dwight Eisenhower for
looking askance at the Dominican strongman. Then there was the
ex-communist Nathaniel Weyl, who wrote for National Review to
defend not only Trujillo's rule but also apartheid in South Africa. In
his view, Trujillo was a nifty leader who "supports religion instead
of trying to extirpate it, who has brought his people order from
chaos and who supported U.S. policies until Washington rebuffed,
reviled and castigated him."[32]

Franco, who ruled Spain for decades, drew Buckley's praise after
he visited it in 1957. In a "Letter from Spain," Buckley extolled the
Generalissimo as "an authentic national hero" who alone had the
fortitude to "wrest Spain from the hands of the visionaries, ideo-
logues, Marxists, and nihilists that were imposing upon her, in the
thirties, a regime so grotesque as to do violence to the Spanish soul,
to deny, even, Spain's historical identity."[33] Other Buckley siblings
harbored oneiric fantasies about Spain. In 1956, after graduating
from Yale, Buckley's younger brother, Fergus Reid Buckley, moved

to Spain and lived there until 1971. "Spain," Reid Buckley wrote, "is an idea, a dream—always—a crusade."[34] In 1984, he wrote a column in *Southern Partisan*, a neo-Confederate magazine, explaining that Asians, Africans, and South Americans, unlike Anglo-Saxons, possessed "no temperament for democracy."[35] To preserve America, it was imperative to keep out the riffraff by closing the southern border. In an old rhetorical trick of the dictator-loving Right, Reid Buckley presented himself as a supposed defender of democracy even as he expressed an atavistic loathing for it as soon as he believed his social status was threatened by non-white immigrants.

It was Bozell who went furthest, heralding Franco as a Christ-like savior. Bozell viewed Franco's Spain as an outpost of Western Christendom, providing a possible redemption for an America that had plunged into decadence and debauchery. It's hard not to suspect that, at least in part, Bozell may have been seeking an escape from his own emotional turbulence. He found comfort in the idea of Franco's Spain, a reassuring sense of order and stability that his own personal life conspicuously lacked. An alcoholic and later a manic-depressive, Bozell valorized Franco's theocratic authoritarianism, embracing political violence in his self-appointed quest to overthrow, as far as possible, rights-based liberalism in the US.

Bozell, who was born in Omaha in 1926, completed his conversion to Catholicism after he met Buckley at Yale. In October 1948 he joined the Conservative Party of the Yale Political Union and sounded Kendallian notes, displaying a disdain for bipartisanship in foreign policy and civil rights legislation. Before attending Yale Law School, he married Buckley's sister, Patricia, with whom he had ten children, all red-haired like both their parents. Toward the conclusion of *McCarthy and His Enemies*, Buckley and Bozell warned that communists were their current prey but "Some day, the patience of America may at last be exhausted, and we will strike out against Liberals."[36]

Some day arrived sooner than later for Bozell. He evinced an eagerness to strike out against liberalism, particularly after he visited Spain in the early 1960s. He was smitten by Franco's readiness to crush dissent. In his writings, Bozell poured scorn on the notion that freedom was a worthy aspiration. In early 1961 he and his family rented a farm near El Escorial, a grand palace-monastery. Living in Spain instilled in him the conviction that the Christian West wasn't simply at odds with liberalism, but in a fight with it to the death. The authoritarian Spanish model was worthy of emulation. The Spanish regime had promoted the power of the Catholic Church and banned other religions. Abortion, contraceptives, and divorce were prohibited by the church. The throne-and-altar conservatism that he witnessed, coupled with a wider medieval piety (and poverty), left him agog. In a September 1962 essay in *The National Review* called "Freedom or Virtue?," Bozell assailed the libertarians in the conservative movement. He asserted that the Founding Fathers offered "not a word suggesting that freedom is the goal of the commonwealth" and that upholding traditional morality and fostering religious virtue, not democracy and liberty, should be paramount. There was no point in arguing with liberals, he suggested, for they wanted to perfect man on earth, an inherently impossible goal that flouted scripture. His invocation of founding fathers serves as a reminder that the dictator-loving Right did not conceive of itself as foreign in nature, but as the faithful defender of the founding of America. It acted as though it had a patent on what constituted Americanism and the true Constitution.

At a Madison Square Garden rally in 1962, Bozell initiated the proceedings with an obscurantist plea for theocratic rule in America. While Senator Barry Goldwater fumed backstage, Bozell droned on about the "inner nature" of liberalism, which was "nothing but secularized Gnosticism trying to establish a paradise in this world." The *New York Times* noted that "Mr. Bozell referred repeatedly to the conservative cause as that of the 'Christian West.' "[37]

For Bozell and a Catholic philosopher named Frederick "Fritz" Wilhelmsen, who taught at the University of Dallas and wrote for *The National Review*, the recondite monarchist movement known as Carlists exerted a strong appeal. The Carlists named Wilhelmsen a Knight of the Grand Cross of the Order of the Outlawed Legitimacy. Both Bozell and Wilhelmsen were taken by the fervor with which the Carlists' armed, red-bereted followers opposed secular liberalism. They were attracted to what is referred to by conservative Catholics as integralism, the union of the church and state—and a doctrine that is being revived today by a faction on the Right. In 1966, Bozell openly advocated theocracy, establishing a Catholic magazine called *Triumph* that would deliver the truths that even *The National Review* shrank from airing. There was no waning of the Middle Ages for Bozell.[38] He complained that his brother-in-law was supplying anodyne "political prescriptions when only a spiritual rebirth can save the West."[39] For Bozell, it was apocalypse now.

On June 6, 1970, he organized the first violent anti-abortion protest in American history, leading a neo-Carlist faction of about two hundred protesters called the Sons of Thunder to attack a student clinic at George Washington University. Bozell himself assaulted a police officer with a five-foot wooden cross. The front page of the Sunday *Washington Post* showed Bozell in handcuffs as he chanted *"¡Viva Cristo Rey!"* ("Long Live Christ the King!"). "I didn't know what it was," a local policeman said, "but it didn't sound good." A year later, Patricia Bozell tried to assault the feminist speaker Ti-Grace Atkinson after she declared during a speech at Catholic University that the Virgin Mary would have benefitted from being "knocked up."[40]

Buckley was chagrined by the militancy of the Bozells. He lamented that he had become "estranged" from Brent, and tut-tutted that *Triumph* served as "an organ of militant anti-Americanism."[41] The Bozells' endorsement of violence to accomplish political aims was disturbing to their former allies. They seemed to be leading conservativism, or at least whoever was prepared to follow them, back into the wilderness. The Sons of Thunder episode turned out to be the high-water mark of Bozell's own activism, but he proved more prescient than Buckley about the ultimate direction of conservatism.[42]

By this time, Franco's Spain had become something of an old reliable on the Right. Africa, though, represented a new frontier. After Belgium left the Congo, its former colony, in 1960, and President John F. Kennedy supported a new, UN-backed government, the Right championed Moïse Kapenda Tshombe, the leader of a breakaway republic called Katanga. His bid for independence from Congo was supported by Rhodesia, South Africa, and Portugal, which depicted him as an anti-communist freedom fighter who could preserve the long-standing privileges that colonial rule had entailed. As the UN sought to unify Congo, Senator Goldwater became a sponsor in January 1962 of an organization called the American Committee for Aid to Katanga Freedom Fighters. It ran a full-page advertisement in the *New York Times* denouncing the UN's alleged war of aggression on Katanga that was signed by a variety of conservative luminaries. James Burnham wrote that the "United States was engaged in a military attack on a peaceful, orderly people governed by a regime that had proved itself the most pro-Western and anti-communist within any of the new nations."[43] *The National Review's* special rapporteur Ernest van den Haag traveled to the region to instruct readers about the UN's war of aggression. He wrote a pamphlet titled "The War in Katanga" that criticized the United Nations. In the January 30, 1962, issue of the *The National Review*, Tshombe himself published an "Appeal to the People of the United States" in which he insisted that they should persuade the State Department to end its "irrational policy toward Katanga and to understand, at long last, that the people of Katanga, animated by the most noble of ideals, will fight to the end to defend their liberty and their right to dispose of their fate." In truth, Tshombe was a corrupt, if irresolute, leader who parked the money that was dispensed to him by the Belgian government and the Union Minière, a mining consortium, in his personal Swiss bank account. His militia was composed of white mercenaries and Belgian officers, and he modeled his presidential guard, with their plumed helmets and swords, on the French Garde Nationale.[44]

None of this unduly perturbed his strange bedfellows in America. Tshombe was a useful club with which to bash the Kennedy administration, and the Right intended to wield it. On March 7, 1962, Bozell and Senators Goldwater and John G. Tower spoke to a crowd of 18,000 in Madison Square Garden at the second Annual Awards Rally of the Young Americans for Freedom (YAF), an organization that had been established with much fanfare in September 1960 at Buckley's Great Elm estate. At the event, red-white-and-blue bunting was draped over the balconies, young women in red-white-and-blue dresses greeted attendees, and behind the speakers was the slogan "Conservative Rally for World Liberation From Communism." Tshombe was supposed to be the recipient of an award celebrating, as YAF put it, "his dedication to the basic principles of freedom and his gallant leadership of his people's struggle," but the Kennedy administration had denied him entry to the country. The crowd booed and hissed when reminded of this fact.

Why was Tshombe the object of such conservative affection? One reason was that the prospect of decolonization in Africa frightened them. Burnham, for example, seems to have viewed matters in the spirit of Lothrop Stoddard—decolonization amounted to a dangerous uprising against white supremacy that would irrevocably weaken, if not destroy, the Christian West. In his lugubrious 1964 book *Suicide of the West*, Burnham sketched horror scenarios about the probable consequences of Africans claiming superiority over their former white masters.[45]

Another reason was that the Right saw Africans as inherently incapable of self-government. Thus Buckley declared that events in the Congo in 1961 suggested that "1) black Africans, with some but insufficient exceptions, cannot handle their own political and economic affairs; 2) they tend to revert to savagery."[46] For Buckley, the Katanga independence movement was a plaything with which to settle scores with liberals back at home for what he saw as the latter's excessively concessive stance on civil rights. It had little, if anything, to do with the issue of African sovereignty.

———

South Africa proved a more enduring interest than the issue of Katanga's fate. In 1960, the *New York Times* editorial page invoked the legacy of Stoddard to argue that where South Africa was concerned, "It is not a rising tide of color or of race that we need to fear. It is rather the rising tide of anger and intolerance. The Government of South Africa stand rebuked before the world because it is stirring up the spirit of violence." Buckley and company, however, channeled Stoddardism.[47]

There was a fundamental similarity between the stance of many conservatives toward South Africa and their view of race relations at home, at a time when the civil rights movement was forcing the federal government to pass new legislation to recognize the citizenship of Black Americans. In the 1960s, Buckley modified his earlier position, stated in a 1957 editorial, that Black Americans should continue to be denied the right to vote. He now maintained that voting rights should be restricted for the uneducated generally.[48]

One of the first mentions of South Africa in *The National Review* came in an editorial comment on April 23, 1960, that asked, "Deadend in South Africa?" Initially, the editors defended apartheid by depicting the problem of race relations as insoluble and therefore hopeless. "It is not a solution to assert that South Africa belongs to the blacks (who, as it happens, moved into the region after the whites)," the editors said, "any more than it is proper to say that the American South 'belongs' to the white man." The editors contended, "the whites are entitled, we believe, to pre-eminence in South Africa."

Perhaps the most revealing example of right-wing thought on South Africa came in a March 9, 1965, column by conservative founding father Russell Kirk. Kirk drew a contrast between the United States and South Africa. In the United States, he wrote, the Warren Court's notion of one man, one vote "will work mischief—much injuring, rather than fulfilling, the responsible democracy for which Tocqueville hoped." But America, Kirk believed, was vigorous enough to survive such folly. South Africa was not: "This degradation of the democratic dogma, if applied, would bring anarchy and the collapse of civilization." Repeating white South African propaganda, Kirk maintained that Blacks were not fit to govern themselves. Only a minority of the various races in South Africa, Kirk wrote, was "civilized." The European "element" had rescued South Africa, and "Bantu political domination would be domination by witch doctors (still numerous and powerful) and reckless demagogues." By the 1970s, apartheid would become increasingly offensive in the public eye, forcing the magazine to emphasize anti-communism as the principal reason for backing the regime in Pretoria. Buckley understood, as Bozell did not, that messaging matters—and that explicit extremism is a hard sell. It is a lesson about the anti-democratic Right worth remembering today.

Chapter 8

THE KIRKPATRICK DOCTRINE

Ambassador Jeane J. Kirkpatrick giving her final press
conference in 1985 at the United Nations, where she
had defended the Argentine junta against Great Britain
during the 1982 Falklands War.

When General Augusto Pinochet led a violent coup in Chile,
which the Nixon administration supported, against the
Socialist president Salvador Allende in September 1973, he became
a hero to William F. Buckley Jr. and his crowd. Here was a Porfirio Díaz in reverse—a military strongman who ousted the Left
to restore order and stability. With his characteristic efficiency,
James Burnham laid down the conservative line on the coup in the
October 1974 *National Review*: "The political choice in Chile was
never democracy versus dictatorship, but a rightwing authoritarian

regime versus the totalist regime to which the victory of the left under existing conditions must have led."[1] Case closed.

The problem, however, was that Pinochet's brutality in liquidating his opponents meant that it wasn't. In October 1974, Buckley received a phone call from the Chilean ambassador to Washington, Patricio Carvajal, asking him to recommend a public relations firm to sanitize Pinochet's reputation. To accomplish this daunting task, Buckley turned to Marvin Liebman, a veteran political activist who was left destitute following a recent and ill-fated venture into London theater and film production. Promoting Chile seemed like a good opportunity to pull himself out of penury. His razzle-dazzle may have failed in show business, but Liebman reckoned that it stood a good chance of persuading Americans that Pinochet was a worthy Catholic, anti-communist leader. (In 1990, Liebman published a memoir, revealing that he was gay and denouncing the Right for its intolerance of minorities.)

Liebman, who dubbed himself "the agitprop of the Right," grew up during the Great Depression in Brooklyn, where communist doctrines, ranging from Trotskyism to Stalinism, attracted many Jewish teenagers. As a fourteen-year-old, he joined the Young Communist League in 1937, hawking the party magazine *New Masses* outside Macy's. Liebman didn't leave his ideological home until after World War II, when he became acquainted with the horrors of the Soviet Gulag and gradually drifted into the conservative orbit during the early 1950s. He turned his talent for ideological combat against his former brethren. He and his new comrades always found it exhilarating to be on the barricades.

This P. T. Barnum of the Right excelled at creating front organizations, including the Committee of One Million to block

China's entry into the UN, the American Committee for Aid to the Katanga Freedom Fighters, the Committee Against the Treaty of Moscow, the Emergency Committee for Chinese Refugees, and the Young Americans for Freedom. "Through this labyrinth of fronts," John Gregory Dunne wrote, "Liebman has been largely responsible for both the respectability of the Conservative Revival and for differentiating it from the lunatic fringe."[2] He raised funds for *The National Review*, worked on the Goldwater and Reagan presidential campaigns, and called Buckley "the most important man in my life."[3]

On October 28, 1974, Liebman met with several Chileans, including Mario Arnello, who became the country's ambassador to the UN, to discuss Chile's image in America. Liebman and his Chilean counterparts agreed to establish an American-Chilean Council funded by American and Chilean businesses. After a car bomb exploded on September 21, 1976, in Washington that killed the exiled Chilean diplomat Orlando Letelier and his American assistant Ronni Moffitt, while injuring her husband Michael, who was sitting in the rear of the automobile, Liebman attempted to dispute Pinochet's responsibility for this act of state terrorism. Documents released in 2015 by the Obama administration confirmed that Pinochet was himself directly responsible for the bombing.[4] The American-Chilean Council and *The National Review*, however, went to great lengths to detach Pinochet from the murders, suggesting that Letelier was "an agent of the USSR" or a Cuban agent. Buckley himself contended that "there are highly reasonable, indeed compelling grounds, for doubting that Pinochet had anything to do with the assassination."

Buckley's writings indicate that he had a real affinity for

Pinochet that transcended anti-communist beliefs. To him, the dictator was a bona fide leader who knew how to exercise power and who looked the part: "In Chile, General Pinochet is archetypically the leader. His portrait is now seen in every government office: standing erect, big-chested, penetrating eyes, the faintest glimmer of suspicion there, coordinating with the slightly arched, light traced moustache: regal, is another way to put it."[5] This panegyric could be seen as prefiguring Trumpist boasts about "broadshouldered" leadership, which, then as now, betrayed an insecurity among those right-wing intellectuals who ridiculed "effete" liberals.

In its November 29, 1976, newsletter, the American-Chilean Council disparaged Pinochet's victims by employing quotation marks around the term "political prisoners." The council took *National Review* writers, including publisher William A. Rusher and Dartmouth English professor Jeffrey Hart, on junkets to Santiago. After Hart wrote an obsequious tribute to Pinochet in *The National Review* called "Chilean Spring" in March 1978, he received a letter from another fan of the dictator—former president Richard M. Nixon. "I only wish that this kind of objective writing," Nixon wrote, "could receive wider distribution in the United States."[6]

Nixon's praise notwithstanding, the scheme to whitewash Pinochet ended up backfiring. In December 1978 the Justice Department charged that the American-Chilean Council, which had been founded to "promote friendship and cooperation" between America and Chile, was, in fact, a front organization secretly funded by Santiago's military dictatorship. The accusation, the *Washington Post* reported, was as simple as it was sweeping: "the Chilean government for the last 3 1/2 years has engaged in a secret and illegal propaganda campaign aimed at making congressmen, journalists, academics and the American public more sympathetic to Chile's military dictatorship."[7] The Justice Department targeted Liebman—just as it had George Sylvester Viereck decades before—on the basis of the 1938 Foreign Agents Registration Act.

Liebman signed a "public consent" agreement that required him to take out newspaper ads in New York and Washington listing the civil complaints of the Justice Department and acknowledging the court's demand that his lobbying organization file amended registration documents.[8] In a press release, however, he protested his innocence and complained that the Carter administration had embarked upon a witch-hunt by deploying the Justice Department against him: "This is a major weapon that the Government has over any citizen or group it chooses to involve in legal proceedings." In his memoirs, Liebman was also unrepentant, stating that "Allende was a close collaborator of Fidel Castro and, if not an agent, certainly a willing pawn in the international communist apparatus aimed at taking over all of Latin America."[9]

Decades later, Jeffrey Hart, a professor of English at Dartmouth College, repeated another mantra of the Right, this one holding that Pinochet was an economic modernizer whose pluses far outweighed any minuses. (Even by the skewed standards of the Right, Hart had a notable thing for dictators: in his 1987 book *From This Moment On*, he asserted that Mussolini had put an end to "political deadlock and leftist riot" with his March on Rome and that his "domestic achievements were substantial.") After dismissing Allende as "elected by a minority," Hart depicted Pinochet in *The Claremont Review of Books* as a wise and perspicuous steward of the economy. "Under Pinochet," wrote Hart, "Chicago-educated economists reformed the Chilean economy, to the immense good of the Chilean people."[10] Hart's encomium to Nobel Prize–winning economist Milton Friedman's influence on Pinochet appeared only a few months before Pinochet, who faced some three hundred outstanding criminal charges, died on December 10, 2006.

That very same month a conservative stalwart who had served President Ronald Reagan in his first term as ambassador to the United Nations also died, prompting the *Financial Times* to comment that "It is somehow fitting that Jeane Kirkpatrick and Augusto Pinochet should die within a week of each other. For it was Kirkpatrick who did most to provide an intellectual justification for American tolerance for Latin American dictators, like Pinochet."[11] Indeed she had.

On April 6, 1980, Kirkpatrick, a professor of government at Georgetown University, met Richard V. Allen, a member of Ronald Reagan's campaign who would become his first national security adviser, at Washington's Madison Hotel. As they prepared to go upstairs to meet candidate Reagan and his entourage, she grabbed Allen by the arm and told him, "Listen, Dick, I am an A.F.L.-C.I.O. Democrat and I am quite concerned that my meeting Ronald Reagan on any basis will be misunderstood." They went to Reagan's suite, where she met William Casey and Edwin Meese. For about an hour Reagan's advisers complained about how a naïve and hapless President Jimmy Carter was failing to stand up to the Soviet threat before turning to the true subject of the meeting—Kirkpatrick's controversial essay in *Commentary* in

November 1979. Titled "Dictatorships and Double Standards," it denounced the Carter administration for sabotaging vital authoritarian allies such as Iran and Nicaragua and maintained that right-wing autocrats, unlike communist dictators, are fully compatible with American interests. Allen had sent him the piece, and Reagan was bowled over by it: "What you gave me to read was extraordinary! Who is this guy Jeane Kirkpatrick?"[12]

"This guy" was a pugnacious woman drawn to the mostly male fields of politics and academia who had to battle her way to prominence. Jeane Jordan, who was born on November 19, 1926, in Oklahoma, became fascinated by totalitarianism early in life. As a graduate student at Columbia University, she studied with the German exile Franz Neumann, whose landmark study *Behemoth* analyzed the composition of the Nazi state. She absorbed the lesson that the extreme Right and Left had trampled over ineffectual liberals in Germany, destroying the Weimar Republic before it ever had a chance to become a stable democracy.[13]

In 1955, she married Evron Kirkpatrick, a University of Minnesota political scientist who decamped to work in Washington at the Office of Strategic Services, and then the State Department. Through her marriage to the older Evron, a Cold War liberal par excellence, she became a member of a high-powered intellectual set that included Willmoore Kendall, Sidney Hook, and Freda Utley. Kirkpatrick had ambitions of her own. After earning her Ph.D. with a study of Juan Peron's Argentina, Kirkpatrick landed a teaching position at Georgetown University and then a yearlong fellowship at the American Enterprise Institute (AEI) in 1977, where she focused on Latin American affairs. As she watched the Carter administration's fumbling attempts to deal with revolutionary upheaval in Iran and Nicaragua, Kirkpatrick began writing a lengthy essay asserting that the administration had lost sight of America's traditional national interests and replaced them with balderdash about democracy and human rights that promoted neither. It was anti-Wilsonianism all over again.

In "Dictatorships and Double Standards," Kirkpatrick attacked Carter by drawing a fundamental distinction between authoritarian and totalitarian regimes. Autocracies, she said, could eventually adopt internal reforms leading to democracy. Totalitarian governments were immutable. American policy should be to ally with the former against the latter. In her words, "Although there is no instance of a revolutionary 'socialist' or Communist society being democratized, right-wing autocracies do sometimes evolve into democracies—given time, propitious economic, social, and political circumstances, talented leaders, and a strong indigenous demand for representative government." Traditional autocracies did not intrude upon the private sphere of family life, while precisely "the opposite is true of revolutionary Communist regimes." Her distinction, echoing James Burnham on Chile, provided Reagan with a handy intellectual justification for cozying up to right-wing regimes and rebel movements, while doubling down on confronting communist ones.

———

Reagan's appointment of Kirkpatrick to the position of American ambassador to the United Nations launched her on a new career that allowed her to unleash her inner conservative. No longer was she an obscure female academic trailing in the wake of her husband and his friends. Instead, her voice carried. Like her intellectually flamboyant predecessor at the UN, Daniel Patrick Moynihan, she used her new post to flay the Third World for wallowing in anti-American, anti-Israel, and pro-communist sentiments. After her appointment was announced, Kirkpatrick was invited to speak to the Bilderberg Group, an elite forum often accused of promoting one-world government. She told her audience that the thing that truly mattered in international relations wasn't the North-South divide or the environment but the clash between the Soviet Union and the United States. One member stood up to declare that her talk "sent shivers down his spine and struck horror into his heart."[14] He wouldn't be the only one.

As Reagan's UN ambassador, Kirkpatrick quickly became a celebrity for her fierce defenses of authoritarian regimes and denunciations of the Soviet Union. With her deep voice, piercing gaze, and no-nonsense mien, she struck a chord with conservative audiences. The *New York Times* called her "a phenomenon in American politics" and speculated that the former academic might even be presidential timber.[15] In the Reagan administration, Kirkpatrick belonged to a faction of hard-liners that included Defense Secretary Caspar W. Weinberger and National Security Advisor William P. Clark. Together, they made life miserable for Secretary of State Alexander Haig, who ended up resigning in June 1982. His replacement, George P. Shultz, also tangled regularly with Kirkpatrick, whom he grew to despise for her hectoring intransigence.

Kirkpatrick was an unabashed defender of right-wing regimes. After El Salvadoran soldiers seized, raped, and shot four American nuns on December 2, 1980, Kirkpatrick stated that "the nuns were not just nuns. They were political activists. . . . The answer is unequivocal. No, I don't think the government was responsible."[16]

Secretary of State Haig chimed in to suggest that perhaps the women had run a roadblock.[17] In June 1981, as she embarked upon a trip to Latin America that included visits to military regimes in Uruguay, Argentina, Chile, and Brazil, Kirkpatrick dismissed the idea of pressing them on human rights. They had "more elements of constitutionalism" than many other countries, she said.[18]

Her fervor for all things authoritarian exceeded even that of her colleagues. When the Argentine junta, headed by General Leopoldo Galtieri, sent 300 marines to the Malvinas, as irredentist Argentines insisted on calling the British-held Falkland Islands, on the morning of April 2, 1982, Kirkpatrick supported the action. She attended a reception the evening of the invasion at the Argentine embassy in Washington as a guest of honor. To the consternation of Haig and Weinberger, she saw it as a perfectly natural move, dismissing as "closet Brits" her colleagues in the Reagan administration who supported Prime Minister Margaret Thatcher.[19] Kirkpatrick met regularly with members of the Argentine regime to apprise them of the administration's diplomatic maneuvers. Indeed, in a testy phone conversation with Kirkpatrick, Haig accused her of being "mentally and emotionally incapable of thinking clearly about the Falklands because of your close links to Latins."[20]

Kirkpatrick had first met Galtieri in the summer of 1981. He may have been presiding over a "Dirty War" that resulted in the disappearance of 30,000 Argentinians, but she was smitten by his eagerness to battle communism. He was a staunch source of support for the Nicaraguan Contras, an insurgency movement that the Reagan administration was determined to back by whatever means necessary. After the Falklands War began, Kirkpatrick told CBS's

Face the Nation that ownership of the islands was in dispute and, indeed, that "if the Argentines own the island, then moving troops into them is not aggression." *New York Times* columnist Anthony Lewis wrote that her comment possessed "all the slippery ingenuity of a third-rate academic treatise."[21] But it was her detractor Haig who ended up flaming out, while Kirkpatrick's views retained their purchase during the Reagan era.

One of Kirkpatrick's earliest meetings as UN ambassador had, in fact, been with a high-ranking South African intelligence official, Lieutenant Pieter van der Westhuizen, and three of his aides. First the Reagan administration denied that the meeting occurred. Then it conceded that it had. "White House Says Mrs. Kirkpatrick Didn't Know South African's Role," read the *New York Times* headline.[22]

The fervor on the Right for South Africa had never abated. In August 1986, Jerry Falwell, the leader of the Moral Majority, announced his support for P. W. Botha: South Africa was "a country that is making progress and is a friend of the West," he said in a speech he gave in Pretoria. When Congress passed the Comprehensive Anti-Apartheid Act in 1986 imposing economic sanctions, Buckley denounced the move.

South Africa had become a losing cause, but others seemed more promising. Conservatives in Congress such as New York's Jack Kemp who had voted for sanctions on South Africa wanted to show that they weren't going wobbly in the fight against communism. So they latched on to another African country whose rebel leader was invited to the 1984 inauguration ceremony of South Africa's Botha as an honored guest and who was widely seen as a pawn of the apartheid regime—Jonas Savimbi, the leader of the National Union for the Total Independence of Angola (UNITA).

In January 1986, Reagan had excited conservatives when he declared in his State of the Union address, "America will support with moral and material assistance your right not just to fight and die for freedom, but to fight and win freedom—in Afghanistan; Angola; Cambodia and Nicaragua." In 1985, Congress had repealed the 1976 Clark Amendment banning aid to paramilitary groups in Angola, but military aid remained stalled. Conservatives were restless. *Commentary* editor Norman Podhoretz exhorted Reagan to do more and complained that liberals who took professions of pro-democracy sentiments "at face value when they come from communists now scoff at an anticommunist such as Savimbi in spite of the fact that, by contrast with communists everywhere, he has done nothing to forfeit his claim to good faith when he speaks of democracy and freedom."[23] But this was wishful thinking. As Sanford J. Ungar noted at the time, there was no cogent reason to see Savimbi as a Western-style democrat. Quite the contrary. "Although Savimbi has been wise enough to alter his pro-Marxist, antiwhite rhetoric when it is expedient to do so," Ungar wrote, "the UNITA slogan remains "Socialism, Negritude, Democracy, and Nonalignment."[24]

When Reagan met with Savimbi, who was dressed in a Nehru jacket, at the White House in January he assured him of his support in UNITA's struggle against the Cuban-backed José Eduardo dos Santos and his People's Movement for the Liberation of Angola, which took power in 1975 after Portugal exited the country. "We want to be very helpful to what Dr. Savimbi and his people are trying to do, and what we're trying to arrive at is the best way to do that," Reagan said. "We want to be very supportive. We're seeking a way to be of help."[25] Chester A. Crocker, the assistant secretary for African affairs, said Savimbi was "one of the most talented and charismatic leaders in modern African history."

Kirkpatrick, who was now back at the American Enterprise Institute, took a leading public role in touting Savimbi. On January 31, 1986, she served as master of ceremonies at the Washington Hilton International Ballroom at the thirteenth annual meeting of the Conservative Political Action Conference. That year's meeting celebrated Savimbi, Contras Comandante Adolfo Calero, and several Afghan mujahideen.[26] With Vice President George H. W. Bush seated to her immediate right at the head table, Kirkpatrick explained that in entering the hotel, she was dismayed to encounter an African National Congress protest and "I thought to myself, we don't need that national liberation movement. . . . Tonight, we'll have some real national liberation movements."

She described Savimbi as a man of "dazzling accomplishments . . . linguist, philosopher, poet, politician, warrior, guerrilla tactician. Savimbi has admirers the world over, and I have long been one of them."[27] After calling Savimbi "one of the few authentic heroes of our times" who wins the hatred of the "real Marxist myth makers," Kirkpatrick said that it was time for Washington to give real assistance to him, the Contras, and "all the other freedom fighters in the world." Kirkpatrick shouted that what Savimbi required were "Real helicopters! Real ground-to-air missiles!" The audience gave her a prolonged standing ovation.

After she presented Savimbi with an award from the American Conservative Union and the Young Americans for Freedom, they chanted, "U-NI-TA! U-NI-TA!" Bush, too, praised Savimbi and others who were "willing to fight and die" for liberty and justice for all. Savimbi himself told the crowd, "I am not a communist. I am a Christian." "If Jonas Savimbi were an American citizen," said Howard Phillips, the chairman of the Conservative Caucus, "he would be the presidential candidate of the conservative movement in 1988."

What transformed Savimbi into the Right's favorite warlord? A good deal of his celebrity was due to a forty-two-year-old swashbuckling American operative named Jack Wheeler, who attended the Washington Hilton event for Savimbi. Known as "the Indiana Jones of the Right," Wheeler traveled the globe, visiting anticommunist movements in Africa, the Middle East, and Latin America. He played an important role in persuading the Reagan White House to champion them as freedom fighters. Thanks to Wheeler, Reagan even referred to the Nicaraguan Contras as the "moral equivalent of the Founding Fathers."

Wheeler had long-standing ties to Reagan. After graduating from UCLA, Wheeler, who grew up in Los Angeles, was introduced to Reagan by his father, Jackson, a local television entertainer, in 1965 and named state chairman of Youth for Reagan during the Gipper's run for governor of California in 1966. A professional adventurer, he was described by Reagan's director of presidential speechwriting, Bently Elliott, as living "the dreams the rest of us talk and write about." Angola became the conservative magic kingdom. Wheeler traveled there in 1983, and reached the conclusion that "Savimbi may very well become the most dynamic and outstanding leader in Africa, if not the entire Third World."[28] Supporting him would liberate Africa from Soviet imperial designs and lead to an efflorescence of democracy across the continent.

Wheeler got Lewis Lehrman, a drugstore mogul and president of Citizens of America, to sponsor a meeting of four guerrilla movements in Jamba, where Savimbi had his headquarters and where the quartet of leaders issued a declaration, "Our struggles are one struggle." A letter from Reagan to Lehrman was read aloud, declaring "Their goals are our goals." Courtesy of Lehrman, each of the rebel leaders received a framed copy of the Declaration of Independence. When he returned to Washington, Wheeler conducted a briefing with slides for Reagan's speechwriting staff about the need to confront Soviet tyranny by aiding desperadoes abroad. "This was not some mundane realignment of the Republican Party; it was, rather, a cosmic realignment of the planet," wrote Sidney Blumenthal. "Now, conservative ideology began at the barrel of a gun."[29]

Savimbi endeared himself to the Right through the work of the Washington lobbying firm of Black, Manafort, Stone & Kelly in 1985. The firm adroitly molded the Angolan authoritarian into an American hero. Key to its efforts was Christopher Lehman, a former Reagan administration national security aide who traveled with Manafort to meet with Savimbi in the African bush, where Savimbi inked a $600,000 contract with the firm. Manafort and Lehmann crafted a plan for Savimbi that was designed to raise his profile with the Reagan administration, Congress, and American media, including coaching him on how best to deal with his critics. "During his 10-day visit," the *Washington Post* reported of Savimbi's trip to America in early 1986, "he had as much exposure on U.S. television networks and in the press as a U.S. presidential candidate."[30] Savimbi was profiled on CBS's *60 Minutes* and ABC

News' *Nightwatch*. "At each opportunity," the *New York Times'*
R. W. Apple wrote, "he sought to picture himself not as a friend
of Pretoria but as the foe of the Soviet-backed Angolan troops and
their Cuban allies."[31]

The Reagan administration continued to back Savimbi when he
visited Washington again in July 1988. He became a campaign issue
as Michael Dukakis, the Democratic nominee for the presidency,
called for cutting off aid to UNITA. Bush, the Republican candidate, was anxious to shore up his bona fides on the Right, which
viewed him with suspicion. Bush met with Savimbi and called him
a "true patriot." Terminating aid would be "an immoral sellout of
a loyal friend and a foreign policy disaster."[32] On a return visit in
early October, Savimbi met with Bush at the White House before
speaking at the Heritage Foundation, where he declared, "We are
not here to promise you that we will be the first, but my heart tells
me that we will be that example of freedom and democracy."[33]

This was preposterous. For all the praise that the Right had
heaped on him, and for all his pious asseverations about promoting
freedom and democracy, Savimbi was a ruthless leader who murdered dissenters within his own ranks, terrorized his country for
decades, and refused to accept the result of a free election.[34] There
were two UNITA movements: "Outside Africa it was a besuited
political movement talking democracy and freedom and fighting
Communism, led by a fluent and charismatic 'Doctor.' In Angola it
was a vicious dictatorship bent on getting to power with whatever
allies it could find."[35]

It wasn't Savimbi who offered an example of freedom. It was
Nelson Mandela. After he was released from prison in 1990, Mandela,
not Savimbi, embodied the values that the American Right purported

to espouse. Mandela, not Savimbi, was the local hero. So much for Kirkpatrick's scorn for the ANC demonstration outside the Hilton Hotel. The Right had willfully backed the wrong freedom fighter.

In supporting guerrillas around the globe, the Reagan administration wanted to undermine the Soviet Union through proxy warfare. In Afghanistan, where the mujahideen inflicted severe losses on the Red Army, the strategy worked, at least to the extent that it drove out the Soviet Union. Support for dissident movements inside the Eastern Bloc, particularly in Poland, helped subvert communist rule as well. But the outcome after 1989 wasn't one that the Right anticipated. It was girded for what was often referred to in conservative circles as (borrowing from John F. Kennedy) a long twilight struggle against an implacable Soviet empire. No one, after all, had depicted totalitarian regimes as immutable more stridently than Kirkpatrick. But after the formal dissolution of the Soviet Union, her fanciful theory of dictatorships collapsed along with it. Soviet premier Mikhail Gorbachev and Russian president Boris Yeltsin radically upended the geopolitical order with their reforming zeal. Almost overnight the Warsaw Pact was disbanded, Eastern Europe liberated, and Germany reunified. America stood at the apex of its power. And while many on the Right said that Reaganism had triumphed, others began to align themselves with a new crop of dictators and tyrants abroad. Now that the Cold War had ended, the Old Right began to stir once more in opposition to the liberal hawks and neoconservatives who claimed victory over the Soviet Union and wanted to go abroad in search of new monsters to slay.

Chapter 9

BACK TO THE FUTURE

Patrick J. Buchanan, campaigning in New Hampshire in 1992, set the stage for a fresh round of dictator worship and repudiation of internationalist elites on the Right.

When Iraqi dictator Saddam Hussein invaded Kuwait on August 2, 1990, the George H. W. Bush administration—after a warning from British prime minister Margaret Thatcher not to go wobbly—moved to expel him. Once Bush and his secretary of state James Baker assembled an international coalition that included the deployment of more than 500,000 American troops in Saudi Arabia and the Persian Gulf, Congress debated a joint war resolution, which the Senate approved on January 12, 1991, by a vote of 52–47. The majority of Democrats voted against it. The Democratic Senate majority leader George J. Mitchell stated that "we must make certain that war is employed only as a last resort." In their opposition to the war, the Democrats were also joined by a fiery apostle of the Old Right: Patrick J. Buchanan.

No sooner did the Cold War reach its terminus than Buchanan, in the spring 1990 issue of *The National Interest*, proclaimed that it was time to return to America First. He said that the US should remove its troops from Europe and play a diplomatic rather than a military role in future border conflicts on the continent, including in Yugoslavia. It should also withdraw from Asia. Foreign aid should be terminated and democracy promotion abandoned. How other countries ruled themselves was their own business. "What we need, is a new nationalism, a new patriotism, a new foreign policy," he wrote, "that puts America first, and, not only first, but second and third as well."[1]

But Buchanan did not leave it there. In attacking the Bush administration's push for war, Buchanan stated on the television show *The McLaughlin Group* that there were "only two groups that are beating the drums for war in the Middle East—the Israeli defense ministry and its amen corner in the United States." Buchanan was reviving an old feud with neoconservatives, whom he regarded as interlopers. That feud went back to 1982, when the neocons scotched the nomination of the troglodytic University of Dallas professor M. E. Bradford, a former supporter of Alabama governor George Wallace, to become chairman of the National Endowment for the Humanities in favor of William J. Bennett, a protégé of neocon godfather Irving Kristol. The Old Right—the so-called paleoconservatives—never forgot (or forgave) this Reagan-era battle over power and patronage.

The paleoconservatives accused the neocons of dual loyalty. In an October 1988 speech at the Heritage Foundation, for example, Russell Kirk stated: "Not seldom it has seemed as if some eminent neo-conservatives mistook Tel Aviv for the capital of the United States—a position they will have difficulty in maintaining as matters drift." The *Washington Times* reported that Midge Decter, the director of the Committee for the Free World, a member of the board of the Heritage Foundation, and wife of Norman Podhoretz, the editor of *Commentary*, called his remarks "a bloody piece of anti-Semitism."

Three years later, when Buchanan accused neocons of doing Israel's bidding to promote a war over Kuwait, *New York Times* columnist A. M. Rosenthal, among others, pounced. "We are not dealing here," he wrote, "with country-club anti-Semitism but with the blood libel that often grows out of it."[2] By the end of 1991, as he announced an insurgent campaign against Bush for the Republican nomination for the presidency, Buchanan came under fire from his former mentor, William F. Buckley Jr., who wrote a 40,000-word essay detailing and criticizing the perennial problem of anti-Semitism on the Right. Buckley not only examined Buchanan's record, but also that of his fellow *National Review* editor Joseph Sobran, who in March 1986 in an essay for the Hillsdale College publication *Imprimis* protested the "diabolization" of Hitler. A paleoconservative who was often likened to H. L. Mencken by his admirers, Sobran ended up being dismissed from *The National Review* in 1993 by Buckley.

Like Sobran, Buchanan never wavered, never apologized, never buckled. Instead, he fought back. His main targets were establishment Republicans—global elites, and Wall Street bankers. Throughout, Buchanan reserved particular animosity for the

the mostly Jewish neoconservatives, many of whom had moved from left to right, lamenting that they had hijacked the Republican party and severed it from its true heritage. They espoused a crusading Wilsonianism that sought to promote democracy abroad rather than the anti-interventionist credo of H. L. Mencken, Albert Jay Nock, and other opponents of entry into the two world wars. Like Mencken and Nock, Buchanan evinced a predilection for eyebrow-raising statements about Jews and Germany that testified to an unhealthy obsession with rewriting history. And like Mencken and Nock, he took a jaundiced view of democracy. An admirer of the southern confederacy and a defender of South Africa, he insisted that America was a "republic," not a "democracy."

Like Buckley, Buchanan was decisively shaped by a Catholic autocrat. His father, William Baldwin Buchanan, was a successful accountant and staunch Anglophobe who tried to toughen up his nine sons by giving them boxing lessons and punishing any infractions with a black leather belt. Pope Pius XII, Francisco Franco, Douglas MacArthur, and Joseph McCarthy were household demigods. In his memoirs, Buchanan recounted, "Before Pearl Harbor, my father's sympathies had been with the isolationists, with Charles Lindbergh and the America First Committee. 'I was all for 'em,' Pop told me. Sending millions of American boys to fight and die in Europe a second time, to pull Britain's chestnuts out of the fire, was something he could not accept. A popular sentiment, 'Let Hitler and Stalin fight it out,' would have summed up his attitude in the late 1930s."[3]

Buchanan admired his older brothers who fought in World War II and returned to tell him that the Germans had been great fighting men. His own martial exploits were confined to fisticuffs in Georgetown and throwing snowballs, along with his chums from Blessed Sacrament, at the "Boston Blackie," a bus that conveyed Black maids to and from the DC suburbs. When the March on Washington took place on August 28, 1963, Buchanan drove to the Mall early in the morning with his brother Buchs. As he later recalled, they encountered "George Lincoln Rockwell, the ex-naval officer and articulate Nazi, who had set up headquarters in Arlington, and whom I had never met."[4]

In a 1977 syndicated column about Hitler, Buchanan expressed admiration for him: "Though Hitler was indeed racist and anti-Semitic to the core, a man who without compunction could commit murder and genocide, he was also an individual of great courage, a soldier's soldier in the Great War, a political organizer of the first rank, a leader steeped in the history of Europe, who possessed oratorical powers that could awe even those who despised him." In a 1982 television interview with Allan Ryan, the former head of the Office of Special Investigations, a Justice Department office that tracked down Nazi war criminals living in America, Buchanan said that it was a waste of money to investigate Nazi war crimes and that he saw no "singularity" about the Holocaust.[5] In 1985, during a stint as White House communications director, Buchanan weighed in on the side of the Third Reich when the Bitburg controversy erupted, urging Reagan to remain steadfast. German chancellor Helmut Kohl invited Reagan to visit a cemetery in Bitburg that turned out to contain the graves of members of the Wehrmacht as well as the Waffen-SS.

NBC News reported that at a White House meeting about the visit Buchanan wrote the phrase "succumbing to the pressure of the Jews."[6] Buchanan denied it.

In 1985, after he resigned from the administration, Buchanan defended John Demjanjuk, a Ukrainian-born autoworker living in Cleveland who was accused of having been a concentration camp guard known as "Ivan the Terrible." Buchanan called him an "America Dreyfus." It turned out that he was not Ivan, but a different guard at Sobibor. In his columns, Buchanan, much like the generation of conservatives immediately after the Second World War had done, consistently referred to the Nuremberg war crimes trials as a form of victor's justice. In essence, he depicted a moral equivalence between Churchill's England and Hitler's Germany. It all came full circle in 1990 when Buchanan defended Saddam Hussein by invoking Hitler's example in the final days of the Third Reich. It was the height of folly, Buchanan wrote, to insist that Saddam Hussein exit Kuwait. His reputation in the Arab world would be toast. "Even Adolf Hitler," Buchanan wrote, "preferred to die, a suicide in his bunker, than agree to such a disgrace"—as though Hitler was not already amply disgraced in April 1945.[7]

Buchanan's own field of battle was American politics. When he hosted several dozen conservative leaders at his home in January 1987 to moot the possibility of running for the presidency, John Lofton, a columnist for the *Washington Times*, shouted from the rear of the room, "Let the bloodbath begin!"[8] Four years later, it did.

After the successful conclusion to the Gulf War, Bush's position looked impregnable as American troops marched down

Constitution Avenue in a victory parade on June 8, 1991. But the hard Right was increasingly disgruntled with Bush's presidency, including his conspicuous retreat on his "no new taxes" pledge. The breaking point came when Bush signed the Civil Rights Act in November 1991, which made it easier for employees to sue their employers for discrimination. Conservatives were infuriated that Bush had indulged this heresy. "Run, Pat, Run!," the influential *New Hampshire Union Leader* urged in a front-page editorial.

At a rally on December 11, 1991, at the New Hampshire state capitol, ten weeks before the first Republican primary, Buchanan announced that he was running for the presidency on a platform of America First. (The other challenger to Bush was the Louisiana neo-Nazi David Duke.) In launching his crusade for the soul of the GOP, Buchanan dismissed Bush as a "globalist" who was prepared to sacrifice American sovereignty on the altar of free trade and was indifferent to the growing economic disparities and hardships endured by the (white) working class.[9] He also depicted Germany and Japan as predators rather than worthy allies. "With a $4 trillion debt, with a U.S. budget chronically out of balance," he asked, "should the United States be required to carry indefinitely the full burden of defending rich and prosperous allies who take America's generosity for granted as they invade our markets?"[10] As he campaigned across New Hampshire to visit diners and commiserate with the white unemployed, Buchanan channeled what *Washington Post* writer Henry Allen sympathetically described as the "yearnings and bewilderments" of a White America mourning the vanished 1950s.[11] Most often, those yearnings expressed themselves as rage and bafflement, and no one was better at expressing them than the Scots Irish brawler Buchanan. Now it was the in prison and six strokes with a four-foot-long, six-inch-wide rat-tan cane. American officials officially protested the stern, archaic punishment, but Buchanan, Buckley, and other conservatives were elated by it. They hailed Singapore and its prime-minister-for-life Lee Kuan Yew as moral exemplars. In a column, Buchanan contended that "It is our moral elite's distance from reality . . . which induce[s] a moral paralysis when it comes to domestic enemies." In contrast to relativistic American liberals, Lee understood "first-hand what happens when bad men are allowed free rein." America, in other words, should look to Singapore for inspiration.

A year later, when he ran a second time for the presidency, Buchanan once again condemned America for trying to meddle in an authoritarian country's affairs. He flew to New Hampshire with a $1,000 filing fee in hand on December 10, 1996, to register for the upcoming primary. The first thing he talked about wasn't immigration or abortion but his sympathy for the marauding Serbs, who had perpetrated genocide against Bosnian Muslims. He blasted Senate Majority Leader Bob Dole for endorsing President Bill Clinton's stationing of American troops in the Balkans to maintain the fragile peace created by the Dayton Accords, which American special envoy Richard Holbrooke had painstakingly negotiated.[14]

At a rally in Manchester, Buchanan declared, "I say to Bob Dole, my old friend: 'Bob, lead this fight to keep us out of Bosnia.' If you can't, Bob, stand aside and I will." A flurry of other Republican candidates, including Senator Phil Gramm and Alan Keyes, agreed. Keyes, a former aide to Jeane Kirkpatrick at the UN, complained that Dole was "acting as Bill Clinton's henchman." After

Buchanan won the New Hampshire primary in February 1996, he received a telegram of congratulations from abroad. The nationalist Russian presidential candidate Vladimir Zhirinovsky wrote to suggest that Jews—"this small but troublesome tribe"—in both Russia and America should be deported forthwith to reservations in the hinterlands.[15]

That Buchanan would receive a message from Russia with love was no accident. In the 1990s, he consistently voiced Moscow's geopolitical line, warning that NATO expansion and intervention in the Balkans were colossal errors. Buchanan was not alone in his apprehensions—realist thinkers such as the diplomat George F. Kennan opposed NATO expansion as well—but Buchanan came at these questions from a distinctive place, not of foreign policy realism (which he claimed to espouse), but outright fervor for Christian nationalist Russia.

It was Moscow's economic debility that had made it possible for the Clinton administration to push for enlarging NATO in 1995 and to launch NATO's Operation Deliberate Force in August of that year to stymie Serbia's incursion into Bosnia. President Clinton engaged in a combination of dexterous diplomacy and muscle-flexing to earn Russian president Boris Yeltsin's acceptance of NATO expansion at meeting in Helsinki in March 1997.[16] Buchanan dismissed Bosnia as a "fictitious country" and lamented that Poland, Hungary, and the Czech Republic had been accepted into NATO, with a second round looming for the Baltic States.

Two years later, Buchanan attacked the Clinton administration for intervening in Kosovo to halt Serbian ethnic cleansing. The seventy-eight-day NATO bombing campaign forced Serbian president Slobodan Milošević's forces to exit Kosovo in June 1999.

"This Balkan war," Buchanan said, "is not America's war." Once again, he wasn't the only critic of that campaign, prompting Robert Kagan to observe that too many "Republicans have adopted a Neville Chamberlain attitude toward the population of Kosovo, yet another distant people whose fate need not concern us."[17] Kagan's evocation of Chamberlain was a staple of neocon discourse, but in the case of Buchanan it was quite accurate. In fact, Buchanan had always supported appeasement.

Buchanan was launching a third wave of revisionism, one that mirrored those that followed the First and Second World Wars. He blamed America first, stating that there was no need for the US to intervene in Europe and that liberal elites were responsible for eviscerating American sovereignty. Buchanan's book *A Republic, Not an Empire* (1999) offered a kind of doxology for the post–Cold War, post-Reagan Right. Buchanan expounded at length on the perils of an America engaged with the rest of the world, condemning international crusades and predicting that America's global hegemony would soon be challenged. In a lengthy historical exegesis, he expressed the traditional conservative grievances about America's path in the twentieth century. After World War I, Buchanan claimed, historians showed how British propaganda had "cleverly suckered" America into a senseless war.[18] Then came the Second World War. The election of 1940, Buchanan wrote, was "among the most dishonest ever held" as neither Franklin Roosevelt nor Wendell Willkie was willing to fess up that they supported going to war.[19] (At least Buchanan was willing to stipulate that it was only "among" rather than "the" most dishonest.) In praising the original America First movement, Buchanan dismissed the notion that it contained insalubrious elements. The reverse was the truth. Those who "were big on war were Wall Street bankers, society groups, commentators, plutocratic newspapers, magazine writers, the intelligentsia, communists, Hollywood, and the party's big contributors." By contrast, the upstanding patriots of America First—small town types and members of local chambers of commerce—wanted "no part of a new war."[20]

Buchanan suggested that Hitler was preoccupied with attacking the Soviet Union, not the United States.[21] It was Roosevelt and his advisers who were the malevolent actors; on the eve of war, they not only accepted, but welcomed the prospect of conflict with Japan. The liberal elite had seized upon World War II to transform America into the world's policeman, Buchanan argued, but with the end of the Cold War, it was time to come home. In touting the virtues of retreat, however, Buchanan never could conceal his admiration for a certain kind of right-wing autocrat abroad. What he really longed for was a kind of internationalism rooted in those small towns and conservative values and in whiteness, whether in the US or in Serbia or Russia or South Africa or elsewhere. The Right had its own internationalist agenda even if it was loath to use that term.

One prospective candidate for the presidency who picked up on—and initially disparaged—Buchanan's unusual history lessons was a loudmouthed Manhattan real estate mogul.[22] Donald J. Trump, who was contemplating running on the Reform Party ticket in 1999, viewed Buchanan as a rival. On a trip to Los Angeles in December of that year, Trump made sure to visit the Simon Wiesenthal Center's Museum of Tolerance in Los Angeles together with his twenty-six-year-old girlfriend Melania Knauss. After perusing the exhibits and declaring, "Good job, Rabbi!" to

Marvin Hier, the museum's director, Trump went on to deliver a conventional statement in the atrium that was directed at Buchanan: "In the 1930s, everyone thought Hitler was a fringe element who could never come to power. History showed otherwise. We must recognize bigotry and prejudice and defeat it whenever it appears." Appearing on *The Tonight Show*, Trump was more distinctive: "He's obviously been having a love affair with Adolf Hitler."[23]

Trump's rebuke notwithstanding, Buchanan received the Reform Party's nomination on August 12, 2000, in Long Beach, California, where he once more zeroed in on Kosovo and the Clinton administration. "Why did we do this?" he asked. "Why did we bomb this little country for 78 days when it never threatened or attacked the United States?" Secretary of State Madeleine Albright, whose family fled to London during the Nazi invasion of Czechoslovakia, declared that America was the "indispensable nation." It had an obligation to stand up for democracy and human rights. Buchanan saw it differently. Washington should leave authoritarians unmolested. Human rights were not America's concern. Its commitments were exceeding its obligations. Overreach was leading to the rise of an American empire that would suffer the dire fate of previous ones.

These were the nostrums that Buchanan preached with metronomic regularity. For the most part, they fell flat. At a moment when American power was unchallenged, the economy booming and the budget balanced, Buchanan seemed like a Cassandra. When Bill Clinton left office in January 2001, he enjoyed a Gallup poll approval rating of 65 percent, a record high for American presidents. Over the next decade, however, the imperialist follies of a Republican, not a Democratic, administration would give Buchanan's arguments real traction on the Right.

In September 2002 a new magazine was launched at the National Press Club by Buchanan, former *New York Post* editorial page writer Scott McConnell, and Greek shipping heir and playboy Taki Theodoracopulos. It was called *The American Conservative*. Washington was in a triumphalist mood as American forces prepared to crush Saddam Hussein's army as part of the George W. Bush administration's global war on terror. But the new magazine's cover story was called, "Iraq Folly: How Victory Can Spell Defeat."

The magazine truly did want to stand athwart history and yell "Stop," as William F. Buckley Jr. had claimed *The National Review* would. In his inaugural column, Theodoracopulos explained, "My main aim is to remind Americans that since we are a predominantly white society rooted in Christianity, our responsibility to immigrants is to bring them into our culture, not the other way around."[24] At a press conference announcing the magazine's birth, Buchanan was asked why he was receptive to "Taki," as he was known, coming to America as a Greek immigrant. Buchanan responded that as far as he knew, Taki had not crossed over the Rio Grande. "I came on a yacht," Taki said. With the Bush administration intent on regime change abroad, the target of the *American Conservative* crew was the neocons. As Buchanan boasted, "We are not neo-anything. We are old church, old right and we believe in the old republic and whenever we hear phrases like 'new world order,' we tend to release the safety catch from our revolvers."[25]

Even before the first issue of the magazine appeared, it was dismissed as at best a curiosity. *The New Republic* crowed that it would become "Buchanan's surefire flop." Liberal hawks and neoconservatives forecast a new Pax Americana. "Over time it has become clear," Franklin Foer wrote, "that on this side of the Atlantic, 9/11 hasn't boosted the isolationist right; it has extinguished it. Instead of America Firstism, September 11 has produced a war on terrorism that has virtually ended conservative qualms about expending blood and treasure abroad." Buchanan & Co. could hardly have selected "a worse time to start a journal of the isolationist right."[26] *Weekly Standard* editor William Kristol, too, was unimpressed. "I don't intend to pay much attention to it," he said. "I think Taki is really a kind of repulsive character, and I'm not a huge fan of Pat's, either."[27]

The National Review agreed. In a sign of how far the Right had drifted from its original moorings and toward neoconservatism, the magazine featured a cover story by David Frum, a former speechwriter for George W. Bush who had coined the phrase "axis of evil" for the president's 2002 State of the Union speech. Frum denounced, as the piece's title put it, "Unpatriotic Conservatives." One of Frum's targets, the paleoconservative columnist Robert Novak, a critic of American policy toward Israel, called it "an attempt to silence people regarded as conservatives, particularly me, who do not agree with positions the administration has taken on some aspects of foreign policy."[28] To this day, the populist Right invokes his essay as a kind of stab in the back, while Frum, on the twentieth anniversary of its appearance, tweeted that "the piece caused a ruckus at the time, but it's been all too sadly proven prophetic."

Frum lashed into the anti-war conservatives as nothing more than modern-day quislings who had made common cause with left-wing and Islamist movements. Accusing them of rejoicing in American defeat, Frum read Buchanan, Novak, and McConnell, among others, out of the movement. Frum took umbrage at Buchanan's charge in *The American Conservative* that through their "arrogance, hubris, and bellicosity," a cabal of neocon writers and government officials had stirred up antagonism against America in Europe and the Middle East. "Since 9/11," wrote Frum, "the paleo-conservatives have collapsed into a mood of despairing surrender unparalleled since the Vichy republic went out of business."[29] He concluded that the paleoconservatives began by hating neoconservatives, moved on to hating George W. Bush, and ended by "hating their country."

Yet two decades on, *The Weekly Standard* was defunct. The editors of *The National Review*, who initially condemned Donald J. Trump as a kind of moral leper, were running tributes to him. And McConnell could deliver a toast at the twentieth anniversary gala dinner of the *The American Conservative* on November 17, 2022, to Buchanan, celebrating his path to victory. McConnell recollected that when he first met a Buchanan campaign staffer at the *New York Post* in 1992 some of his ideas—opposing free trade and attacking NATO—"seemed nuts to me," but "now of course these ideas are more mainstream. . . . They form more or less the bedrock of conservative populism, which is an international movement."[30]

How did it happen? How did Frum and others end up in the wilderness as apostates? And how did the Old Right reemerge triumphant?

A large part of the answer is that the Iraq War did indeed become synonymous with the very arrogance, hubris, and bellicosity that Buchanan had condemned. In this instance, at least, Buchanan's old campaign button—"Pat's Right"—was prescient. The neocons were a victim of their own success. They got the war they wanted.

It was the neocons who had provided George W. Bush with the conceptual framework, following the 9/11 attacks, for a sweeping campaign for regime change in the Middle East. In 1997, for instance, Robert Kagan published an article in *Commentary* that revisited Jeane J. Kirkpatrick's essay on dictators and double standards. Kagan said that it was flawed. According to Kagan, "we could and should be holding authoritarian regimes in the Middle East to higher standards of democracy, and encouraging democratic voices within those societies, even if it means risking some instability in some places."[31] When I visited Kirkpatrick at her office at the American Enterprise Institute shortly after Kagan's essay appeared, she was indignant. As part of an older generation of neocons, she was more inclined to embrace authoritarians as a force for stability. The new generation, represented by Kagan and William Kristol, was not. She regarded the push for war in Iraq by the George W. Bush administration with misgivings.

As the Bush administration engaged in a massive public relations push to sell the Iraq War, the hypertrophied language from neocons such as Max Boot also helped set the stage for a backlash. With his paeans to the British imperial era, Boot almost made it too easy for the Old Right. "Afghanistan and other troubled lands today cry out for the sort of enlightened foreign administration once provided by self-confident Englishmen in jodhpurs and pith helmets,"

Boot declared in the October 15, 2001, *The Weekly Standard*. Nor was this all. Further victories beckoned. "Once we have deposed Saddam," he predicted, "we can impose an American-led, international regency in Baghdad, to go along with the one in Kabul. With American seriousness and credibility thus restored, we will enjoy fruitful cooperation from the region's many opportunists, who will show a newfound eagerness to be helpful in our larger task of rolling up the international terror network that threatens us."[32]

When the war turned into a debacle, a few critics on the Right were unsparing. They saw the war—based on deceptive government propaganda about weapons of mass destruction and an imminent threat—as a quasi-Wilsonian endeavor that flouted traditional conservative strictures about utopian crusades. William F. Buckley Jr. was among the critics. He still had enough Albert Jay Nock in him to dub the war an unmitigated disaster, returning to the Old Right's traditional hostility toward military adventurism abroad. It was Buckley who had originally welcomed the Democratic neocons to the conservative movement in the early 1970s. Now, when queried about the neocons by the *New York Times*' Deborah Solomon, he said, "I think those I know, which is most of them, are bright, informed and idealistic, but that they simply overrate the reach of U.S. power and influence."[33]

Then there was Congressman Ron Paul, who ran for the Republican nomination for the presidency in 2008 and 2012. Paul was a traditional libertarian conservative whose anti-globalist stands were not dissimilar to those of third-party candidate H. Ross Perot in 1992. He was also something of a fuddy-duddy. But in bashing away at military intervention and neocons, Paul appealed to younger voters and helped to foster a populist insurgency.

Nevertheless, the neocons did not really experience a reckoning in the GOP itself during the 2008 or 2012 presidential campaigns, when Senator John McCain and Governor Mitt Romney, respectively, were the Republican candidates. Both were foreign policy hawks. Both had numerous neocon advisers. Both backed the war. And both went down to defeat.

After Kagan published an essay in 2014 in *The New Republic* criticizing President Barack Obama's foreign policy, "Superpowers Don't Get to Retire," Obama invited him to the White House to discuss it. When the *New York Times* profiled Kagan, he said that the deleterious consequences of Obama's hesitation about deploying military power had "vindicated to some degree" the neoconservatives. Kristol added, "The sort of desire to say 'Neocon! Neocon! Neocon!' has moved out a little bit to the fringe."[34]

Not exactly. In April 2016 I saw firsthand the inroads that Trump was making when the Ethics and Public Policy Center held a lavish fortieth-anniversary dinner at the St. Regis Hotel in Washington to honor House Speaker Paul Ryan. Kristol was the master of ceremonies. Eugene Scalia and his wife were sitting next to me, and she explained to me that her only regret about her father-in-law, Justice Antonin Scalia, was that he wasn't conservative enough. When Kristol told the audience that Donald Trump had just won the New York Republican primary, there were loud groans. Kristol went on to note, jocularly, that Trump had referred to him as "dopey" and the editor of a "slightly failing magazine."

But as the primaries continued, it didn't seem like a laughing matter. In February, Trump had already attacked George W. Bush and the Iraq War in the South Carolina primary. Trump's accusation that Bush lied about weapons of mass destruction got most of the attention. But he also made clear his fondness for Russia. After Florida governor Jeb Bush said that it was "ludicrous" to consider Russia a partner in the fight against terrorism, Trump responded, "Jeb is so wrong."[35]

Only a few weeks earlier, Vladimir Putin had convened with his spy chiefs and senior ministers during a special meeting of Russia's national security council to authorize a multiagency operation to assist the "mentally unstable" Trump.[36] Putin established a new working group that included Defense Minister Sergei Shoigu and Federal Security Bureau head Alexander Bortnikov to execute it. The top-secret Kremlin plan—No. 32–04\vd—deemed Trump the "most promising candidate" and called, among other things, for creating "media viruses" and cyber-hacking on behalf of Trump.

At the same time, Trump began his own effort to condition the Republican party to accept and even adopt his fawning view of Russia and Putin. Trump converted his pro-authoritarian sentiments into a weapon with which to bully any dissenters in the GOP into submission. In schooling the Republican faithful, Trump took a large swath of the party back in time.

Throughout the campaign, Trump returned repeatedly to the theme that Russia was misunderstood by the West. In December 2015, on MSNBC's *Morning Joe*, for instance, Trump made his veneration of Putin, who had recently termed him "brilliant," plain. Trump dismissed host Joe Scarborough's warning that Putin murdered journalists and political opponents without compunction as so much piffle. "I've always felt fine about Putin," Trump said. "He's a strong leader. He's a powerful leader."

In addition to his professions of admiration for Putin, Trump threatened to withdraw from NATO and depicted Russia as facing the same Islamic terrorist threat as America. It was time to join forces with the Kremlin. In July, at the Republican National Convention in Cleveland, Trump and his campaign manager Paul Manafort—the onetime propaganda chief for Jonas Savimbi and, more recently, a lobbyist for the Russian-backed Ukrainian president Viktor Yanukovych, who fled to Moscow after a spontaneous revolution overthrew him in 2014—eviscerated a proposed amendment to the Republican platform on supporting Ukraine. One platform committee member remarked, "This is another example of Trump being out of step with GOP leadership and the mainstream in a way that shows he would be dangerous for America and the world."[37] But the GOP would capitulate to Trump rather than Trump capitulating to the GOP.

Nothing seemed to dent Trump's confidence in the Kremlin. He continued to flaunt his Putin idolatry. He wasn't fazed by the serial revelations of his ties to Russia. Rather, Putin's pursuivant exploited the accusations to subdue the GOP further.

On May 10, 2017, one day after firing FBI Director James Comey over "this Russia thing," now-President Trump met with Russian foreign minister Sergey Lavrov and ambassador Sergei Kislyak in the Oval Office, where he divulged highly classified information to his Russian guests on the terrorist group Islamic State that had not even been shared with America's closest allies.[38] Trump's supporters in Congress didn't see anything wrong with the meeting. In July, Trump thanked Putin for evicting American diplomats from Moscow, claiming that "We'll save a lot of money."

None of it seemed to matter. Trump's summit meeting in Helsinki in July 2018, where the American president sided with Putin against his own FBI over allegations of Russian attempts to influence the American election? A brief flap. The Mueller Report? With the aid of Attorney General William P. Barr, Trump turned it to his advantage, explaining to his followers that it was merely the latest installment in the ongoing saga of the Deep State's nefarious attempt to abort his presidency. The Senate 2020 Intelligence Committee report on the 2016 election detailing Russian interference and contacts with the Trump campaign? More fodder for his "Russia hoax" claim.

During his presidency, Trump, as far as possible, sought to sabotage NATO and undermine Ukraine, whose president he unsuccessfully tried to coerce into launching an investigation of Biden for his own political advantage, leading to his first impeachment trial and acquittal in February 2020. Once more, he could present himself as a victim to his followers.

The public narrative today, largely shaped by Trump's lackeys, is that he was "innocent" of any "collusion," that Democrats and centrists overreached in their accusations. So it has become easy to forget how strange it was to see a president of the United States profusely and repeatedly praise any foreign nation—and authoritarian Russia in particular. In lavishing praise on Putin and other dictators, however, Trump wasn't creating a new style of right-wing politics. Instead, he was building on a long-standing tradition.

In February 2017, a month after Donald J. Trump's inauguration, Christopher Caldwell, a senior fellow at the Claremont Institute, delivered a speech about Putin at the Hillsdale College National Leadership Seminar in Phoenix, Arizona. Caldwell, who was an editor at *The American Spectator* in the 1990s before moving to *The Weekly Standard*, spent the 2000s writing about an increasingly multicultural France. In a sense, Caldwell was Trumpian before there was a Trump. Unlike Roger Kimball, the editor of *The New Criterion*, who complained in 2016 that "For many of us, what is most troubling about Donald Trump is not his particular views or policies—much though we might disagree with them—but rather the aroma of populist demagoguery and menace that surrounds him," Caldwell embraced conservative populism early on.[39]

He advanced a coherent case for nationalism, arguing that attempting to create a multicultural society, or acceding to demands for one, was a mistake. When riots took place in France in 2005, for example, Caldwell said that the government needed to take a much harder line against Muslims. "Pouring new energy into their traditions, rather than diluting them," he wrote, "may be what the moment demands of the French, including the minorities among them."[40] That a crackdown would likely have been a surefire recipe for exacerbating rather than calming tensions seemed to bother him not at all. In his 2009 book *Reflections on the Revolution in Europe*, Caldwell expanded his critique. Muslims, he said, had come to constitute an "adversary culture" (a term he borrowed from the literary critic Lionel Trilling, who had employed it in the 1960s to describe disaffected American intellectuals) that menaced the European way of life (whatever that was). Caldwell was applying a high-gloss finish to old-fashioned fears.

In his Hillsdale address, Caldwell began by explaining that he wasn't intent on telling anyone what to think about the Russian dictator (a term, incidentally, he never used to describe Putin) but

how to think about him. He went out of his way to deride Western "globalist leaders" for pretending that sovereignty was passé.
Putin didn't. "Vladimir Vladimirovich," Caldwell affirmed, "is
not the president of a feminist NGO. He is not a transgender-
rights activist. He is not an ombudsman appointed by the United
Nations to make and deliver slide shows about green energy. He is
the elected leader of Russia—a rugged, relatively poor, militarily
powerful country that in recent years has been frequently humiliated, robbed, and misled."[41] It was a remarkably charitable view of
a Russian president who had crushed Chechnya, invaded Georgia
and Crimea, threatened the Baltic States, stomped out dissent and
trampled on civil rights at home. Caldwell elided Putin's human
rights record in Russia, declaring that any evidence connecting him
to killings of political opponents was "circumstantial" but "merits
scrutiny." To Caldwell, Putin was a great leader, "the preeminent
statesman of our time. On the world stage, who can vie with him?
Only perhaps Recep Tayyip Erdoğan of Turkey."

When Caldwell's musings appeared in 2017 in Hillsdale's *Imprimis* magazine, they received a rave notice from Patrick Buchanan in
The American Conservative. Nine years earlier Buchanan had asked,
"Is Vladimir Putin a paleoconservative?" Now his answer was plain
enough. Maybe it was Barack Obama's America, Buchanan suggested, that was the new evil empire. Buchanan felt certain that
the Russian leader had the right stuff. After all, Putin had allied
himself with nationalists, populists, and traditionalists in the West
against liberal progressives. He was opposed to gay and transgender
rights. He rejected a Wilsonian New World Order led by America.
"Putin," Buchanan wrote, "puts Russia first."[42]

Putin and Erdoğan weren't the only authoritarians to receive Caldwell's benison. Another was Viktor Orbán, the prime minister of Hungary. Orbán's meticulous construction of an illiberal democracy in Hungary brings to mind Edward Gibbon's description of Augustus as a "subtle tyrant." Orbán did not launch wars or assassinate his opponents. Instead, he followed a different course, creating what has become a model for conservative Americans aiming for regime change at home. After he was returned to power in 2010, Orbán gradually tightened the tourniquet on Hungarian democracy, relying upon a parliamentary supermajority to undermine the independent judiciary and tilt the electoral system in his favor. For good measure, he promulgated a higher education law in 2017 to drive out the Central European University from Budapest for supposedly promoting "gender ideology." The law also curbed any teachings about sexuality and gender in public schools. For Orbán, as one former Hungarian diplomat put it to me, illiberalism is "an acquired taste"—a convenient formula for the Hungarian prime minister, who denounced Soviet tyranny as a youth, to retain power.

Caldwell argued that Orbán had been calumniated by globalist elites in Brussels and Washington who failed to recognize his singular gifts. Like Buckley enthusing about Pinochet, Caldwell depicted Orbán as a political titan. "He is blessed," Caldwell wrote, "with almost every political gift—brave, shrewd with his enemies and trustworthy with his friends, detail-oriented, hilarious."[43] The character reference was a prelude to identifying Orbán's greatest asset—his contempt for liberalism, a malignant force that if left unchecked would end in the destruction of Hungary itself. Caldwell hailed Orbán's speech in 2015 at the village of Kötcse opposing a liberal immigration policy. Caldwell saluted it—as though Orbán were the Winston Churchill of the twenty-first century and Kötcse were Fulton, Missouri, where the British leader spoke of an iron curtain descending across Europe. As Orbán spoke, Caldwell wrote, hundreds of thousands of Muslims were "marching" out of Asia Minor, across the Balkans and into the "heart of Europe." Were they an invading army that was "marching" toward Budapest? Or were they desperate refugees whose plight was exploited to solidify his rule over Hungary?

No matter. Orbán had installed his own iron curtain around Hungary and Caldwell marveled at it. Caldwell's enthusiasm for all things Hungarian came as something of a jolt to his former allies in *The Weekly Standard* orbit. In *Twilight of Democracy*, a memoir of her time on the Right, Anne Applebaum anathematized Caldwell, Roger Kimball, and former *National Review* editor John O'Sullivan as ideological heretics for jettisoning Reaganite optimism for populist nationalism.[44] Whereas Kimball had seen Trump as trailing an "aroma of populist demagoguery" in the spring of 2016, by that fall Trump had become "a breath of fresh air."[45] O'Sullivan, who describes himself as an "old classical liberal of a conservative disposition," became the founder and president of the Danube Institute, a think tank in Budapest located next to the prime minister's building and funded by Orbán's Fidesz party.[46] A skillful polemicist who assisted former British prime minister Margaret Thatcher with her memoirs, O'Sullivan was an astute pick for the post. With his extensive connections in the conservative universe, he became Orbán's conduit to the American Right.

One of the marquee intellectuals O'Sullivan attracted to his institute was Rod Dreher, the author of *The Benedict Option*, a call for Catholics to withdraw from wider society, as Pope Benedict did, and embrace religion and tradition. In 2018, Dreher visited Budapest, where he spoke at the institute and asserted the West was in a state of imminent "civilizational collapse." Drawing on the work of Notre Dame professor Patrick Deneen, Dreher pointed the finger at the atomizing consequences of liberalism that Orbán wisely sought to resist.[47] Since then, Dreher has become a visiting fellow at the Danube Institute where his aim is to reach out and build a network of conservatives sympathetic to Hungary.

It's not proving a particularly difficult task. A number of other Catholic intellectuals, too, have developed something of a man-crush on Orbán. Sohrab Ahmari is an émigré from Iran and a lapsed neoconservative and former member of the *Wall Street Journal* editorial page whose career has had a somewhat vertiginous aspect. In 2016 he wrote an essay for *Commentary* called "Illiberalism; The Worldwide Crisis." After Trump defeated Hillary Clinton in 2016, he wrote another essay, this one titled, "The Terrible American Turn Toward Illiberalism."

But it was Ahmari himself who made a turn. During the Trump presidency, he adopted what he had previously abhorred. Writing in *Tablet*, James Kirchick observed, "He has . . . become representative of a new intellectual and political redoubt on the American Right, one that is fundamentally pessimistic about the country, its people, its values, and its role in the world, imbuing his dizzying personal odyssey of the last 10 years with a broader cultural salience."[48] In 2019, Ahmari helped to draft an open letter that appeared in *First Things* praising Trump's election and condemning the "fetishizing" of individual liberty and "tyrannical liberalism." Orbán's Hungary, which Ahmari had previously lambasted as a writer for *Commentary*, now became a subject of fulsome praise. In a 2019 column for the *New York Post*, he denounced the idea of Radio Free Europe broadcasting into Hungary. According to Ahmari, "What Washington's 'defend-democracy' types really fear is that Hungary has become less liberal—not less democratic."[49] This was a rhetorical sleight of hand. The refrain of Ahmari and others was that limiting individual rights was tantamount to expanding them—for the conservative slice of population that bridled at gay and transgender rights. In his provocative new book *Tyranny, Inc.*, Ahmari criticized corporate capitalism as part of what one critic has termed a movement back to an "un-modern America."[50]

Dismantling American democracy itself was the aim of the new authoritarians who had succumbed to the Hungarian rhapsody. Another recent convert to Catholicism, Harvard Law School professor Adrian Vermeule, has called for a radically different interpretation of the US Constitution. "It is just not true that liberal democracy," he observed, "is the *sine qua non* of a just political order."[51] Vermeule, who grew up in Cambridge, Massachusetts, is as purebred a product of Harvard as they come. His mother, Emily, taught archeology at Harvard and he earned both his undergraduate and law degrees at Harvard. Vermeule has nothing but contempt for traditional conservatism, which he has described as a stalking horse for a well-funded libertarian legal movement.[52] Instead, he has called for "an illiberal legalism that is not 'conservative' at all, insofar as standard conservatism is content to play defensively within the procedural rules of the liberal order."[53] Vermeule is the foremost American exponent of integralism, the belief that the state and society are coterminous with religion. There is a good dose of nostalgia for the Habsburg empire among the American champions of integralism; "Catholic intellectuals are to the New Right," one pundit has observed, "as Protestants were to the evangelicals and Jews to the neoconservatives."[54] Eduard Habsburg, archduke of Austria and the great-great-great-grandson of Franz Joseph I, wrote an integralist primer, complete with a foreword by Viktor Orbán, highlighting the seven principles that guided the Habsburg dynasty—"Get Married," "Be Catholic!," and so on—that he offered as lifelines from the past for the turbulent present.[55] Indeed, former House Speaker Newt Gingrich, whose wife Callista was Trump's ambassador to the Vatican, stated that the Habsburg rules for governing "are as applicable today as they have been for centuries."

What else captivates Orbán enthusiasts? *New York Times* opinion columnist Ross Douthat noted that it was not merely Orbán's opposition to immigration but also his antipathy to "wokeness" that appealed to American conservatives. Unlike Trump, who had talked big but never taken effective measures to curb liberal overreach, Orbán was actually doing something to oppose the Left's totalitarianism.[56] Emulating Orbán in targeting the Ivy League or Silicon Valley would be a good thing as long as it didn't lead to financial corruption. That it might also impinge on freedom and liberty was not mentioned by Douthat. "Some version of this impulse," Douthat wrote, "is actually correct."[57]

In February 2020, Orbán declared at a National Conservatism Conference in Rome that Hungary was replacing democracy with

CONCLUSION

The American Right's affection for Vladimir Putin and Viktor Orbán involves a queasy mixture of credulity, posturing, and personal financial considerations. The real-world consequences became manifest on February 21, 2022, when Putin—after weeks of warnings from the Biden administration that were met with fierce denunciations and expressions of disbelief from the Trumpian Right—invaded Ukraine. The action triggered an international outcry and sent American conservatives into overdrive to defend Putin and his paladins. Once more the Right claimed that the US was getting it all wrong. No matter that conservatives refused to believe that Putin would invade, trusting the dictator more than their own government. Self-reflection was out of fashion, especially post-Trump.

Revisionism remained rampant. The arguments of its heralds went something like this: America had antagonized Putin by pushing to extend NATO and constantly braying about human rights. Ukraine was part of Russia's legitimate sphere of influence.

And America's European allies were mendicants bilking it rather than paying for their own defense. It was old wine in new bottles. The complaint about NATO was not about foreign policy realism. It was rooted in real admiration for Putin—for his disdain for LGBTQ rights, for his support for the Russian Orthodox church, and for his cult of masculinity.

One former military officer expressed deep disdain for American foreign policy and sympathy for Russia. No sooner did Putin invade than Retired Army Colonel Douglas A. Macgregor stated on Fox News that America should "absolutely" allow the Russian dictator to conquer Ukraine.[1] His unrestrained fervor for Russia prompted former Representative Liz Cheney to call him "part of the Putin wing of the GOP."[2] A West Point graduate, Macgregor was a squadron operations officer during the first Gulf War and the author of an innovative book on military strategy, *Breaking the Phalanx*. After retiring from the US military in 2004, Macgregor published regularly in conservative outlets and appeared on Fox News to defend Putin and Russia.

In November 2020, Trump appointed him senior advisor to the acting secretary of defense as part of the administration's abortive push to exit Afghanistan overnight.[3] In May 2021, Macgregor stated that the Biden administration was seeking to alter the racial composition of America: "The idea is that they have to bring in as many non-Europeans as possible in order to outnumber the numbers of Americans of European ancestry who live in the United States. That's what it's all about. And I don't think there's any point in questioning it. That is the policy. . . . It is a deliberate policy to enact demographic change."[4]

Macgregor's comments were often rebroadcast on Russian

television. This decorated officer initially said that resistance to the Russian army was an exercise in futility and would only prolong the agony of Ukraine. Once the Right was forced to admit reality—that Putin's forces had, in fact, invaded Ukraine—it quickly regrouped around the claim that Putin's authoritarian war machine would simply overwhelm Ukraine. Macgregor was one of many on the Right who clung to the contention that Ukraine represented a lost cause. When Biden had denounced Russian predatory ambitions in a March 2022 speech in Warsaw, he was simply indulging in the "ideology of moralizing globalism" popular in Washington and European capitals, but his attempt to impose a "Carthaginian peace" was doomed to failure.[5] In November 2022, Macgregor suggested that the Biden administration was engaging in war propaganda. It was concealing the truth from the American people that Ukraine could never stymie, let alone defeat, Russia. Moscow had built up an overwhelming force. Russia was the victim of the West. Macgregor explained on March 15, 2023, that "the truth is coming out that this war was not started by Russia. That Russia begged us not to try and drag Ukraine into NATO. We ignored Russia."

For Trump and his MAGA acolytes, supporting Russia and disparaging Ukraine amounted to the continuation of a war by other means on the Biden administration and the deep state. The old legends about the First World War were conscripted into service. One writer in *The American Conservative* thus alleged that just as the First World War had been sold by "proto-neoconservatives" as a rapid engagement, so Americans were sleepwalking into a third world war: "Americans should ignore the state-sponsored propaganda (creepily similar to that which led up WWI), wake up . . . and do all they can to end support for this cruel war before we face a Great War–like conflagration or worse."[6] Republican presidential candidate Vivek Ramaswamy stated that he would visit Putin in Moscow, hand over a third of Ukraine's territory on a silver platter, and persuade the Russian tyrant to sever his ties with China in return.[7] Representative Matt Gaetz and eleven other Republican lawmakers proposed a "Ukraine Fatigue Resolution."[8] It called for terminating all military and financial aid to Kyiv. Meanwhile, Congresswoman Marjorie Taylor Greene stated on the cable network Real America's Voice that the notion that Putin entertained any further designs on Europe was a bunch of "lies." In her view, "The whole point that we're over there in Ukraine is ridiculous. We are paying for . . . a proxy war with Russia, when I've never seen Putin actually show in any detail his plans to invade Europe."[9] Why Putin would have shared any plans for invading Europe was left unexplained. In any case, were the Right to get its way, American aid to Ukraine would come to an abrupt terminus— and its prophecies of a Ukrainian debacle would likely be fulfilled.

———

No American journalist was a more impassioned supporter of the Russian war effort than Tucker Carlson. He admired Putin for his swagger, for his decisiveness, for his defense of Christian values, for being an all-around great leader. In 2017, Carlson pooh-poohed the idea that there was anything uniquely evil about Putin: "He's not Saddam Hussein, he's not Adolf Hitler, he's not a danger to the United States." Two years later he offered that it would be wise to take Russia's side should a war break out between Russia and Ukraine. Putin, he said, does not hate America as much as American liberals do. When Carlson interviewed a variety of Republican candidates for president at the Family Leadership Summit in Iowa in July 2023, including the hapless former vice president Mike Pence, he engaged in a fresh inversion of reality, depicting Zelensky, not Putin, as the true dictator—a corrupt and odious leader who was persecuting Christians inside Ukraine.

When Carlson appeared at the Heritage Foundation's fiftieth anniversary celebration—the same one described in this book's introduction—as a keynote speaker in May 2023, he was in an expansive mood. He reminisced about starting to work at the think tank's old journal *Policy Review* in August 1991, the month that the Soviet Union collapsed. He offered that it had not occurred to him that America would end up succumbing to the very totalitarianism that existed in the USSR, but then proudly noted that there wasn't any special courage in his own willingness to challenge it. "I'm paid to do that," he said. "I can have any opinion I want."

But Carlson's sudden ouster from Fox News that week, complete with a report from *Rolling Stone* that the network had compiled a secret dossier of kompromat on him, indicated otherwise. Russian foreign minister Sergey Lavrov weighed in at the United Nations, calling Carlson's defenestration a "curious decision" that raised doubts about America's commitment to freedom of speech. It was a comment that suggested that this master dissembler had managed to learn something new about bad faith from the American Right.

Carlson's respect for Putin's Russia was mirrored by his enthusiasm for Orbán's Hungary. He even traveled to Hungary in August 2021 and January 2022 to broadcast his show, then the most popular prime-time cable news program, from Budapest. His goal was to help persuade American conservatives that Hungary could serve as a model for America. He conducted a lengthy interview with Viktor Orbán that focused on family values and immigration.

Carlson admired Orbán's efforts to boost the Hungarian birthrate, much as Mussolini had aspired to in Italy. One of his last guests was that close adviser to Orbán, his namesake Balázs Orbán. Carlson described him "as one of the smartest people who has ever talked about politics."

With its Republican governor Ron DeSantis also in thrall to the tiny Eastern European nation, the state of Florida has been converted into a laboratory for testing out illiberal doctrines and legislation imported from abroad. DeSantis met in Tallahassee with Hungarian president Katalin Novák in April 2023, the same month that the Hungarian parliament passed a federal law attacking same-sex families for violating the "constitutionally recognized role of marriage and the family." The Florida legislature introduced ten anti-LGBTQ bills in the first half of 2023 as well as a bill titled "Information Dissemination" that would require bloggers writing about DeSantis to register with the state's Office of Legislative Affairs or its Commission on Ethics. It also passed legislation banning the use of public funds for critical race theory and gender studies at public universities.

DeSantis's assault on academic freedom was reminiscent of the playbook that William F. Buckley Jr. first outlined in *God and Man at Yale*, not to mention Orbán's methods. In 2017, the Fidesz party ratified a bill that drove the Central European University from Budapest to Vienna, a move that DeSantis emulated in taking over New College. In the introduction to his presidential campaign book, *The Courage to Be Free*, DeSantis explained his methods plainly: "What Florida has done is establish a blueprint for governance that has produced tangible results while serving as a rebuke to the entrenched elites who have driven our nation into the ground." Sounding like a product of the New Left in the 1960s, DeSantis denounced the "ruling class" of progressives who controlled big business, corporate media, Big Tech companies, and universities. Though he didn't mention Woodrow Wilson by name, he condemned a cadre of experts running an administrative state who viewed the average citizen with contempt and believed in the "wholesale social engineering" of American society, with themselves in charge. There is a highly selective side to whom DeSantis—himself a graduate of Yale and Harvard Law School—and his ideological brethren deem part of the elite. Someone like Supreme Court Justice Clarence Thomas may have graduated from Yale Law School, DeSantis claimed, but is somehow separate from the elite because he rejects its ideology, tastes, and attitudes (though given recent revelations of Thomas's junkets with the billionaire Harlan Crow—a collector of Nazi memorabilia—that assessment seems wide of the mark as well).

Attacking the so-called deep state has become a mainstay of the Right. Orbán had succeeded in taking control of the machinery of state in Hungary, and American conservatives were taking note. "Either the deep state destroys America," Trump declared at a March 2023 rally, "or we destroy the deep state." The architect of a plan to liquidate it is Russ Vought, who served as Trump's director of the Office of Management and Budget. Vought, who is the president of the Center for Renewing America, a haven for Trumpism, has proposed an executive order known as "Schedule F" that would transform tens of thousands of federal bureaucrats into political appointees. Trump endorsed Schedule F in the waning months of his presidency but ran out of time to implement it. President Biden rescinded it on January 22, 2021, declaring that it "undermined the foundations" of the civil service, which is supposed to be independent, apolitical, and staffed with the experts needed to run a modern nation safely and effectively. In targeting the bureaucracy, conservatives would be carrying out the vision of Buckley, McCarthy, Kendall, and others who first warned about the need to subdue the liberal malcontents who had insinuated themselves into permanent positions in government. Were a Republican president to enact Schedule F, he or she would put paid to an independent civil service, turning it into the plaything of an unrestrained president. Trump-supporting organizations that would locate and vet the bureaucratic loyalists needed to replace current federal employees include the Heritage Foundation, America First Legal, and the Conservative Partnership Institute. Everything from the Justice Department to the Federal Communications Commission would come under the direct sway of the president.[10] As Senator J. D. Vance put it, "I think that what Trump should do, if I was giving him one piece of advice: Fire every single mid-level bureaucrat, every civil servant in the administrative state, replace with our people."[11] Then it would be time "to do what Viktor Orbán has done."[12]

In May 2023, the Conservative Political Action Conference held a "United We Stand!" meeting in Budapest to celebrate the strengthening ties between Hungarian and American conservatives. Hundreds of Americans attended, including a delegation from the Heritage Foundation as well as journalists and legislators. The conference took place in the Bálna center along the Danube, with the

Hungarian federal parliament looming across the river. I planned to go. Before traveling to Hungary, I went to some lengths to obtain an official press pass and was promised one by the Hungarian Center for Fundamental Rights, which was co-hosting the meeting. When I arrived at the Bálna, I walked through a gateway arch that bore the slogan, "Woke Free Zone" on it. But at the reception desk I was instructed, "We are full." The putative opponents of cancel culture had, in effect, canceled me. I headed off to get some breakfast and wound up at Scruton V.P., an airy café named after the conservative British philosopher Roger Scruton that regularly hosted events about how to combat the insidious woke Marxist Left. On the wall next to me hung a small, framed quotation from Scruton: "Causes should be distinguished from reasons: causes explain, reasons justify." Well, yes. But it wasn't an admonition that the Bálna attendees themselves appeared to be adhering to very closely.

As I live-streamed the conference in my hotel room, I watched as various speakers inveighed against a new totalitarian regime that had allegedly arisen in Brussels to supplant the old Soviet threat, a regime (as they put it) not dissimilar to the liberal one that had ensconced itself in Washington, where a regnant elite, ruling class, deep state, and so on were seeking to upend traditional morality and enmesh the West in a destructive war against Vladimir Putin's Russia. At the outset of the conference, Victor Orbán declared that it was imperative to stand against the woke liberals who threatened everything good and true and noble. The following day a video of Donald Trump was beamed in that featured the forty-fifth American president hailing the "freedom-loving patriots" at the conference, who understood the imperative to "stand together to defend our borders, our Judeo-Christian values, our identity and our way of life."

I may have been denied the chance to join in the celebration of illiberalism, but I met with Balázs Orbán at an outdoor café next to the Bálna, where he graciously instructed me on how to mix a proper Hungarian spritzer. "Our ties have never been closer," he told me about Hungary's relations with the GOP. He quizzed me intently on the prospects of various GOP candidates and seemed glum when I explained that I figured that Trump could capture the nomination but was unlikely to defeat Biden in a general election. As we talked, Michael Anton stopped by to introduce himself to Orban. The last time I had seen Anton—who wrote the "Flight 93" essay in September 2016 under the pseudonym "Publius Decius Mus" in *The Claremont Review of Books*, declaring that it was imperative to rally behind Trump no matter what—was at the Marriott Marquis hotel in downtown Washington in April 2022 at an "Up From Chaos" conference, an "emergency meeting" held by Trumpian conservatives to address the fallout from Putin's invasion of Ukraine. Their fundamental argument, which had been previewed in a manifesto titled "Away from the Abyss" appearing in the then-new magazine *Compact* (co-edited by Sohrab Ahmari), was that helping Ukraine was hurting it by fostering the illusion that it could defeat an almighty Russia. "Ukraine is a corrupt country," Helen Andrews, a senior editor at *The American Conservative*, said at the emergency meeting. "Come and get me." (Andrews, who wrote an essay defending Rhodesia in 2017 in *The National Review*, praised the former East Germany as a bastion of traditional family values in May 2023.)[13]

At the Budapest conference, an even more strident tenor

prevailed as the former Arizona Republican candidate for governor Kari Lake demanded that America "turn off the money spigot. I say we should invest in protecting our borders, not Ukraine's." This fit neatly with Victor Orbán's party line. In May 2023, Orbán attended the Qatar Economic Forum, where he declared that there was no way the "poor Ukrainians" could win the war. His solicitude was touching. In retaliation for the European Union sanctioning the Hungarian bank OTP as a war sponsor, Hungary blocked a new tranche of European military support for Ukraine.

After the CPAC conference ended, I walked to the House of Terror, which Balázs Orbán had recommended I visit. The museum contained exhibits about the Nazi-backed Arrow Cross Party and the Soviet-supported Hungarian Communist Party. A Soviet T-54 tank dominated the atrium. The museum's director general, Mária Schmidt, had spoken at the CPAC conference, stating that "we want to preserve our own culture, we want to hold on to our language, our roots, our traditions, our identity. We don't tolerate people crawling under our duvets and interfering in our private lives." I was curious to see what political messages, if any, the museum sought to convey. As it turned out, the exhibits were quite moving, detailing the torture and killings that the Nazis and Communists each conducted in the chambers of the dank and gloomy building.

The real propaganda resided in the museum's bookstore, where I acquired two volumes by Schmidt, one titled *Language and Liberty* and the other *From Country to Nation*. The Democratic Party in America, she wrote in the first book, represents "urbanites, those in need of state welfare allowances, African Americans, minorities, non church-goers, those from single-parent families and the liberal intellectual and media elite." Progressives, Schmidt wrote in *From Country to Nation*, want to eviscerate the idea of the traditional nation and prostrate themselves before racial minorities. Having repudiated Nazism and communism, Hungarians were not about to sacrifice their freedom on the altar of a liberal elite that was "championing self-denigration and uncritically copying the West." Instead, Hungary represented the "last fortress" of European (read: white Christian) culture.

While traveling on a train from Budapest to Vienna, I leafed through this mishmash of bombast, truculence, and resentment. It struck me as resembling the debates about liberalism and nationalism that took place in fin-de-siècle Vienna, the capital of the Austro-Hungarian Empire, where the kind of national populism that Orbán represents was first espoused by Karl Lueger, the city's charismatic mayor. Like Orbán, Lueger was an opportunist who began as a liberal before founding his own anti-Semitic Christian Social Party in 1893.[14] A populist demagogue who was known as "the uncrowned king of Vienna," he championed the working class and a Greater Austria. The Zionist leader Theodor Herzl fantasized about dueling Lueger.[15] Adolf Hitler, who lived in a men's flophouse during his formative years in Vienna, was a fan. "I regard this man as the greatest German mayor of all times," Hitler wrote in *Mein Kampf*. "If Dr. Lueger had lived in Germany, he would have been ranked among the great minds of our people." The historian Carl E. Schorske observed that Lueger helped develop "a concept of life and a mode of action, which, transcending the purely political, constituted part of the wider cultural revolution that ushered in the twentieth century."[16]

How much has changed? As I glanced through the local

newspapers at breakfast in Vienna, I came across an article in the *Kurier* about the Freedom Party, a repository of unrepentant Nazis after 1945, whose latest political efforts included demonizing immigrants and denouncing "state-subsidized transvestite shows" in Vienna.[17] After setting off on a walk to visit Lueger's statue, I encountered several women at a memorial to Austrians who had resisted enlistment in Hitler's *Wehrmacht*. They held a banner declaring, "Asylum is a human right. Absent human rights no democracy." Next, I came upon a plaque to the Austrian novelist Stefan Zweig affixed to the house where he was born in November 1881. Zweig, who fled Austria in 1934, committed suicide in Petrópolis, Brazil, together with his young second wife Lotte, in February 1942, despairing of Nazi hegemony over Europe and the bleak future of Western democracy.

Finally, I arrived at the imposing Lueger monument, which was erected in 1926. Its plinth was smeared with red spray-painted graffiti calling Lueger a Nazi and declaring the statue itself a *Schande*, or disgrace. An installation called "Lueger Temporary" by the artists Nicole Six and Paul Petritsch was situated next to the monument. It was made of light lath wood painted different colors and it traced the contours of various memorials to Lueger. A sheet of paper attached to the installation contained a brief commentary in German on Lueger, noting that he was a combination of populist, racist, and anti-Semite, "very much beloved and worshipped by many." Someone scribbled in German in large red ink on the placard, "Just like today!!"

The parallels are hard to overlook. In refurbishing old arguments about nationalism, elites, and sovereignty, the new authoritarians—from Budapest to Washington, from Moscow to

ACKNOWLEDGMENTS

In one form or another, I have been preoccupied since childhood with the collision between liberalism and totalitarianism. That preoccupation was largely the product of my own family history. Both my parents were born in the Third Reich. My mother grew up in Freiburg and my father emigrated from Kassel in May 1940 by himself as a six-year-old to America on the SS *Conte di Savoia*, which he boarded in Genoa (Italy did not enter the Second World War until June 10, 1940). Having spent an inordinate amount of time reading and writing about German history, I couldn't help but see some disquieting similarities between Weimar Germany and America. In writing this book, it became clear to me that America's anti-democratic traditions are more robust than I had presumed.

My profuse thanks to Liveright's Dan Gerstle, a model of editorial acuity who carefully guided this book to completion. Sarah Despres and Oscar Heilbrunn watched with curiosity and affection as I plunged headlong into the thickets of past political controversies. Over the years, I have come to owe Sam Tanenhaus, who helped me to disentangle the history of the Right, more intellectual debts than I can hope to repay. At an early juncture, Geoffrey Kabaservice, a scholar of conservatism nonpareil, laid down the law over lunch at the Cosmos Club, providing valuable guidance about structuring the book. Conversations with Joshua Tait about Spain and Franco were especially helpful. Melinda Haring, who appears to have overcome her disappointment that I am not a Russian agent, offered indispensable good cheer and wise counsel. Christian Caryl supplied vital insights into the Putin regime. Ambassador John Herbst shaped my thinking about the true traditions of American realism and foreign affairs. I was the surprised and happy recipient of a vital historical pamphlet by Harry Elmer Barnes that Jennifer Schuessler unearthed. Sidney Blumenthal and John B. Judis each offered cogent advice and enthusiastic support. Matt Seaton, an editor at *The Atlantic* and formerly *The New York Review of Books*, skillfully edited several essays of mine that nudged me in the direction of writing this book. I am grateful to all for their help. Any errors that may remain are of course my responsibility.

NOTES

INTRODUCTION

1. Patricia Sullivan, "Konstantin Simis," *Washington Post*, December 17, 2006.
2. Julia Davis, " 'Get Rid of the Video!': Putin Crony Freaks Out in Live TV Flop Over Zelensky Clip," Daily Beast, December 22, 2022.
3. Adrian Karatnycky, "Putin's American Cheerleaders," *Wall Street Journal*, January 6, 2023.
4. Pyotr Kozlov, "Why a Soviet-American Thinker Moderated Putin's SPIEF Panel," *Moscow Times*, June 20, 2023.
5. Dimitri K. Simes, "Richard Nixon: A Reappraisal," *Christian Science Monitor*, August 8, 1984.
6. Ben Smith, "Divorce for Nixon Center, Foundation," *Politico*, April 19, 2011.
7. Betsy Swan, "Maria Butina: Private Messages Reveal Accused Russian Spy's True Ties to D.C. Wise Man," *Daily Beast*, August 29, 2018 (updated April 26, 2019).
8. Josh Rogin, "Dimitri Simes flew too close to Trump, and his think tank got burned," *Washington Post*, May 2, 2019.
9. See George Thomas, " 'America Is a Republic, Not a Democracy,' Is a Dangerous—And Wrong—Argument," *The Atlantic*, November 2, 2020.
10. Patrick Deneen, *Regime Change: Toward A Postliberal Future* (New York: Penguin, 2023).

CHAPTER 1: COURTING KAISER WILHELM

1. Cited in Robert K. Massie, *Dreadnought: Britain, Germany, and the Coming of the Great War* (New York: Simon & Schuster, 1991), 136.

2. Miranda Carter, "What Happens When a Bad-Tempered, Distractible Doofus Runs an Empire?" *The New Yorker*, June 6, 2016.

3. See Isabel V. Hull, *Absolute Destruction: Military Culture and the Practices of War in Imperial Germany* (Ithaca, NY: Cornell University Press, 2013), esp. "Part 1. Suppression Becomes Annihilation."

4. John C. G. Röhl, *The Kaiser and His Court: Wilhelm II and the Government of Germany*, paperback edition (Cambridge: Cambridge University Press, 1996), 210–11.

5. To Hitler's great annoyance, "Otto Habsburg in exile and Maximilian and Ernst Hohenberg loudly spoke out against him, condemning his Nazi Party, exposing and denouncing the abhorrent racism he sought to legitimize." James Longo, *Hitler and the Habsburgs: The Fuhrer's Vendetta Against the Austrian Royals* (New York: Diversion Books, 2018), 119.

6. Michael Kazin, *War Against War: The American Fight for Peace, 1914–1918* (New York: Simon & Schuster, 2017), xv–xvi.

7. Patrick Allitt, *The Conservatives: Ideas and Personalities Throughout American History* (New Haven, CT: Yale University Press, 2009), 146.

8. Spencer, Richard [@RichardBSpencer]. "I co-founded The HL Mencken Club, along with Paul Gottfried, William Regnery, and others, in 2008, after a sort of 'conservative purge' took place at a small paleo organization called The Association of Philosophy and Letters, which had been run by Gottfried and Claes Ryn." Twitter, August 20, 2018. Marion Elizabeth Rodgers suggests that Mencken would have viewed the appropriation of his name by these figures with distaste, if not revulsion, in "The Alt-Right Loves H.L. Mencken. The Feeling Would Not Have Been Mutual," *Reason*, September 12, 2018.

9. Cited in Marion Elizabeth Rodgers, *Mencken: The American Iconoclast* (New York: Oxford University Press, 2005), 159.

10. Cited in Marion Elizabeth Rodgers, "H. L. Mencken: The German-American from Baltimore," lecture, The Society for the History of Germans in Maryland, https: //loyolanotredamelib.org/php/report05/articles/pdfs/Report47-03-Mencken-Marion-Rodgers.pdf.

11. Cited in Douglas C. Stenerson, *H. L. Mencken: Iconoclast from Baltimore* (Chicago: University of Chicago, 1971), 52.

12. I. A. R. Wylie, *The Germans* (Indianapolis: Bobbs-Merrill Company, 1911), 4.

13. Rodgers, "H. L. Mencken."

14. Carlin Romano, "The Scourge of Baltimore," *The Nation*, November 7, 2002.

15. Rodgers, *Mencken: The American Iconoclast*, 133.

16. Quentin Taylor, "Mencken's Nietzsche: A Centenary Observance," *Modern Age* (Winter 2014).

17. Alfred Kazin, "H. L. Mencken and the Great American Boob," *Menckeniana*, no. 99 (1986), 2.

18. Ellery Sedgwick, "HLM, Ellery Sedgwick, and the First World War." *Menckeniana*, no. 68 (1978), 1–4.

19. H. L. Mencken, "Free Lance," *Evening Sun*, May 10, 1915.

20. H. L. Mencken, "Free Lance," *Evening Sun*, July 9, 1915.

21. "A Neutral Is Outraged by a Violation of Neutrality," *Evening Sun*, September 4, 1914.

22. "The Overrated Germans," *Evening Sun*, August 12, 1915.

23. Quoted in Oleg Panczenko, "Some Notes on Mencken in the First World War." *Menckeniana*, no. 215 (2016), 10.

24. Rodgers, *Mencken: The American Iconoclast*, 166.

25. Edgar Kemler, *The Irreverent Mr. Mencken* (Boston: Little, Brown, 1950), 88.

26. Cited in Kemler, *The Irreverent Mr. Mencken*, 131.

27. Kemler, 147.

28. Ido Oren, *Our Enemies & US: America's Rivalries and the Making of Political Science* (Ithaca, NY: Cornell University Press, 2003), 32.

29. John Higham, *Strangers in the Land: Patterns of American Nativism 1860–1925* (New York: Atheneum, 1973), 197.

30. Charles Thomas Johnson, "The National German-American Alliance, 1901–1918: Cultural Politics and Ethnicity in Peace and War" (Ph.D. diss., Western Michigan University, 1997), 196.

31. Tom Reiss, "The First Conservative," *The New Yorker*, October 24, 2005.

32. Cited in Elbert Gertz, *Odyssey of a Barbarian: The Biography of George Sylvester Viereck* (Buffalo, NY: Prometheus Books, 1978), 19.

33. Clifton James Child, *The German-Americans in Politics, 1914–1917* (Madison: University of Wisconsin Press, 1939), 141.

34. Cited in Johnson, "The National German-American Alliance, 1901–1918," 216.

35. Gustavus Ohlinger, *Their True Faith and Allegiance*, foreword by Owen Wister (New York: Macmillan Company, 1916), 124.

36. Rodgers, *Mencken: The American Iconoclast*, 175.

37. John Maxwell Hamilton, *Manipulating the Masses: Woodrow Wilson and the Birth of American Propaganda* (Baton Rouge: Louisiana State University Press, 2020), 177.

38. Cited in Hamilton, *Manipulating the Masses*, 98.

39. Ronald Steel, *Walter Lippmann and the American Century* (Boston: Atlantic Monthly Press, 1980), 126.

40. "Viereck Used A Code In Letters To Germany," *New York Times*, July 27, 1918.

41. "Viereck Expelled by Authors' League," *New York Times*, July 26, 1918.

CHAPTER 2: MENCKENIZED HISTORY

1. Cited in John B. Duff, "German-Americans and the Peace, 1918–1920." *American Jewish Historical Quarterly* 59, no. 4 (1970), 444.

2. Samuel Flagg Bemis, "First Gun of a Revisionist Historiography for the Second World War." *The Journal of Modern History* 19, no. 1 (1947), 55.

3. Cited in Joachim Riecker, *Hitlers 9. November: Wie der Erste Weltkrieg zum Holocaust führte* (Berlin: WJS Verlag, 2009), 51.

4. Selig Adler, *The Isolationist Impulse: Its Twentieth Century Reaction* (New York: Abelard-Schuman, 1953), 90.

5. Cited in Warren I. Cohen, *The American Revisionists: The Lessons of Intervention in World War 1* (Chicago: University of Chicago Press, 1967), 85.
6. Albert Jay Nock, *Memoirs of a Superfluous Man* (New York: Harper, 1943), 60.
7. Francis Neilson, *How Diplomats Make War*, reprint second edition (San Francisco: Cobden Press, 1916), 13.
8. Michael Wreszin, "Albert Jay Nock and the Anarchist Elitist Tradition in America," *American Quarterly* 21, no. 2 (1969), 174.
9. Albert Jay Nock, *The Myth of a Guilty Nation* (New York: Ben Huebsch, 1922), 22–23.
10. Nock, *The Myth of a Guilty Nation*, 49.
11. "Prince Wilhelm, 69, Is Dead in Germany," *New York Times*, July 21, 1951.
12. Cited in Terry Teachout, *The Skeptic: A Life of H. L. Mencken*, paperback edition (New York: Perennial, 2003), 9.
13. On Barnes's career and influence, see Justus D. Doenecke, "Harry Elmer Barnes." *The Wisconsin Magazine of History* 56, no. 4 (1973), 311–23. In discussing Nazi Germany, Barnes referred to the "alleged extermination" of Jews in concentration camps and "doings, real or alleged, at Auschwitz." See Richard Bernstein, "Untwisting Revisionism on the Holocaust," *New York Times*, June 21, 1988. In 1994, Willis Carto, a right-wing political activist, founded *The Barnes Review*, an anti-Semitic journal named after Harry Elmer Barnes that published an issue in 2014 titled "In Defense of Adolf Hitler."
14. Harry Elmer Barnes, "Revisionism and the Historical Blackout," *Perpetual War for Perpetual Peace* (Caldwell, ID: Caxton, 1953). *Heritage History*, https://www.heritage-history.com/site/hclass/secret_societies /ebooks/pdf/barnes_blackout.pdf.
15. Frederick Bausman, *Facing Europe* (New York: Century Co., 1926), 88.
16. Bausman, *Facing Europe*, 98.
17. Cohen, *American Revisionists*, 44–45.
18. Bausman, *Facing Europe*, 6.
19. Kathryn S. Olmsted, *The Newspaper Axis: Six Press Barons Who Enabled Hitler* (New Haven, CT: Yale University Press, 2022), 43.
20. Adler, *The Isolationist Impulse*, 91.
21. Charles Grant Miller, "Anglicized Histories Swept from New York Schools," *San Francisco Examiner*, June 24, 1923.
22. Jerald A. Combs, *American Diplomatic History: Two Centuries of Changing Interpretations* (Berkeley: University of California Press, 1986), 135.
23. "Says Britain Seeks to Conquer America," *New York Times*, October 20, 1927.
24. Bruce W. Dearstyne, "Lessons from the History Textbook Wars of the 1920s," *History News Network*, Columbian College of Arts & Sciences, The George Washington University (n.d.).
25. Frederick Bausman, "Under Which Flag?," *The American Mercury* (October 1927).
26. Jill Lepore, "Fixed," *The New Yorker*, March 22, 2010.
27. Higham, *Strangers in the Land*, 272.

NOTES

CHAPTER 3: MUSSOLINI'S VICARS

1. Leonard Dinnerstein, *Anti-Semitism in America*, paperback edition (New York: Oxford University Press, 1994), 79.
2. Andy Ware, "President Harding Pushed for Racial Equality in the Deep South 100 Years Ago," *Marion Star*, October 26, 2021.
3. Geoffrey Kabaservice, *The Guardians: Kingman Brewster, His Circle and the Rise of the Liberal Establishment* (New York: Macmillan, 2004), 23.
4. Adam S. Cohen, "Harvard's Eugenics Era," *Harvard Magazine* (March–April 2016).
5. Dexter Perkins, *Yield of the Years: An Autobiography* (Boston: Little Brown and Company, 1969), 28.
6. T. Lothrop Stoddard, *The French Revolution in San Domingo* (Boston: Houghton Mifflin, 1914), 348.
7. Matt Lebovic, "The White Supremacist Influencer Beloved by President Harding—and Hitler," *Times of Israel*, January 18, 2021.
8. Daniel Okrent, *The Guarded Gate: Bigotry, Eugenics and the Law That Kept Two Generations of Jews, Italians, and Other European Immigrants Out of America* (New York: Scribner, 2019), 231.
9. Charles C. Alexander, "Prophet of American Racism: Madison Grant and the Nordic Myth," *Phylon*, no. 1 (1962): 73–90.
10. T. Lothrop Stoddard, *The Rising Tide of Color Against White Supremacy* (New York: Scribner's, 1923), 183.
11. W. L. Courtney, "The Crisis of the Ages," *Daily Telegraph*, October 22, 1920.
12. Joseph W. Bendersky, *The "Jewish Threat": Anti-Semitic Politics of the U.S. Army* (New York: Basic Books, 2000), 26.
13. Robert Vitalis, *White World Order, Black Power Politics: The Birth of International Relations* (Ithaca, NY: Cornell University Press, 2015), 195.
14. Vitalis, 198.
15. Cited in Michael Rogin, *Blackface, White Noise: Jewish Immigrants in the Hollywood Melting Pot*, paperback edition (Berkeley: University of California Press, 1996), 89.
16. Ian Frazier, "When W. E. B. Du Bois Made a Laughingstock of a White Supremacist," *The New Yorker*, August 19, 2019.
17. Benjamin M. Welton, "The Anglo-Saxons—Stoddard and Lovecraft: Ideas of Anglo-Saxon Supremacy and the New England Counter-Revolution," *Madison Historical Review* 18, 2021.
18. Ruth Ben-Ghiat, *Strongmen: Mussolini to the Present*, paperback edition (New York: W. W. Norton, 2021), 22.
19. Ben-Ghiat, 27.
20. Patrick Bernhard, "Blueprints of Totalitarianism: How Racist Policies in Fascist Italy Inspired and Informed Nazi Germany," *Fascism* 6 (2) 2017, 127–62. doi: https://doi.org/10.1163/22116257-00602001.
21. Cited in John P. Diggins, *Mussolini and Fascism: The View from America*, paperback edition (Princeton, NJ: Princeton University Press, 1972), 206.

22. Wreszin, *The Superfluous Anarchist*, 90.
23. Irving Babbit, *Democracy and Leadership*, intro. by Russell Kirk (Carmel, IN: Liberty Fund, 1979), 337.
24. Cited in Wreszin, The *Superfluous Anarchist*, 93.
25. Babbitt, *Democracy and Leadership*, 19.
26. Babbitt, 338.
27. Cited in Victor C. Ferkiss, "Ezra Pound and American Fascism," *The Journal of Politics* 17, no. 2 (1955), 186.
28. Katy Hull, *The Machine Has a Soul: American Sympathy with Italian Fascism*, (Princeton, NJ: Princeton University Press, 2021), 8.
29. Hull, 9.
30. Richard Washburn Child, *A Diplomat Looks at Europe* (New York: Duffield and Company, 1925), 203.
31. George Barton, "Richard Child's Good Opinion of Mussolini," *Philadelphia Inquirer*, January 2, 1926.
32. Victor Shultz, "A Case History," *Des Moines Register*, December 9, 1928.
33. Richard Washburn Child, "Italy's Fascisti Under Fire," *Courier-Journal*, December 20, 1924.
34. Hull, *The Machine Has a Soul*, 62–63.
35. "Full Text of Mussolini's Speech Outlining His Plans for a Greater Italy," *New York Times*, May 29, 1927.
36. Lothrop Stoddard, "Realism: The Challenge of Fascism," *Harper's Magazine* (October 1927).

CHAPTER 4: AN INTELLIGENT FASCISM

1. Gilliam Borckell, "Wealthy Bankers and Businessmen Plotted to Overthrow FDR. A Retired General Foiled It," *Washington Post*, January 13, 2021.
2. Frederick N. Rasmussen, "Mencken Saw Conventions in Harsh Light," *Baltimore Sun*, July 31, 2004.
3. See Murray N. Rothbard, *The Betrayal of the American Right*, edited with an introduction by Thomas E. Woods Jr. (Auburn, AL: Ludwig von Mises Institute, 2007), 12.
4. "New Deal Spending Assailed by Ritchie," *New York Times*, June 30, 1935.
5. Kemler, *The Irreverent Mr. Mencken*, 281.
6. Gary Younge, "The Fascist Who 'Passed' for White," *The Guardian*, April 4, 2007.
7. "Boy Evangelist Dennis to Lecture," *Washington Post*, March 8, 1905.
8. Gerald Horne, *The Color of Fascism: Racial Passing, and the Rise of Right-Wing Extremism in the United States* (New York: New York University Press, 2006), 18.
9. "Honduran Decency," *Time*, February 2, 1925.
10. "Nicaragua Asks Our Intervention," *New York Times*, September 10, 1926.
11. C. Gerald Fraser, "Lawrence Dennis, 83; Advocated Fascism," *New York Times*, August 21, 1977.

12. "Charges Renewed by Dennis against State Department," *Washington Post*, March 11, 1927.

13. Lawrence Dennis, "Recognition, Revolution and Intervention," *Foreign Affairs* (January 1931), 208.

14. Dennis, 216.

15. Dennis, 219.

16. James Rorty, "The Native Anti-Semite's 'New Look': His Present 'Line' and His Prospects," *Commentary*, November 1954.

17. "Capitalism Doomed, Say Fascist and Red," *New York Times*, March 5, 1934.

18. Cited in Horne, *The Color of Fascism*, 54.

19. Lawrence Dennis, *The Coming American Fascism* (New York: Harpers, 1960), 241.

20. R. L. Duffus, "Mr. Dennis and His 'American' Fascism," *New York Times*, January 5, 1936.

21. Hart, 152.

22. Horne, *The Color of Fascism*, 61.

23. Lawrence Dennis, *The Dynamics of War and Revolution* (New York: Weekly Foreign Letter: 1940), 125.

24. Friends of Democracy, *Joe Kamp: Peddler of Propaganda and Hero of the Pro-Fascists* (Kansas City, MO: Friends of Democracy, Inc., n.d.), Florida Atlantic University Digital Library, https://fau.digital.flvc.org/islandora/object/fau%3A32455/datastream/OBJ/view.

25. Gil Troy, "She Was the 1930s' Steve Bannon," *Daily Beast*, February 4, 2017.

26. Amy Danielle Dye, "The Powers of Perception: An Intimate Connection with Elizabeth Dilling," Electronic Theses and Dissertations, Paper 1861 (2009), 13.

27. Quoted in Glen Jeansonne, *Women of the Far Right: The Mothers' Movement and World War II* (Chicago: University of Chicago, 1996), 13.

28. Quoted in Jane Mayer, *Dark Money: The Hidden History of the Billionaires Behind the Rise of the Radical Right* (New York: Anchor Books, 2017), 37.

29. Michelle M. Nickerson, *Mothers of Conservatism: Women and the Postwar Right* (Princeton, NJ: Princeton University Press, 2012).

30. Nickerson, 23.

31. Zach Honoroff, "Who Is Elizabeth Dilling, and Why Is Glenn Beck a Fan?" *History News Network*.

32. Jeansonne, *Women of the Far Right*, 75.

33. Zach Honoroff, "Who Is Elizabeth Dilling, and Why Is Glenn Beck a Fan?," *History News Network*.

34. Troy, "She Was the 1930s' Steve Bannon."

35. A. J. Clements, " 'The Franco Way': The American Right and the Spanish Civil War, 1936–9," *Journal of Contemporary History* 57 (2), 2022, 341–64.

36. Quoted in Austin J. Clements, "General Washington Goes to Guernica: Pro-Franco Americans and the Spanish Civil War," *Global History Blog*, February 11, 2021.

37. Zachary D. Carter, *The Price of Peace: Money, Democracy, and the Life of John Maynard Keynes*, paperback edition (New York: Random House, 2020), 375.

38. Ralph Lord Roy, *Apostles of Discord: A study of organized bigotry and disruption on the fringes of Protestantism* (Boston: Beacon Press, 1953), 222.

39. "Urges Economy on Hoover," *New York Times*, May 17, 1932.

40. "Hart Scores Roosevelt," *New York Times*, October 4, 1937.

41. David Austin Walsh, "The Right-Wing Popular Front: The Far Right and the American Conservative Movement from the New Deal to the 1960s" (Ph.D. diss., Princeton University, 2017), 70. Walsh's careful study emphasizes Hart's significance for the Right before and after World War II.

42. Michael E. Chapman, *Arguing Americanism: Franco Lobbyists, Roosevelt's Foreign Policy, and the Spanish Civil War* (Kent, OH: Kent State University Press, 2011), 127.

43. Chapman, 152.

44. Merwin K. Hart, *America—Look at Spain* (New York: P. J. Kenedy & Sons, 1939), 75.

45. Hart, 87.

46. Hart, 102.

47. Hart, 200.

48. Toni L. Kamins, et al., "Jews Seek War, Finance Communism, Gen. Moseley Tells Philadelphia Rally," *Jewish Telegraphic Agency*, March 20, 2015.

49. "Moseley Proposes Use of the Army to Drive Out Reds," *New York Times*, June 1, 1939.

50. "Moseley Depicts a 'World Jewry,'" *New York Times*, June 2, 1939.

51. Washington declared, "Against the insidious wiles of foreign influence (I conjure you to believe me, fellow-citizens) the jealousy of a free people ought to be constantly awake, since history and experience prove that foreign influence is one of the most baneful foes of republican government."

52. "Dies & Hart," *Time*, January 1, 1940.

53. "Sheean & Hart," *Time*, January 22, 1940.

54. Quoted in Arnold Forster, *A Measure of Freedom* (New York: Doubleday, 1950), 66.

55. "Union League Gets 'Americanism' Plea," *New York Times*, September 20, 1940.

56. "We, the People," *New York Times*, September 21, 1940.

CHAPTER 5: DEMOCRACY UNDER FIRE

1. "Address by Hon. Robert H. Jackson Attorney General of the United States At a Meeting of The Law Society of Massachusetts, Boston City Club, Boston, Massachusetts, October 16, 1940," Robert H. Jackson Center, accessed June 12, 2023.

2. "Ickes Hits Takers of Hitler Medals," *New York Times*, December 19, 1938.

3. "M. K. Hart Demands That Ickes Recant," *New York Times*, December 19, 1940.

4. Leo P. Ribuffo, *The Old Christian Right: The Protestant Far Right from the Great Depression to the Cold War* (Philadelphia: Temple University Press, 1983).

5. Bradley W. Hart, *Hitler's American Friends: The Third Reich's Supporters in the United States*, paperback edition (New York: Thomas Dunne Books, 2018), 17.

6. "Ex-Rep. Martin Dies, 71, Is Dead; Led Un-American Activities Unit," *New York Times*, November 15, 1972.

7. Walter Goodman, foreword Richard H. Rovere, *The Committee: The Extraordinary Career of the House Committee on Un-American Activities* (New York: Farrar, Straus and Giroux, 1968), 26.

8. "Great Interviews of the 20th Century: Adolf Hitler Interviewed by George Sylvester Viereck." *Guardian*, September 17, 2007.

9. Phyllis Keller, *States of Belonging: German-American Intellectuals and the First World War* (Cambridge, MA: Harvard University Press, 1979), 176.

10. Toni L. Kamins, et al., "Viereck Called Chief Nazi Propagandist in U.S.," *Jewish Telegraphic Agency*, March 20, 2015.

11. Keller, *States of Belonging*, 178.

12. George Sylvester Viereck, *The Kaiser on Trial* (Richmond, VA: William Byrd Press, 1937), xvi.

13. "Double Exposure," *Time*, June 16, 1941. For more on Wirsing's activities, see Max Weinrich, *Hitler's Professors*, 2nd ed. (New Haven, CT: Yale University Press, 1999), 59.

14. Hart, *Hitler's American Friends*, 101.

15. Lewis Wood, "Strempel Links Stewart to Cash," *New York Times*, March 18, 1947.

16. Kevin Duchschere, "Did a Nazi Sympathizer Once Represent Minnesota in the U.S. Senate?" *StarTribune*, February 17, 2023.

17. Hart, *Hitler's American Friends*, 103.

18. Hart, 104.

19. "German Day Rally Splits with Nazis," *New York Times*, October 3, 1938.

20. Eric Pace, "Ex-Rep. Hamilton Fish, Roosevelt Foe, Dies at 102," *New York Times*, January 20, 1991.

21. Hart, *Hitler's American Friends*, 108.

22. "Not Fish, But Foul," *Time*, January 26, 1942.

23. Sayers and Kahn, 188.

24. Olmsted, *The Newspaper Axis*, 50–51.

25. "Hearst Is Quoted as Hailing Nazi Vote," *New York Times*, August 23, 1934.

26. "The Press; Hearstwhile Nazi," *Time*, January 21, 1946.

27. Olmsted, *The Newspaper Axis*, 53.

28. Nickerson, *Mothers of Conservatism*, 23.

29. Cited in Jeansonne, *Women on the Far Right*, 45.

30. Jeansonne, 57.

31. "Women Form Group to Keep Out of War," *New York Times*, September 20, 1939.

32. "Laura Ingalls Drops Peace Pleas Over Capital, May Lose License," *New York Times*, September 27, 1939.

33. Cited in Jeansonne, *Women of the Far Right*, 68.
34. Kirstin Fawcett, "The Famed American Aviatrix Secretly on the Nazi Payroll." HistoryNet, March 4, 2022.
35. "W. R. Davis Is Found Guilty in Oil Trial," *New York Times*, October 18, 1938.
36. For an illuminating discussion of Hoover's visit and the 1940 GOP convention, see John Lukacs, "Herbert Hoover Meets Adolf Hitler," *The American Scholar* (Spring 1993).
37. James A. Hagerty, "Hoover Bids for Nomination to Fight New Deal," *New York Times*, June 26, 1940.
38. "A Congressman Tried to Get Convention to Back Isolationism Records State—Hamilton Fish Denies German Connection," *New York Times*, May 27, 1956.
39. "Lothrop Stoddard To Cover European War," *Washington Post*, September 26, 1939.
40. Lothrop Stoddard, *Into the Darkness: Nazi Germany Today* (North Gaven: Dead Authors Society, 2023), 189.
41. Stoddard, 195–96.
42. Lynne Olson, *Those Angry Days: Roosevelt, Lindbergh, and America's Fight Over World War II, 1939–1941* (New York: Random House, 2013), 237.
43. "Nazi Honor to Ford Stirs Cantor's Ire," *New York Times*, August 4, 1938.
44. Derek Leebaert, *Unlikely Heroes: Franklin Roosevelt, His Four Lieutenants, and the World They Made* (New York: St. Martin's Press, 2023), 280.
45. "President Defines Lindbergh's Niche," *New York Times*, April 26, 1941.
46. "Lindbergh Called Nazi Tool by Ickes," *New York Times*, July 15, 1941.
47. "Lindbergh Seeks Roosevelt Inquiry," *New York Times*, July 18, 1941.
48. "Byrd Scores Sowers of Seeds of Disunity," *New York Times*, October 9, 1941.
49. "Ickes Says Nation Must 'Decide' Now," *New York Times*, October 21, 1941.
50. Ollie Gratzinger, "This Week in Pittsburgh History: Attack on Pearl Harbor Hits Home and Ends a Movement," *Pittsburgh Magazine*, December 5, 2022.
51. Sayers and Kahn, 242.
52. Olson, *Those Angry Days*, 435.
53. "Viereck Publisher Is Out of Business," *New York Times*, November 18, 1941.
54. "Fish Shouts 'Lie' At Viereck Trial," *New York Times*, February 21, 1942.
55. "Axis Agents: Safeguard for Viereck," *Time*, March 16, 1942.
56. James E. Chinn, "Dennis Calls Sedition Trial 'Corny Farce,'" *Washington Post*, May 19, 1944.
57. "Seditionists On Trial—The Poison of Hatred," *Chicago Defender*, April 29, 1944.
58. Maximilian St. George and Lawrence J. Dennis, *A Trial on Trial: The Great Sedition Trial of 1944* (Chicago: National Civil Rights Committee, 1946), 402.

CHAPTER 6: AMERICA FIRST, LAST, AND ALL THE TIME

1. "Second Supplemental Appropriation Bill, 1945," *Congressional Record—House*, vol. 91 (May 16, 1945), 4675.
2. "Hostile Audience Hears Hart Blast at Marshall Plan," *Harvard Crimson*, February 5, 1948.
3. "Merwin Hart Says Poster Made to Get HSU Roused," *Harvard Crimson*, March 21, 1939.
4. Quoted in Forster, *A Measure of Freedom*, 67.
5. "Senator Langer, 73, G.O.P. Rebel, Dead," *New York Times*, November 9, 1959.
6. Kathryn S. Olmsted, *Real Enemies: Conspiracy Theories and American Democracy, World War I to 9/11* (New York: Oxford University Press, 2009), 65.
7. Felix Belair Jr., "McCormick Leans to Taft or Bricker," *New York Times*, September 22, 1946.
8. Nicole Hemmer, *Messengers of the Right: Conservative Media and the Transformation of American Politics* (Philadelphia: University of Pennsylvania Press, 2016), 36.
9. Henry Regnery, *Memoirs of A Dissident Publisher* (New York: Harcourt, Brace, Jovanovich, 1979), 9.
10. Regnery, 12.
11. Regnery, 13.
12. Deborah E. Lipstadt, *Denying the Holocaust: The Growing Assault on Truth and Memory* (New York: The Free Press, 1993), 67.
13. John P. Jackson Jr. focuses on a "Nazi transmission belt" among postwar publishers on the Right in "The Pre-History of American Holocaust Denial," *American Jewish History*, vol. 105, nos. 1/2 (January/April 2021).
14. George Morgenstern, *Pearl Harbor: The Secret Road to War* (New York: Devin-Adair, 1947), 13.
15. Alden Whitman, "Lindbergh Says U.S. 'Lost' World War II," *New York Times*, August 30, 1972.
16. Henry Regnery, "Historical Revisionism and World War II," *Modern Age* (Summer 1976).
17. William Henry Chamberlain, *America's Second Crusade*, paperback edition (Chicago: Regnery, 1950), 285.
18. Chamberlain, 345.
19. "Historian Says Wilson Shaped War Plans in 16," *Washington Post*, December 13, 1934.
20. Quoted in Julia Boyd, *Travelers in the Third Reich: The Rise of Fascism: 1919–1945* (New York: Pegasus Books, 2018), 250.
21. "Germany Now Strongest Bulwark in Europe Against Communism and War, Tansill Says," *Washington Post*, November 17, 1936.
22. "American University Dismisses Professor with Nazi Leanings," *Washington Post*, March 9, 1937.
23. Tansill's study remains an object of interest for some conservatives, with one

citing it as "far and away the best study of American policy in this period." David Gordon, "Can You Trust Robert Kagan?," *Modern Age* (Spring 2023).

24. *Time*, "The South: Rebel Yell," June 16, 1947.

25. "Charles Tansill, Historian, Is Dead," *New York Times*, November 14, 1964.

26. John Beaty, *The Iron Curtain over America* (Dot Connector Book Library, 2016).

27. Quoted in Bendersky, *"Jewish Threat,"* 409.

28. Beaty, *The Iron Curtain*, 54.

29. Beaty, 102.

30. In 1954, the Board of Trustees condemned Beaty for anti-Semitism. He had published a pamphlet called "How to Capture a University" that asked whether students were to be guided by B'nai B'rith, Moscow, or "assorted devotees of the little world power which usurps the name 'Israel'?" See, "S.M.U. Professor Accused of Anti-Semitism," *Harvard Crimson*, June 17, 1954.

31. Regnery, *Memoirs of a Dissident Publisher*, 41.

32. Russell Kirk, "Odyssey of a Liberal," *New York Times*, April 19, 1970.

33. Freda Utley, *Odyssey of a Liberal: Memoirs* (Washington, DC: Washington National Press, Inc., 1970), 80.

34. Utley, 235.

35. "Freda Utley, Writer on Asia, Dies at 79," *Washington Post*, January 25, 1978.

36. Freda Utley, *The High Cost of Vengeance* (Chicago: Regnery, 1949), 2.

37. Utley, 183.

38. Delbert Clark, "Western Rule in Germany," *New York Times*, July 10, 1949.

39. Ted Morgan, *Reds: McCarthyism in Twentieth-Century America*, paperback edition (New York: Random House, 2004), 361.

40. Morgan, 361.

41. Utley, *The High Cost of Vengeance*, 185.

42. Cited in Morgan, *Reds*, 363.

43. Quoted in Morgan, 363.

44. David Oshinsky, *A Conspiracy So Immense: The World of Joe McCarthy*, paperback edition (New York: Oxford University Press, 2005), 75.

45. Carter, *The Price of Peace*, 374.

46. Morgan, *Reds*, 365.

47. Oshinsky, *A Conspiracy So Immense*, 77.

48. Oshinksy, 78.

49. Walter H. Waggoner, " 'Mock Trials' of Malmedy Nazis by U.S. Army Scored by Senator," *New York Times*, April 21, 1949.

50. Drew Pearson, "Malmedy Set Precedent for Korea," *Washington Post*, November 26, 1951.

CHAPTER 7: MONSTERS ABROAD

1. "Religion: Chiang's Testimony," *Time*, April 26, 1943.

2. Ibid.

3. Ibid.

4. Quoted in Walter Isaacson and Evan Thomas, *The Wise Men: Six Friends and the World They Made* (New York: Simon and Schuster, 1986), 475.

5. Robert E. Herzstein, *Henry R. Luce, Time, and the American Crusade in Asia* (Cambridge: Cambridge University Press, 2006), 11.

6. Rothbard, *The Betrayal of the American Right*, 152.

7. Richard H. Rovere, foreword by Arthur M. Schlesinger Jr., *Senator Joe McCarthy* (Berkeley: University of California Press, 1996), 10.

8. "Businessman Here Is McCarthy Source," *New York Times*, April 8. 1950.

9. "Goodwin Admits Role in Charges," *New York Times*, April 11, 1950.

10. John A. Adams Jr., foreword by James L. Buckley, *William Buckley, Sr.: Witness to the Mexican Revolution, 1908–1922* (Norman: University of Oklahoma Press, 2023), 127.

11. Jeet Heer, "National Review's Bad Conscience," *The New Republic*, July 29, 2015.

12. John B. Judis, *William F. Buckley, Jr.: Patron Saint of the Conservatives* (New York: Simon and Schuster, 1988), 44.

13. Quoted in Judis, *William F. Buckley, Jr.*, 131.

14. Christopher Owen, *Heaven Can Indeed Fall: The Life of Willmoore Kendall* (Lanham, MD: Lexington Books, 2021), 81.

15. Owen, 105.

16. Thomas Kaplan and Paul Needham, "William F. Buckley '50 Dies At 82," *Yale Daily News*, February 28, 2008.

17. Carter, *The Price of Peace*, 379.

18. Alvin S. Felzenberg, *A Man and His Presidents: The Political Odyssey of William F. Buckley Jr.* (New Haven, CT: Yale University Press, 2017), 56. The editorial page of the *Washington Post* observed, "Senator Benton's compilation is a notable piece of research. It is useful, too, as an expression of indignation and disgust." "Indictment," October 2, 1951.

19. Cited in Geoffrey Kabaservice, "The Tea Party's Godfather," *The National Interest* (May–June 2014).

20. William F. Buckley Jr., "The Party and the Deep Blue Sea," *Commonweal*, January 25, 1952.

21. Geraldine Fitch, "Formosa, Last Hope of Asia," *The Freeman*, September 10, 1951.

22. From the outset, Eisenhower was viewed with antipathy by the Right. See Albert Friendly, "The Hate Merchants Are Out to Get Ike, *Washington Post*, April 20, 1952.

23. "Letter, Senator Joseph McCarthy to President Eisenhower re James B. Conant as High Commissioner in Germany, February 3, 1953" [DDE's Papers as President, Name Series, Box 22, McCarthy Joseph; NAID #16660398], Dwight D. Eisenhower Presidential Library, Museum & Boyhood Home, accessed June 12, 2023.

24. William F. Buckley Jr., and L. Brent Bozell, prologue by William Schlamm, *McCarthy and His Enemies: The Record and Its Meaning* (Chicago: Henry Regnery Press, 1954), 4. James Rorty and Moshe Decter noted that "some of

McCarthy's neophyte intellectual spokesmen and sophisticated apologists hanker to make a totalitarian of him," but that he was simply too erratic to rise to the challenge. See *McCarthy and the Communists* (Boston: Beacon Press, 1954), 111.

25. "McCarthy To Demand 'Blockade,'" *New York Times*, December 27, 1954.

26. Joyce Mao, *Asia First: China and the Making of Modern American Conservatism* (Chicago: University of Chicago Press, 2005), 145.

27. Samuel Bennett, "'A Critic Friendly to McCarthy': How William F. Buckley, Jr. Brought Senator Joseph R. McCarthy into the American Conservative Movement between 1951 and 1959" (2019). MSSA Kaplan Prize for Use of MSSA Collections. 20.

28. *A Moral Temper: The Letters of Dwight Macdonald*, edited with an introduction by Michael Wreszin (Chicago: Ivan R. Dee, 2001), 248.

29. "M'Carthy Praises Role Of M'Arthur," *New York Times*, February 23, 1956.

30. Antonio Oliveira Salazar, "Be Resolved to Fight," *The National Review*, December 29, 1956.

31. Cited in Owen, *Heaven Can Indeed Fall: The Life of Willmoore Kendall*, 156.

32. Nathaniel Weyl, "Myopia on Latin America," *The National Review*, May 20, 1961.

33. William F. Buckley Jr., "Yes, and Many Thanks—But Now the War Is Over," *The National Review*, October 26, 1957.

34. Joshua Tait, "Long Before Hungary, the Right Was Fixated on Another Country," *The Bulwark*, January 24, 2022.

35. Paul Vitello, "F. Reid Buckley, Novelist and Columnist, Dies at 83," *New York Times*, April 16, 2014. Also see Sam Hodges, "Buckley Brother Prefers to Take Quiet Approach," *Chicago Tribune*, February 25, 1985.

36. Buckley and Bozell, *McCarthy and His Enemies*, 333.

37. Peter Kihss, "18,000 Rightists Rally at Garden," *New York Times*, March 8, 1962.

38. Nicholas von Hoffman, "'Crusader' Bozell Means It Literally," *Washington Post*, May 22, 1966.

39. L. Clayton Dubois, "The First Family of Conservatism," *New York Times Magazine*, August 9, 1970.

40. Quoted in Judis, *William F. Buckley, Jr.*, 321.

41. William F. Buckley Jr., *Cruising Speed: A Documentary* (New York: G.P. Putnam's Sons, 1971), 236.

42. Kevin Michel, "A Struggle Between Brothers: A Reexamination of the Idea of a Cohesive Conservative Movement Through the Intellectual Life and Personal Conflict Surrounding L. Brent Bozell" (2009). MSSA Kaplan Prize for Use of MSSA Collections. 3.

43. James Burnham, "The Tangle in Katanga," *The National Review*, December 30, 1961.

44. Brian Urquhart, "Character Sketches: Mobutu and Tshombe—Two Congolese Rogues, *UN News*, United Nations, accessed June 12, 2023.

45. James Burnham, foreword by John O'Sullivan, introduction by Roger

Kimball, *Suicide of the West: An Essay on the Meaning and Destiny of Liberalism* (New York: Encounter Books, 2014), 267–69.

46. Quoted in Judis, *William F. Buckley, Jr.*, 185.
47. "The Rising Tide," *New York Times*, April 3, 1960.
48. Judis, *William F. Buckley, Jr.*, 191.

CHAPTER 8: THE KIRKPATRICK DOCTRINE

1. Quoted in Judis, *William F. Buckley, Jr.*, 370.
2. John Gregory Dunne, *Quintana & Friends* (New York: Henry Robbins, 1978), 60.
3. Phil McCombs, "Revelation from a Right-Winger," *Washington Post*, July 9, 1990.
4. Jeet Heer, "When Will National Review Apologize for Cooperating with Murderous Dictator Augusto Pinochet?," *The New Republic*, October 9, 2015.
5. "Chile: Settling Down," Washington Star Syndicate, Released February 10, 1977. https://cumuluscanto.hillsdale.edu/Buckley/index2.html#1680798 942428_19.
6. Letter, Richard M. Nixon to Jeffrey Hart, March 20, 1078, Jeffrey Peter Hart papers, box 1, Hoover Institution Library & Archives.
7. Kenneth Bredemeier, "Justice Dept. Says Group Illegally Lobbies for Chile," *Washington Post*, December 19, 1978.
8. "A Public Relations Firm Takes Out an Ad," *New York Times*, December 23, 1979.
9. Marvin Liebman, *Coming Out Conservative: An Autobiography* (San Francisco: Chronicle Books, 1992), 214.
10. Jeffrey Hart, "Our Literature of Extremes," *The Claremont Review of Books* (Spring 2006).
11. "Pinochet, Kirkpatrick and Thatcher," *Financial Times*, December 11, 2006.
12. Richard V. Allen, "Jeane Kirkpatrick and the Great Democratic Defection," *New York Times*, December 16, 2006.
13. Peter Collier, *Political Woman: The Big Little Life of Jeane Kirkpatrick* (New York: Encounter Books, 2012), 23–24.
14. Collier, 113.
15. Jane Rosen, "The Kirkpatrick Factor," *New York Times Magazine*, April 28, 1985.
16. Raymond Bonner, "The Diplomat Who Wouldn't Lie," Politico, April 23, 2015.
17. Clifford Krauss, "How U.S. Actions Helped Hide Salvador Human Rights Abuses," *New York Times*, March 21, 1993.
18. Edward Schumacher, "Latins Get Taste of Kirkpatrick Style," *New York Times*, August 5, 1981.
19. Christopher Hitchens, *Blood, Class, and Empire: The Enduring Anglo-American Relationship*, paperback edition (New York: Nation Books, 2004), 104.

20. Mary McGrory, "Not All Falklands Fighting Is Between British and Argentines," *Washington Post*, June 1, 1982.

21. Anthony Lewis, "Ideology and Ignorance," *New York Times*, April 15, 1982.

22. Francis X. Clines, "White House Says Mrs. Kirkpatrick Didn't Know South African's Role," *New York Times*, March 25, 1981.

23. Norman Podhoretz, "Savimbi's Promise," *Washington Post*, January 29, 1986.

24. Sanford J. Ungar, "Jonas Savimbi: Big Welcome for a Bad Bet," *Washington Post*, January 26, 1986.

25. Terence Hunt, "Reagan Tells Savimbi He Wants to Be Very Helpful," *Associated Press*, January 30, 1986.

26. Michael Hill, "Legacy of an Angolan Opportunist," *Baltimore Sun*, March 3, 2002.

27. Phil McCombs, "The Salute to Savimbi," *Washington Post*, February 1, 1986.

28. Jack Wheeler, "Fighting the Soviet Imperialists: UNITA in Angola," *Reason*, April 1983.

29. Sidney Blumenthal, "Jack Wheeler's Adventures with the 'Freedom Fighters,'" *Washington Post*, April 16, 1986.

30. Patrick E. Tyler and David B. Ottaway, "The Selling of Jonas Savimbi: Success and a $600,000 Tab," *Washington Post*, February 9, 1986.

31. R. W. Apple, "Red Carpet for a Rebel, Or How a Star Is Born," *New York Times*, February 7, 1986.

32. Bill McAllister and David B. Ottaway, "Reagan Vows Support of Angola Rebels," *Washington Post*, July 1, 1988.

33. Jonas Savimbi, "The Coming Winds of Change in Angola," *Heritage Report*, October 1, 1989.

34. Nicholas D. Kristof, "Our Own Terrorist," *New York Times*, March 5, 2002.

35. Richard Dowden, "Not As Nice As He Looked: America Loved Jonas Savimbi Because He Said He Fought for Freedom. Now Democracy Doesn't Suit Him, What Will the West Do?," *The Independent*, October 15, 1992.

CHAPTER 9: BACK TO THE FUTURE

1. Patrick Buchanan, ed. Owen Harries, *America's Purpose: New Visions of U.S. Foreign Policy* (San Francisco: ICS Press, 1991), 34.

2. A. M. Rosenthal, "Forgive Them Not," *New York Times*, September 14, 1990.

3. Patrick J. Buchanan, *Right from the Beginning* (Boston: Little Brown, 1988), 30.

4. Buchanan, 302.

5. "Group Criticizes Buchanan Over Views on Nazi-Hunting," *Washington Post*, April 10, 1985.

6. Eleanor Randolph, "Buchanan's Jottings Cited 'Pressure' of Jews, NBC Says," *Washington Post*, May 3, 1985.

7. Patrick Buchanan, "Has He Provoked the Eagle's Last Scream?," *Daily Press*, August 19, 1990.

8. Buchanan, *Right from the Beginning*, 3.

9. Robin Toner, "Buchanan, Urging New Nationalism, Joins '92 Race," *New York Times*, December 11, 1991.

10. E. J. Dionne, "Buchanan Challenges Bush with 'America First' Call," *Washington Post*, December 11, 1991.

11. Henry Allen, "The Iron Fist of Pat Buchanan," *Washington Post*, February 17, 1992.

12. Michael Ross and James Gerstenzang, "Buchanan Rally Boils Over in Georgia," *Los Angeles Times*, March 3, 1992.

13. John Dillin, "Buchanan Enters Fray, Chides Bush," *Christian Science Monitor*, December 12, 1991.

14. Maria L. La Ganga, "Dole's Rivals Seek to Exploit Bosnia Stance," *Los Angeles Times*, December 11, 1995.

15. "Zhirinovsky to Buchanan: Exile Jews," *UPI*, February 22, 1996.

16. M. E. Sarotte, *Not One Inch: America, Russia, and the Making of Post-Cold War Stalemate* (New Haven, CT: Yale University Press, 2021), 268.

17. Robert Kagan, "Kosovo and the Echoes of Isolationism," *New York Times*, March 24, 1999.

18. Patrick J. Buchanan, *A Republic, Not an Empire: Reclaiming America's Destiny* (Washington, DC: Regnery, 1999), 253.

19. Buchanan, 270.

20. Buchanan, 275.

21. Buchanan, 259.

22. Natalie Schreyer, "The Trump Files: When Donald Called Out Pat Buchanan for Bigotry," *Mother Jones*, August 17, 2020.

23. Matt Labash, "A Chump on the Stump," *Washington Examiner*, December 20, 1999.

24. Peter Carlson, "On a Right Wing and a Player," *Washington Post*, September 26, 2002.

25. Carlson, "On a Right Wing."

26. Franklin Foer, "Buchanan's Surefire Flop," *The New Republic*, July 11, 2002.

27. Carlson, "On a Right Wing."

28. Barbara Matuswo, "The Conversion of Bob Novak," *The Washingtonian*, June 1, 2003.

29. David Frum, "Unpatriotic Conservatives," *The National Review*, March 25, 2003.

30. "Toast by Our Founding Editor, Scott McConnell—20th Anniversary Gala," *The American Conservative*, November 30, 2022.

31. Robert Kagan, "Democracies and Double Standards," *Commentary*, August 1997.

32. Boot, a stern critic of Trump and the MAGA movement, recanted his previous blind faith in neoconservatism in "What the Neocons Got Wrong," *Foreign Affairs*, March 10, 2023.

33. Deborah Solomon, "The Way We Live Now, 7/11/04: Questions for William F. Buckley; Conservatively Speaking," *New York Times*, July 11, 2004.

34. Jason Horowitz, "Events in Iraq Open Door for Interventionist Revival, Says Historian," *New York Times*, June 15, 2014.

35. Jim Newell, "Donald Trump Says George W. Bush Lied about WMDs, Is to Blame for 9/11," *Slate Magazine*, February 14, 2016.

36. Luke Harding, Julian Borger, and Dan Sabbagh, "Kremlin Papers Appear to Show Putin's Plot to Put Trump in White House," *Guardian*, July 15, 2021.

37. Josh Rogin, "Trump Campaign Guts GOP's Anti-Russia Stance on Ukraine," *Washington Post*, July 18, 2016.

38. Greg Miller and Greg Jaffe, "Trump Revealed Highly Classified Information to Russian Foreign Minister and Ambassador," *Washington Post*, May 15, 2017.

39. Roger Kimball, "How Hayek Predicted Trump with His 'Why the Worst Get On Top,'" PJ Media, May 5, 2016.

40. Christopher Caldwell, "France Must Maintain Ideals," *Financial Times*, November 11, 2005.

41. Christopher Caldwell, "How to Think About Vladimir Putin," *Imprimis*, March 2017.

42. Patrick J. Buchanan, "Is Putin the 'Preeminent Statesman' of Our Times?," *The American Conservative*, March 31, 2017.

43. Christopher Caldwell, "Hungary and the Future of Europe," *The Claremont Review of Books* (Spring 2019).

44. Anne Applebaum, *Twilight of Democracy: The Seductive Lure of Authoritarianism* (New York: Doubleday, 2020), 161–65.

45. Gabriel Schoenfeld, "Expose Trump's Enablers," *New York Daily News*, October 31, 2016.

46. John O'Sullivan, "Hungary's Emergency Law Is Flawed—But It Doesn't Herald 'Dictatorship,'" *The National Review*, April 3, 2020,

47. Tom Szigeti, "American Religious Writer and Journalist Rod Dreher Holds Talk on the 'Benedict Option' in Budapest," *Hungary Today*, March 27, 2018.

48. James Kirchick, "When the Pope Hits Your Eye Like a Big Pizza Pie, That's Ahmari," Tablet, February 2, 2022.

49. Sohrab Ahmari, "Why Western Elites Should Stop Lecturing Hungary," *New York Post*, October 2, 2019.

50. Becca Rothfeld, "The New Conservative Arguments for an Un-Modern America," *Washington Post*, July 28, 2023.

51. Brooke Masters, "Adrian Vermeule's Legal Theories Illuminate a Growing Rift among US Conservatives," *Financial Times*, October 13, 2022.

52. Adrian Vermeule, "There Is No Conservative Legal Movement," *Washington Post*, July 6, 2022.

53. Adrian Vermeule, "Beyond Originalism," *Atlantic*, March 31, 2020.

54. Dominic Green, "Archduke Eduard von Habsburg's Advice to Modernity," *Washington Examiner*, June 8, 2023.

55. Eduard Habsburg, *The Habsburg Way: Seven Rules for Turbulent Times* (Manchester, NH: Sophia Institute Press), 2023.

56. Ross Douthat, "Why Hungary Inspires So Much Fear and Fascination," *New York Times*, August 7, 2021.

57. Ibid.
58. The National Conservative movement is the brainchild of the American-Israeli political theorist Yoram Hazony who has been described as the "leader of the New Right most interested in a compensatory cult of unity, energy, and purity." James M. Patterson, "Is the New Right Fascist?," *Religion & Liberty* (Summer 2023).
59. Valerie Hopkins, "Campus in Hungary is Flagship of Orban's Bid to Create Conservative Elite," *New York Times*, June 28, 2021.
60. Ana Luiza Albuquerque, "Hungary's Plan to Build an Army of U.S. Intellectuals," *Foreign Policy*, May 19, 2023.
61. Matthias Meisner, "Kaderschmiede des Illiberalismus," *Der Tagesspiegel*, May 16, 2023.

CONCLUSION

1. Aaron Blake, "Fox News's Jennifer Griffin Fully Loses Her Patience with Fox's Ukraine Punditry," *Washington Post*, February 28, 2022.
2. As David Atkins has observed, American conservatives profess neutrality in the conflict over Ukraine but in fact adore the doctrines that Putin and Orbán are peddling. "Trump, DeSantis Say They Just Want Peace in Ukraine. Don't Fall for It.," *Washington Monthly*, March 29, 2023.
3. Steve Benen, "Before Exiting, Trump Finds Another Radical Voice to Help Lead Pentagon," MSNBC, November 12, 2020.
4. Andrew Kaczyinski and Em Steck, "Trump Appointee on West Point Board Spreads Conspiracy that Biden is Replacing White People of European Ancestry," *KFile*, CNN, May 28, 2021.
5. Douglas Macgregor, "Washington's Carthaginian Peace Collides with Reality," *The American Conservative*, November 29, 2022.
6. George O'Neill, "Death of a Myth," *The American Conservative*, March 9, 2023.
7. Alexander Ward and Ari Hawkins, "We Get Some Specifics on Ramaswamy's Ukraine Plan," *Politico*, June 8, 2023.
8. "Matt Gaetz Leads 11 Lawmakers in Introduction of 'Ukraine Fatigue' Resolution to Halt U.S. Aid to Ukraine," press release, *Matt Gaetz, Congressman, FL-01*, February 9, 2023.
9. Graig Graziosi, "Marjorie Taylor Greene Says Claims Putin Wants to Extend Invasion Further into Europe Are 'Lies,'" *The Independent*, March 16, 2023.
10. Jonathan Swan, Charlie Savage and Maggie Haberman, "Trump and Allies Forge Plans to Increase Presidential Power in 2025," *New York Times*, July 17, 2023.
11. Cited in James Pogue, "Inside the New Right, Where Peter Thiel Is Placing His Biggest Bets," *Vanity Fair*, April 20, 2022.
12. Dana Milbank, "How Reactionary Is MAGA? Try the First Century B.C.," *Washington Post*, September 7, 2022.

13. Helen Andrews, "What Soviet Nostalgia Gets Right," *Compact Magazine*, May 25, 2023.

14. Gordon Brook-Shepherd, *The Austrians: A Thousand-Year Odyssey* (New York: Carroll & Graff, 1996), 101.

15. Derek Penslar, *Theodor Herzl: The Charismatic Leader* (New Haven, CT: Yale University Press, 2020), 70.

16. Carl Schorske, *Fin-de Siecle Vienna: Politics and Culture* (Cambridge: Cambridge University Press, 1981). Also see Robert D. Kaplan, "Austria: Second Try," *The Atlantic* (September 1990) for an illuminating discussion of Lueger and Vienna.

17. Yannik Bogensperger, "Brathendlduft und deftige Wortwahl," *Kurier*, May 2, 2023.

ILLUSTRATION CREDITS